# An Introduction to the Ethics of Social Media

# An Introduction to the Ethics of Social Media

Douglas R. Campbell

HACKETT PUBLISHING COMPANY
INDIANAPOLIS

Copyright © 2025 by Hackett Publishing Company, Inc.

All rights reserved
Printed in the United States of America

28  27  26  25          1  2  3  4  5  6  7

For further information, please address
 Hackett Publishing Company, Inc.
 P.O. Box 44937
 Indianapolis, Indiana 46244-0937

www.hackettpublishing.com

Cover and interior designs by E. L. Wilson
Composition by Aptara, Inc.

Cataloging-in-Publication data can be accessed via the Library of Congress Online Catalog.
Library of Congress Control Number: 2025933254

ISBN-13: 978-1-64792-235-1 (pbk.)
ISBN-13: 978-1-64792-241-2 (PDF ebook)
ISBN-13: 978-1-64792-242-9 (epub)

The paper used in this publication meets the minimum requirements of American National Standard for Information Sciences—Permanence of Paper for Printed Library Materials, ANSI Z39.48–1984.

∞

# Contents

Acknowledgments — vii

Introduction — 1
Chapter 1: Privacy — 7
Chapter 2: The Attention Economy — 37
Chapter 3: Nudging — 57
Chapter 4: Echo Chambers and Polarization — 83
Chapter 5: Misinformation — 107
Chapter 6: Cancel Culture: Online Shaming and Caring — 131
Chapter 7: Friendship — 153
Chapter 8: Quitting — 173
Conclusion — 197

Bibliography — 199
Index — 209

# Acknowledgments

This book is dedicated to the memory of my mother, Susan Rose Caluori.

I am very grateful for all the support that I received while writing this book. I especially thank Jolene Bielicki, Rachel O'Keefe, Julia Atack, Maria Truss, and Sally and Maila Harrison for their support in different ways throughout the writing process. I thank Frank, Emily, and Scott Campbell, too.

I am grateful also to the University of Toronto for giving me the opportunity to design a course on the ethics of social media. I am equally grateful to Alma College's top-notch philosophy department for the opportunity to continue teaching the course.

There is no way that this book would exist without my lovely students across the years. There are too many to list here. A woefully incomplete list of students who have earned my undying gratitude for their interesting discussions and written work includes Eoin Knight, Dani Crews, Morgan Henson, Sandra Choueiri, Kendrix Imafidon, Jla Johnson, Humza Khan, Shruti Sood, Hala Kayed, Justin Cheptea, Lindsay Davies-White, David Ingalls, Minahil Syed, and Julia Viele.

I have special intellectual debts to pay to every scholar that I have cited in this book, without whom this work would not have been possible, especially Lavinia Marin, Cass Sunstein, and Kathryn Norlock.

Lastly, I want to thank Jeff Dean, Jacob Stump, and Nilou Davoudi for their excellent comments on drafts of this book, as well as Hackett for publishing *An Introduction to the Ethics of Social Media*.

The third chapter of this book adapts my article "Nudging and Social Media: The Choice Architecture of Online Life" published in 2022 in *Giornale Critico di Storia Delle Idee* 2: 93–114.

The fourth chapter of this book adapts roughly 2,000 words from my article "In Defense of (Some) Online Echo Chambers" published in 2023 in *Ethics and Information Technology* 25 (3): 1–11.

The sixth chapter of this book adapts roughly 2,000 words from my article "Cancel Culture, Then and Now: A Platonic Approach to the Shaming of People and the Exclusion of Ideas" published in 2023 in *Journal of Cyberspace Studies* 7 (2): 147–66.

# Introduction

Philosophers have developed the field of applied ethics to apply moral concepts to difficult ethical issues that arise in particular areas of our existence. There are environmental ethics, business ethics, medical ethics, and so on. The ethics of social media is one such part of applied ethics. Many of the ethical issues that this book discusses are also treated by philosophers working in the field of information ethics, which gets its name from the fact that it is concerned with information technology.

It is appropriate to talk about the ethics of social media, rather than information ethics, because doing so highlights more precisely what we are talking about—ethical issues that have arisen or become more prominent on account of social-media sites and apps, such as Facebook, Instagram, TikTok, X, LinkedIn, and many others. There is also the fact that many of the topics considered in this book, such as the value of online friendships, really do not have much to do with what people ordinarily mean when they talk about information technologies, such as search engines.

The largest obstacle to the ethics of social media is the set of thought-terminating clichés that surround the subject in popular media and discourse. When we say "thought-terminating cliché," we have in mind those brief slogans that we usually roll out to end a conversation without engaging with much of the substance of what we are replying to. Some familiar thought-terminating clichés are "It is what it is," "God works in mysterious ways," and "Boys will be boys." When we talk about the ethical issues generated by Facebook and Instagram, we might hear that such technologies are just tools or that they can be used for good or bad.

These are particularly pernicious clichés because there does seem to be something true about them. The latter, for instance, cannot possibly be *wrong*. After all, social-media apps *can* be used for good or for evil. When I teach the ethics of social media to students, I clarify on the first day of class that the course is not designed to relentlessly drag social-media apps through the mud. On the contrary, some of the chapters of this book, just like many of the lectures in my class, highlight the good things about social-media platforms: for instance, friendships on these platforms have real value, and they provide a community to people who are vulnerable and might not be able to meet like-minded people offline. All we need to do to establish that social-media apps can do good is point to worthy crowdfunding opportunities. By the same token, this book's Table of Contents provides a list of many harmful things associated with social media, including echo chambers, misinformation, and violations of our privacy.

What makes it a thought-terminating cliché to say that social-media platforms can be used for good or for bad is that it does not really settle any ethical issues. It is equivalent to shrugging and saying "It is what it is." When people debate nuclear disarmament, someone might similarly say that nuclear weapons can be used for good or for bad, but even if we grant that point, we still want to know the answer to specific questions, such as how likely it is that they will be used well, what we should do about them in light of their potential for good and for bad, what using them well entails, and what risks we run by disarming or not disarming. Moreover, we should say *something* about the particular goods and evils that these things *do* cause. Similarly, if we are considering the use of fossil fuels, we would not be satisfied by knowing all the good things that come from having an easily available fuel source. We would want to know about all the bad things that arise from fossil fuels, and then whether the good outweighs the bad.

At this point, we run into the other thought-terminating cliché, which is the claim that social-media apps are merely tools. Since they can be used for good or for evil, how we use them is up to *us*. Of course, there is, yet again, something true about this. I can use TikTok to bully someone or I can use TikTok to advertise an important crowdfunding campaign. That is up to me.

The problem is that social-media technologies are *not* tools in the same way that hammers and saws are. This is an important philosophical point that will not really become clear until the end of Chapter 3, but I shall outline the basics now. Some tools, such as hammers, are inert and passive. They are waiting for us to use them as we see fit. In contrast, social-media platforms *act on us*. Specifically, they nudge us. This means that they are designed to promote the likelihood of some behaviors and choices on our part. Most often, this means that they are designed to get us to spend more time on their platforms and to get us to reveal more information about ourselves.

Social-media platforms simply *cannot* be neutral. They are built with design values in mind, and countless millions of dollars go into building every aspect of apps to promote the likelihood of certain behaviors without coercing you. Everything is designed with the values of the designers as guides, even the color of the notification symbol. (Red, it turns out, is much more effective at getting you to click than blue is.)

Throughout this book, we will discuss more of these design values. For instance, one of them, called *consumer sovereignty*, values prioritizing content that the designers believe you would be most likely to click on and consume. (They infer from your clicking behaviors that it is content that you *want* to see.) This rather innocent-seeming value gives rise to communities in which users are shown only content that they already agree with. This creates a bias: users' beliefs grow more intense because they are shown only corroborating points of view and are never acquainted with the evidence against them.

If we keep our eyes on these considerations—which are mere previews of deeper discussions that unfold on the following pages of this book—then it is appropriate for us to ask how social-media technologies affect *us*. Once we ask this question, we can see that it is mistaken to say that social-media platforms are merely tools. In certain senses, they use us. (Chapter 2 will even bring to light the way that we, and our attention specifically, are the commodities being traded in a transaction between a platform and some advertiser.) Even putting aside philosophical discussions of nudges and design values, each of us can pause and reflect on the way that spending time on social-media platforms changes us: it might make us feel more anxious and lonely, or it might make us feel happy and more connected to other people. Either way, we are not describing tools as we might be when we are talking about hammers or saws.

There is an insight from ancient philosophers that we might profitably learn from today, namely, that the things that we use are active in a way that we downplay when we call them mere tools. Plato, the ancient Athenian philosopher, recognized this point when he talked about how pleasures affect our conception of what is real and valuable. They lure us into changing our beliefs.[1] Even more relevant to the present discussion is the ancient Confucian philosopher Xunzi, who argued that ritual and music can rework human nature itself. For Xunzi, humans are by nature bad, but we can change our nature through deliberate effort and hard work. The path to changing human nature is marked by sages, who invented practices and certain kinds of music to help bring about the desired change.[2] Yet, in the minds of many ordinary people today, who and what we are does not change when we pick up any so-called tool. According to a view that is common today, we might be using social-media apps badly on Monday, but we could just as easily be using them well on Tuesday if only we have the right intention and mindset.

This is overlooking the way that social-media apps are designed to get you in one mindset and keep you there indefinitely.

When I talk about this common view, I have in mind the popular discussions about social media in the news and, perhaps unsurprisingly, on social-media platforms themselves. I do not mean to attribute this common view to philosophers. The burgeoning field of the ethics of social media is rich and exciting, as I am sure that this book will confirm.

Each chapter of this book is designed to facilitate discussion around a different topic within the ethics of social media. I consider multiple points of view, and I have put together an annotated bibliography at the end of each chapter, which is supposed to simultaneously provide a list of further readings and substantiate the claims made in the chapter. I have also provided sets of cases to think through at the end of each chapter. I have chosen real cases because applied ethics is at its most valuable when thinkers work with actual cases. They give us an opportunity to see what philosophy can do when it turns its attention to the day-to-day problems that affect us, and I think that the result of wrestling with these problems will be a more acute sensitivity to what social-media technologies do, both for us and against us.

I shall conclude this introduction with a brief mention of my own experience with the ethics of social media. As a graduate student working on ancient philosophy at the University of Toronto, I became aware of discussions in the media about echo chambers and misinformation. I felt that these discussions were important but that they were not particularly well conducted. Part of the problem with the conversations was certainly due to the fact that the subject was (and still is) new: these technologies are new, and we have not yet developed the necessary social antibodies to protect against some of their harms. ("Social antibody" is a term, discussed in Chapter 2, that refers to the way that society spontaneously develops rules and norms to help it deal with threats, as our own immune systems do with the threats that they encounter.) The problem was also partly due to the fact that philosophers had not yet had their contributions to these discussions fully appreciated. My hope is that by introducing to students and other interested readers the ethics of social media, more people will benefit from the richness of philosophical analyses of these problems.

At the same time as I was noticing these discussions in the media, I attended a talk at a meeting of the American Philosophical Association by Professor Kathryn Norlock, who was discussing whether it is possible to consent to the terms and conditions of use of what was then called Twitter. Her talk convinced me that philosophers have a lot to contribute to these discussions. Later that year, I designed and taught my course on the ethics of social media at the University of Toronto for the first time. Now I have moved to Alma College, where I still teach the course every year, and I find that each new cohort of students visits the various ethical problems in new ways. This book represents the culmination of years of work teaching students: presenting the material concisely and lucidly to them, choosing topics that speak to what they are experiencing online, and compiling cases that are both philosophically relevant and thought-provoking.

## Notes

1. See Plato's *Phaedo* 83b–c.
2. See *Xunzi*, chaps. 19, 20, and 23.

# Chapter One: Privacy

People share all sorts of information on social-media sites: information about their vacations, jobs, children, religious identities, menstrual cycles, sexual preferences, and so on. Sometimes we share that information with every other user indiscriminately; other times, we share it with only a chosen few. Sometimes we do not even know that we are sharing it, such as when we download an app on our smartphone, and we, unbeknownst to us, give the owners of the app access to all of the photos and information on our device. At other times, we do not directly give the owners a piece of information at all, but we give other information from which the owners can *infer* the information that we have not given access to. In some cases, a company will advertise to us that we should use their products because they are *not* selling our information to a third party; then, it will turn out that the company *is* selling our data and simply lied to us about it.

Some people react with horror when hearing that a company collected their data and then sold it. Others react with horror upon hearing that it was collected in the first place. Some just don't care. For this latter group, it is not obvious whether privacy is worth caring about, and it is open to us to wonder whether it has any value at all. We might say that there is a right to privacy that is being violated—but before we can talk about what it might mean to respect that right and what it might mean to violate it, we should discuss whether the people who do not care about privacy in the first place are correct.

Mark Zuckerberg has said that there is a mere social norm for preferring privacy, implying that there is no right to privacy. What he means is that people only ever held a preference to refrain from sharing personal information with others and that this preference is eroding as society changes. Specifically, Zuckerberg said: "People have really gotten comfortable not only sharing more information and different kinds, but more openly and with more people." He elaborated by explaining that this "social norm is just something that has evolved over time."[1] People have gotten more accustomed to sharing information online, and so their objections have gotten quieter. There is no moral barrier to overcome. Instead, all that needs to happen is for those who still care about privacy to no longer care about it, and time will be enough to take care of that.

7

## 1. The Nature and Value of Privacy

Philosophers have staked out a different position on this question.[2] In the eyes of many philosophers, one reason why privacy has moral importance and is not merely a social norm is that not having control over the flow of personal information can have dire consequences for a person's life. There are many countries, for instance, in which being gay is a crime that carries extremely severe penalties. The same goes for people with unpopular political or religious views. The anonymity provided by the internet is particularly important for protecting people, and one of the internet's virtues is that it allows people to discuss ideas without the fear of being easily tracked by authorities. The demotion of privacy to a mere preference or social norm, rather than the foundation of the security of many political dissidents in authoritarian regimes, overlooks this virtue.

We can draw analogies to other domains of human life in which privacy is important. Consider a medical context, for instance, in which the protection of the information concerning a patient's HIV diagnosis is crucial. Such a diagnosis can be stigmatizing, and patients do not want that information circulating freely. They want to control that personal information because it can have major consequences for their lives. Regardless of whether there is a general social norm concerning the flow of personal information, it is clear that it can be harmful to indiscriminately let people know this information, and it is wrong to cause such harm.

Notice that so far, I have defended the value of privacy by pointing to cases in which people *have something to hide*, such as when they criticize an authoritarian regime or receive a sensitive medical diagnosis. Yet, the protection of our privacy is something that we all have a right to, even when we do not have something to hide, but we have to dig deeper to see why. First, we have to think about the important role that control of the flow of personal information plays in all of our social relationships. Each one of us feels comfortable sharing different kinds of information with our friends, family members, doctors, colleagues, and so on. We might never tell our colleagues about our sexual orientation, but it might be common knowledge among our friends.

We might use a piece of information as a way of inviting someone into our lives. For example, I might tell my colleague Ria details of my personal life as a way of signaling that I do not want to be merely colleagues, but I want to be *friends* with her now. Similarly, there are some things that we just do not tell our colleagues; when we reflect on why, it is because they are our colleagues, not our friends or family. Control of the flow of personal information is an important part of regulating and developing our social relationships. The variety of social relationships that we have requires careful and subtle finessing to maintain, and we tend to limit the flow of information appropriately. Think about how we know exactly when to withhold some information from even our closest family members and friends, but then we go to the doctor's office and we share that information freely. Without this ability to discriminate between cases in which we should and should not share some information, we would lose an important tool for differentiating our relationships. If we keep in mind that the sharing of some information is how we signal to different people the nature and closeness of the bonds that we have, then we begin to see how important it is that we can keep a tight rein on the flow of personal information.

This approach to privacy cannot be reduced to the approach that stresses the harms entailed by revealing some information, such as political dissidents living under an oppressive regime. Of course, the two are not mutually exclusive: we can believe that the right to privacy is part of our right to manage social relationships, while also acknowledging that some people are in extraordinary circumstances in which the exposure of certain information could precipitate harmful outcomes. While the two approaches are compatible, they are based on distinct considerations. The first approach is based on the duty to avoid *harming* someone. The second approach is based on the respect that we ought to have for someone's **autonomy**.[3]

Autonomy is the capacity or power that we have to direct our lives as we see fit. It is our ability to *self-determine*. I like to explain to students that if we imagined our lives as a blank canvas, our autonomy would be our ability to paint on the canvas whatever or however we wished. When we develop plans for our lives, we are expressing our autonomy. One important moral principle is that we ought to respect people's autonomy. In practice, this means that we have a moral duty to respect people's plans for their lives, even if we think that the plans are self-destructive (and, generally, even if they really are self-destructive). For instance, if I decide that I want to avoid talking to my neighbors for no good reason, Jolene can try to talk me out of it or persuade me that I am going to suffer some negative consequences from severing my neighborly ties. Ultimately, though, Jolene is morally required to respect my plan for my life.

Naturally, there are all sorts of philosophical problems in the vicinity. For instance, some people are under the age at which we generally think people develop the ability to properly determine their lives. Until that age, we defer to their parents' judgments. It is not clear what to do if a child expresses a preference for a medical treatment that their parent objects to, especially if the child is able to reason articulately and is close to the age of majority. Similarly, it is obvious that some conditions impede a person's efforts to determine their life in a way that we have to respect. For instance, an ill person might be conscious but unable to understand the actual nature of their illness or appreciate the consequences of a possible treatment plan. To the extent that they lack this sort of insight, there might not be a duty for us to respect their plan but rather a duty to promote their well-being. What to do in these cases and how to even identify these cases are thorny problems.

When it comes to privacy online, our concern for children and people who are unable to make certain kinds of decisions is different. That is not to say that there is no concern for them or that the challenges they face in medical contexts vanish in the online context. For children in particular, we might reasonably worry about the way that some kids have an online presence from the time they are born: parents of a newborn baby might set up an Instagram profile on the way home from the hospital and continue to update it for years. By the time the child comes to understand what is being done, years of photos and videos have been shared with countless strangers. We might be accustomed to deferring to the judgments of parents when children are not yet able to form plans of their own, but what the parents have done to the privacy of their child might strike us as *wrong*.

However, generally, our concern for children and people who are unable to make decisions on their own is different because the landscape online is so different. Some groups of people are unable to self-determine because of something *internal* to them, for example, a sick person who cannot appreciate the consequences of a proposed action due to their illness. In online contexts, the threat to our privacy is not internal. The source of the threat is external to us, preventing us from giving our **informed consent** to any release or withholding of personal information.

Consent is the permission that we give other people to act on us. Accordingly, consent is important in ethics because it can change what would be considered assault into tackling during a sports match, and it can change what would be stealing into borrowing. It is specifically informed consent that transforms these actions.

Informed consent is at the heart of the respect for autonomy. If I tell my doctor that I agree to a surgery, but I have no idea what the surgery is or what the risks are, I have *consented*, but it is clearly not the morally important kind of consent. The *informed* part of "informed consent" is important because of my autonomy, that is, my ability to make plans for my life. Doctors need my informed consent because they ought to respect my plan. If I plan to be a soccer player, and the doctor conducts a surgery on me that causes me to lose my ability to walk, after *failing* to inform me about this risk, the doctor has not respected my autonomy. The duty to get my consent in the first place followed from the duty to respect my autonomy. The consent means nothing if I am unable to authorize the surgery in the context of my plans because I do not know how the surgery relates to those plans.

Of course, none of this is simple. There are questions concerning how much information we need to know, and when we are talking about the online selling and buying of people's data, we ought to keep in mind that the buyers of our personal data are constantly changing. That means that the information we might use to shape our decisions is constantly changing. The models of privacy that we shall turn to shortly will help us answer these questions. For now, I want to highlight the way that the threat to our privacy online comes from the fact that we are kept in the dark about who is doing what with what information of ours. This impedes our ability to give informed consent. There are even cases in which people are *lied* to about whether their data is being collected and sold at all. In such an environment, *nobody* can give their informed consent.

Before we turn to specific models of privacy in online contexts, there is one more philosophical view that I want to discuss: the so-called **simplifying hypothesis**.[4] So far, we have mostly treated the right to privacy as one that follows from our ability to develop social relationships as we see fit, which in turn follows naturally from our autonomy, which is our ability to determine our own lives. It is a *right* because we are morally entitled to have our autonomy respected. The simplifying hypothesis is an attempt to tell us what the right to privacy precisely amounts to. It is called "simplifying" because it maintains that the right to privacy is a cluster of rights: the right to privacy does not exist in itself, but there is a set of simpler rights that the right to privacy consists in.

The value of the simplifying hypothesis is that it further lays out for us why we have a right to privacy. It tells us that this right exists on account of other, basic rights that we independently believe in.

Consider an analogy with the right to private property. You own a television and therefore have a right to it. If someone steals it from you, the thief has violated that right. When we ask what the right to private property *is* or *consists in*, we find that it can be framed as the cluster of several other rights. For instance, it involves the right to do with your television as you see fit: destroy it, cover it up with a towel, lend it out to someone else, and so on.

The simplifying hypothesis says that the right to privacy exists in a similar way. The right to privacy is or consists in a set of other rights. For example, you own your elbow, which means that you have the right to cover it up or expose it, in addition to several other rights, such as the right to destroy it. You own the photographs on your wall, which means that you have the right to cover them up and ensure that nobody looks at them. Accordingly, if someone uses an X-ray to see through the walls of your house and through the covering on top of the photographs, your rights have been violated. The right to privacy specifically concerns your personal information. If someone tortures you to get information about Plato's *Republic*, that violates your right not to be tortured, but it does not violate your right to privacy. If someone tortures you to discover which book you read at night, that does violate your right to privacy.

The simplifying hypothesis relies on *autonomy*. So did the argument that highlighted the importance of privacy in managing our social relationships. The simplifying hypothesis adds to our understanding the insight that we might not be able to spell out exactly what the right to privacy is because it does not exist independently of other, simpler rights. It is an important contribution to the discussion of privacy because it clarifies the nature of this right.

The question that we shall now turn to concerns how we protect and respect people's privacy in practice, especially in online and social-media contexts. We can appreciate how thorny this question is by attending to two offline cases. In one case, a married couple is loudly fighting about their sex life and neighbors overhear it, thereby learning personal information that the couple did not wish anyone to know. While the couple might be embarrassed, few people would say that the neighbors violated anyone's rights. In the second case, a married couple is fighting about their sex life, but they have moved to the basement and are not talking loudly at all, so there is little chance of their conversation being overheard. If a stranger uses a listening device to eavesdrop on their argument, it is undeniable that the right to privacy has been violated. In order to explain why the right to privacy is respected in one instance and violated in the other, despite the fact that in both cases the same information is obtained against the wishes of the people who own that information, we need some philosophical accounts, which are called *models* in the relevant academic literature.

Before we turn to those models, consider two quick points. The first highlights important considerations here: the importance of the flow of personal information for maintaining diverse social relationships and the importance of control and informed consent. It is crucial that we keep in mind that differences in social-relationship contexts affect the appropriateness of sharing and withholding different kinds of information. This will matter because social-media sites tend to erase distinctions between relationships: strangers, colleagues, mortal enemies, friends, family members, and future employers are all among the audience that we have when we post on Instagram. Control and informed consent are just as important, to the extent that we ought to respect other people as entities capable of forming their own life plans and to the extent that information is required to properly form their own life plans.

Notice that none of these considerations depend on a social norm or a preference to withhold information from people. None of these points would be undermined if people in society cared less about privacy. On the other hand, a society where people care less and less about respecting other people's autonomy is a society that is shirking its moral duties.

This leads me to the second and final point before moving on: I doubt that people actually care less about privacy these days. I doubt that because there is some interesting polling data which indicates that people *are* concerned about their personal information; they just do not know what to do about it. A 2019 poll by the Pew Research Center found that 81 percent of Americans believed that the potential risks of data collection by businesses outweighed the benefits; 66 percent said the same concerning the potential risks of data collection by the government.[5] The same poll found that 79 percent reported being concerned about how their data is used by companies; 64 percent said the same about the government. Part of the problem appears to be the fact that people feel they have *no control* over the collection of data: 81 percent said that they have very little or no control over data collected by businesses; 84 percent said the same about the government. The perceived lack of control is exacerbated by the lack of information with 59 percent saying that they have little or no understanding about how businesses use the data they have collected; 78 percent said the same about the government.

The picture painted by this polling data reinforces the view that people are concerned about their privacy, but they feel that they cannot really control the flow of personal information, nor do they really understand how the collected information is used. The behavior that leads people such as Mark Zuckerberg to conclude that people do not care about privacy appears to, in fact, be the behavior of people who feel like they are not in control. Our personal information will be collected anyway, by means poorly understood and for purposes unknown to us, so it does not matter how *we* act with regard to it.

Now that we understand the moral basis of the right to privacy as well as people's general feelings toward the collection of information by businesses and governments, let us turn to models of privacy.

# 2. Models of Privacy

Two of the most important models of privacy are the **restricted access/limited control (RALC) model** and the **contextual-integrity (CI) model**. These two models will be the focus of what follows, but first I want to discuss an older model that was historically influential.

## 2.1 Non-intrusion Model

We can talk about *the* non-intrusion model or a cluster of related models, but the central idea is that the right to privacy is the right to be left alone (or "let alone," as it was originally articulated). This model was developed in 1890 by Samuel Warren, an influential American lawyer, and Louis Brandeis, who later became a justice on the Supreme Court of the United States.[6] Through Brandeis's place on the Supreme Court, this view of privacy achieved historical importance and influenced American jurisprudence. Brandeis's dissent in *Olmstead v. United States*, a 1928 case that involved the wiretapping of private phone conversations, became famous later in the century. The majority opinion in the 1972 *Eisenstadt v. Baird*, written by Justice William Brennan, which established the right of unmarried couples to have contraceptives, was also influenced by Brandeis's conception of privacy. Brennan's majority opinion famously declared the right to privacy entails freedom from unwarranted intrusion by the government. Hence, this model is sometimes called the "non-intrusion model."

## 2. Models of Privacy 15

Whether there is one view of privacy here or a large family of views makes no difference for our purposes. The non-intrusion model of privacy captures the sense that when someone violates our privacy, we are being invaded. Imagine someone peering into your purse when you are looking the other way, or someone breaking into your house when you are not home and looking at the contents of your drawers. The simplifying hypothesis says, plausibly, that these actions are wrong because several rights are violated at the same time: we have a right to not have our purse opened without our permission; we have a right not to have our stuff rifled through without our permission; we have the right to prevent people from looking in our drawers; and so on. The non-intrusion model *improves* this analysis because it captures the feeling that we have after having our privacy violated: we feel that we have been invaded. After all, not every violation of a right is accompanied by such a feeling.

There is no doubt that Brandeis and Warren capture something important about privacy, but the problem with their view is that it fails to provide us with any meaningful description of how to respect someone's privacy. The state of privacy that they describe is something like being perfectly alone. They often discuss *solitude* and sometimes even the need to *retreat from the world*. The problem is that this does not tell us anything about controlling the flow of personal information. Their view implies that having privacy respected looks like being completely inaccessible and left alone. However, what we need is a description of what it means to respect privacy in situations in which we *are* accessible to other people, the government, and businesses.

The last point to mention is that we do not want to confuse secrecy with privacy. When some information is secret, few people know it. The fewer who know, the more secret it is. When many people learn that information, we might decide that it is no longer a secret after all. In contrast, some information can be private even if a great many people know it. For instance, someone's sexual orientation might be *private* but not a *secret*. "Private" in this context means something like "controlled by the person who is the subject of that information." The non-intrusion model, by not recognizing any notion of controlling the flow of personal information, talks about secrecy as if it were privacy.

## 2.2 The RALC Model

According to the restricted access/limited control (RALC) model of privacy, respecting someone's privacy is a matter of restricting access to their information by giving them *limited*, rather than absolute, control over that information.[7] Consider yet another analogy with medical information. A hospital respects our privacy with regard to our medical information by restricting access to that information—for example, by preventing the public from seeing it—and giving us limited control over that information. Now, we do not have (and the RALC model says that we do not *need*) absolute control: few people would feel that their privacy is being violated by having a nurse read their medical information at a hospital.

The reader might be wondering what the RALC model says about *why* the hospital should do this. The RALC model does not have an answer to that question because it is designed to answer another question instead. To learn why hospitals ought to respect the privacy of patients, consult the content from earlier in this chapter on harm and autonomy. The RALC model, in contrast, is designed to tell us what respecting someone's privacy looks like in practice. It tells us that it looks like restricting access to personal information and giving someone limited control.

Of course, the first question that we should answer is about the nature of the limited control. The clearest reason why we should *not* have absolute control is simply that it is impractical. Imagine if a hospital tried to respect the privacy of the patients by giving them absolute control over their medical information. The patient would be quickly inundated with requests for the release of information, and the hospital staff's functioning would grind to a halt. Now compound that with the difficulty of letting the patient also have the ability to *retract* that information.

Instead, the RALC model says that we need to give someone only limited control. Limited control consists in letting someone have three abilities: choice, consent, and correction. In this context, choice is the ability to select between different levels of access to the information: we decide generally how restricted the access is going to be. Consent is our ability to waive restrictions that might be put on the flow of information by default. For instance, I ought to be able to *consent* to Amazon tracking my browsing preferences if I want to. Correction is our ability to amend our preferences as well as amend the personal information itself: both of these reflect a level of control that we ought to have over our information.

Let me give some online examples. We shall start by talking about **data mining** and then cookies, before moving on to general observations about online practices related to privacy and then to the next model.

To *mine* data is to extract patterns from large sets of data. For instance, TikTok collects data from its users. Let's say that it collects data about how many cat videos you watch and how old you are. For the sake of this discussion, let's assume that TikTok collects only these two pieces of data. TikTok will then aggregate, or put together, this information for all of its users into one large dataset, which developers will *mine* useful patterns from the data. They might decide, for instance, that people who are sixteen years old watch lots of cat videos. Accordingly, they will show sixteen-year-old users cat videos; after all, TikTok wants to maximize the amount of time that users spend on their app. (The morality of nudging users to spend more time on a social-media app is discussed at length in Chapter 3.) Conversely, the data-miners might discover that eighty-one-year-olds do not generally watch cat videos. So, the app will refrain from showing those users cat videos.

The RALC model has multiple objections to data mining as a practice. Most seriously, the problem with data mining is that social-media sites collect *way* more data than merely our age and how many cat videos we watch, and as time progresses, data-miners become profoundly proficient at extracting useful patterns of data. The patterns are so useful that they are quite *lucrative*. "Company X is selling our data" usually means that a company, such as Amazon, has collected sufficiently large amounts of data from users that it believes other entities will pay to have access to the patterns that can be inferred from their datasets. (Amazon claims that it does not *sell* your personal information, but it *does* share it with some of its partners, such as Starbucks, Eddie Bauer, T-Mobile, and so on.) In the infamous Cambridge Analytica scandal, data that was collected on Facebook was mined for political purposes; the data was used to help inform Donald Trump's presidential campaign, Ted Cruz's senatorial campaign, and the Brexit referendum.[8]

It is not obvious that this practice results in your being *harmed*, but that is not the end of the moral story because the right to privacy is not grounded exclusively in a duty to avoid harm. The problem with data mining is that it violates the RALC model's requirement that people have at least limited control over the flow of their personal information. By doing so, it violates our autonomy.

In many cases, we are not told that our data will be mined in the first place, let alone given an opportunity to consent. This problem is made worse by the fact that even if we agree to let Facebook collect some information about us, data mining is a process built on getting *more* information about us than what we initially shared. This is an absolutely crucial point in understanding the moral objection to data mining: I might reveal to Facebook five pieces of information about me, but let's say that I specifically do *not* want them to know my political affiliation. However, when Meta sells my personal information to some political firm, there is nothing stopping them from inferring (with a startling degree of reliability, especially as data-mining techniques improve) my political affiliation. In fact, the value of the political firm's purchase lies in its ability to do this with my personal information. This is a process over which I have *no* control; therefore, the RALC model says that my privacy is being violated.

A similar morally objectionable technology is the **cookie**. We should think of cookies as packets of information—text files, really—that are generated by a website's server, sent to your browser when you are on that website, and then sent back to the website's server.[9] Imagine that you are on Amazon's site: the server generates a cookie, sends it to your browser, and then your browser sends it back. When they are sent to your browser, cookies collect information. This information allows how sites such as Amazon and Facebook are able to tailor advertisements to you based on your browsing history. Of course, e-commerce sites have access to other information too. Amazon can look at how many science-fiction books you have ordered on Amazon in the past, for instance.

The underlying technology of the internet is anonymous. The TCP/IP is the chief communication protocol around which the internet is organized, and it is anonymous. The early days of the internet were marked by pervasive anonymity. Cookies are the technology that changed that fact. Cookies let sites track you and learn about your browsing history. They go hand in hand with data mining because there is a real financial incentive to use cookies. Meta wants to sell space on their apps to advertisers. Meta *could* take what we might call the "billboard approach": showing the same advertisement to everyone who uses the Facebook app. On the other hand, Meta could use cookies to determine who has a browsing history of looking for furniture to buy, and then show advertisements for furniture stores to *fewer* Facebook users but ensure that they are *highly interested* users. This is an example of how Facebook uses cookies to increase the value of the advertisement space on their own app, but companies also collect data in cookies and then simply sell that data to third-party buyers.

The RALC model objects to cookies in pretty much the same ways that it objects to data mining. Much of the time, we are not asked for our consent at all. Thanks to the General Data Protection Regulation (GDPR) in Europe, users are now sometimes greeted with a pop-up on websites that asks for permission for that site to use cookies. The RALC model approves of the gesture, but there is no meaningful kind of *informed* consent. Many users agree without even knowing what a cookie is. (Imagine if a surgeon considered it informed consent when a patient agreed to a surgery without the surgeon explaining even the basics.) If users want to educate themselves, websites will sometimes have a policy concerning cookies that is available for reading. When we read the policies, we see that they contain virtually none of the information that we would reasonably want included. Too often, we find boilerplate sentences of the form "We use cookies to provide you with more relevant advertisements." They do not even tell us what information is being collected. Again, imagine if a hospital did that with our medical information.

Sometimes, people assume that by reading the terms and conditions of use, they will be fully informed. This is a deeply implausible view of informed consent. First, keep in mind the medical analogy: we would object if a doctor, trying to get our informed consent, gave us a medical textbook to read. Second, the terms and conditions are often designed to *discourage* us from reading them: they are filled with technical and legal vocabulary that non-experts do not understand. Again, in medical settings, we expect that doctors will make their reasoning transparent to the patients, whereas online terms and conditions of use are often designed to be opaque.

The most prominent reason why the terms and conditions of use cannot provide someone with the information required for informed consent is what I have been alluding to for some time now: companies lie. None of the most egregious cases of privacy violations in the past decade would have been avoided if people had read the terms and conditions. Sometimes, companies lie by presenting a kind of half-truth. For instance, Meta claims that it does not sell user data. In a sense, that *is* true. Yet, Meta *does* let third-party apps access that data, which led to the Cambridge Analytica scandal in 2018, and Meta has ways of profiting from the data that it keeps and does not sell. In 2012, it was reported that Google had been tracking the browsing habits of people using Apple's Safari browser without consent; Google had claimed otherwise to users, saying that Safari's privacy settings would prevent this, but allegedly, they knew that the privacy settings would not and were exploiting that fact in order to get a clearer picture of people's browsing habits.[10] In 2023, Google settled a five-billion-dollar class-action lawsuit that alleged users were being tracked even when using Google's Chrome browser in so-called incognito mode after being misled into thinking otherwise.[11]

Sometimes, governments get in on the action too. For instance, in 2016, it was reported that AT&T had been selling users' information to local law-enforcement agencies. Taxpayer money was being spent to buy information that AT&T had been collecting and storing for years. Needless to say, this was not in the terms and conditions of use. In fact, the involved parties had gone to great lengths to ensure that this program was never discovered. Non-disclosure agreements were signed. Special devices were used so that defense lawyers and the public would never discover the program. It was agreed that court cases would be dropped if there was a chance that the program would be revealed in court.[12]

The RALC model would approve of none of this because it requires that access to our personal information be restricted and that we be given limited controls over the flow of personal information.

Many of the steps that could be taken to rectify this situation are easy. Corporate morality would be greatly improved if companies made the revelation of personal information something that we *opted in to* instead of making it the default, as is ubiquitous today. Similarly, if companies ask for our consent, they should say what information they want from us and why they want it. The RALC model has an important commitment that I have not yet had the chance to emphasize: *the onus is on the one who wants us to consent*. We should not have to do our own research. Doctors and hospital staff inform us and ask us for our consent. It completely subverts the nature of the relationship that we are accustomed to in medical contexts and elsewhere for a website to expect us to know what cookies are and what information of ours the cookies are collecting. Needless to say, in light of the examples just presented, *doing our own research* is futile in this environment where companies lie and hide important information.

As we conclude our look at the RALC model, let me clarify that there is nothing wrong with revealing personal information if that is what we choose to do. There may be reasons to reveal our personal information. For instance, it might lead to better e-commerce outcomes. Someone might grow weary of constantly being shown the same advertisement on YouTube for the same iPhone game when they are a college professor with no interest in iPhone games. I might want to have my browsing history tracked in order to show me advertisements more relevant to my life. There might even come a time when I am provided with a financial incentive for letting sites track me: they stand to make so much money from tracking me that *I* think I should get a slice of that pie in exchange for my consent. Now, that would really reflect a view of informed consent as shared decision-making.

## 2.3 The Contextual-Integrity (CI) Model

The first thing that needs to be said about the contextual-integrity (CI) model is that it is best seen not as a competitor to the RALC model but as a kind of partner.[13] We can appreciate the value of the CI model if we think of it as dealing with cases that feature individuals, whereas the RALC model works best in situations featuring surveillance, by which I mean large-scale data collection by companies and governments. This distinction might be rough and shaky in a few respects, but when we start going over some examples, it will be clearer that the CI model is valuable in cases that are different from data mining and cookies.

Whereas the RALC model enshrines notions of control and informed consent into what we consider respect for privacy, the CI model is built around the idea that privacy is valuable because it is crucial for our ability to manage and develop a variety of social relationships. The CI model says that no one rule that governs the flow of information and is meant to apply universally can be successful because what is acceptable and appropriate changes in each situation. Respecting privacy requires us to respect *contextual integrity*: the rules that are particular to each context. This dependence on context follows from what we find valuable about privacy: the fact that it is integral to the difference between our various relationships. After all, it is acceptable for my doctor to tell the radiologist about my medical status, but it is unacceptable for my mother to tell strangers about it. That is because the medical *context* is different from the situation with my mother.

The CI model says that there are different *kinds* of rules that vary from context to context. There are diverse CI models, but here we shall explore one of the earliest and most influential versions. This version says that there are **rules of** *appropriateness* and **rules of** *distribution*. Rules of appropriateness govern what types of information are appropriate or suitable to share in a certain context. For instance, it is appropriate for my doctor to tell my gastroenterologist about colon cancer in my family history in order that the gastroenterologist can try to detect colon cancer in me, but it is wrong for my doctor to share my HIV status. My HIV status is just not the sort of thing that my gastroenterologist needs to know. Now whether the divulgence of that information is appropriate depends on other features of the context that can quickly change. If it turns out, somehow, that HIV status *can* matter to the work done by the gastroenterologist, then it becomes appropriate to share that information.

This aspect of the CI model is meant to capture the sense that we permit other people to discuss us, but what they can share about us depends on the features of the context. When our parents go to the grocery store and run into a former neighbor, they might share information about how our careers are going, but we typically draw the line at letting them share information about how messy our divorce is. Of course, the CI model does not indicate that it is always wrong to share information about our divorce and always permissible to share information about our careers. We might, after all, be quite touchy and sensitive about our jobs, and we might have told our parents to stay silent about it. These are features of the context that determine the rules of appropriateness.

Then there are rules that govern the *distribution* of information. These are trickier to understand than the rules governing appropriateness. It may be that even if it is permitted to share information in a certain context, there are better or worse ways to go about it. This is what the rules of distribution tell us: *how* we should and should not spread information in a certain context and across certain contexts.

For example, let's say that a wife is talking to her friends about her sex life with her husband. Let's also assume that the rules of appropriateness in this context are such that she is not doing anything wrong. (There *are* contexts in which this might be wrong: perhaps she and her husband had discussed with their therapist that she was not allowed to discuss their sex life with her friends any longer.) However, let's further specify that she discusses it with her friends on a blog. This blog is not password-protected: anyone can stumble upon it, although she *intends* for it to be read only by her friends. She is allowed to discuss her sex life with her friends, but she is going about it in a way that violates the privacy of her husband. *His* personal information is being shared carelessly, and she thus violates the norms of distribution. Each of us can come up with more examples ourselves: just think about a hospital being careless with our medical information. We allow them to have that type of information, but we expect them to deal with it seriously.

The CI model objects to the way that social-media sites are set up with respect to privacy. This time, I do not mean the way that social-media companies collect and sell our data, although the CI model may object to those practices as well. Instead, I have in mind the way that social-media sites have no respect for differences between contexts. Our various relationships are crammed together: we talk to our colleagues, friends, family members, and strangers all at once whenever we post on X or Instagram. Apps that give us some way of restricting access to our profiles do a better job than apps that do not, but, even then, most often the sole

## 2. Models of Privacy

distinction is between those whom we have permitted to follow our accounts and those we have not. Social-media sites either give us no ability to restrict access to our media or they give us the ability to restrict access in a clumsy, ham-fisted way. (There is something funny about an app presenting us with the opportunity to restrict access to our media while also sharing that same information, and more, with third-party buyers.) These sites include nothing like the careful nuances of the contextual integrity of day-to-day life in which I would permit my parents to share information about my divorce in a grocery store with *this* neighbor but not *that* neighbor, and I would also want my parents to carefully moderate the volume of their voice. My parents might comply with the rule of appropriateness by sharing that information with the right neighbor but violate the rule of distribution by yelling it too loudly.

Respecting privacy is like walking a tightrope. The CI model objects to the tendency of social-media apps to blend every kind of social context. It is hard to think of any precedents in human history for this sort of disrespect for the contextual integrity of privacy: nothing seems similar in either the scope or ease with which information can be shared.

Consider the user interface of these apps from the point of view of the CI model. Of course, on the back end, there are egregious privacy-rights violations, but even on the front end, which is what users see when they post, there are problems. Sites are designed to obscure how many people we are talking to. Some sites even have generic post-to-everyone-with-an-internet-connection features that look identical to direct-messaging features. Even the phrase "I will post something on this subreddit" obscures the reality that the post can become shared in news articles around the world. We might be assured that we have the ability to delete that post, but the post can be archived on the internet forever.

An early episode in the internet's history, the Jennicam, illustrates the erosion of the thin lines between each context. In 1998, Jennifer Ringley set up webcams throughout her house and let people on the internet watch her 24/7 as she invented *life-streaming*. There were no boundaries: people could watch her eat, sleep, work, have sex, and so on. You can imagine how low-quality the streams were in the late 1990s, but even as technologically inferior as it was to today's streaming sites, we can see in the Jennicam the anticipation of reality television, social-media apps' glimpses into the personal lives of strangers, and Twitch streaming. (Twitch streaming today does place some limitations on what a person can stream: for instance, sleep-streaming was a fad at one point, but it was eventually banned on the grounds that streams should be interactive.) Whereas we might invite only very special people to glimpse into these parts of our lives, the Jennicam let complete strangers into intimate parts of her life.

This is why the CI model is better at talking about privacy among individuals, rather than among businesses and governments: there are subtleties to the relationships we have with particular individuals that we expect other people to attend to before they release our information. My often-used example of parents in the grocery store reflects this fact. We should not deny that the RALC model could similarly object to these practices, nor should we deny that the CI model could object to data mining, which violates both the rules of appropriateness, since third-party buyers should not have access to my personal information if I have not consented to that, and the rules of distribution, since backroom deals that companies want to keep secret are not the proper venues for facilitating the sharing of anyone's personal information. The most profitable way to interpret the CI model is simply as pointing out the distinction between the two kinds of rules and the way that they are context-dependent.

Here is an example that illustrates what the CI model does the best job of explaining. This case is particularly old by the internet's standards, since it happened in 2004, but is worth a look. This is the story of *The Washingtonienne* blog. The blog was used as a diary by a woman living and working in Washington, DC, as a staffer for a US senator. Many of her living expenses were paid for by various married men, including some who were government officials, in exchange for her romantic companionship. She posted about these things as a way of updating her friends on her life. She took no precautions to restrict access to the blog, but she used only initials to refer to the names of her lovers, and she never used her own name. Eventually, tabloids found the blog, and they discerned her identity and the identities of her lovers. The tabloids widely reported on the affairs.

The CI model says a few things about this case. First, the woman's privacy was not violated by the tabloids. This is an important aspect of the CI model: *you generally cannot violate your own privacy*. This is not the claim that it is impossible for someone to mislead you or manipulate you into violating your own privacy, which might be the case with the way that social-media apps' interfaces are designed in misleading ways. If a blog is not password-protected (or otherwise restricted), it is *not* inappropriate for anyone, including tabloids, to stumble upon it and report on its contents. The moral rules here change in accordance with the context: if the blog had been restricted, and the journalists discovered its contents by somehow hacking into it, then that would be a violation of the privacy of the blogger. Since that was not the case, the journalists did not wrong her by accessing and publicizing her blog.

Second, and in contrast, the privacy of the men *was* violated. She did not ask them for permission to share details about the affairs, and they were not even aware she was doing it. It might be permissible to share details of one's sex life with friends, but the rules of distribution were violated by the fact that she was so careless with identifying information. This reveals another aspect of the CI model: *the rules of distribution exist to protect third parties.* The men were morally entitled to have their personal information treated better because of considerations related to their autonomy. Again, the moral rules change with the circumstances: if the men had been informed and given permission to the blogger to post details about the affairs, their privacy would not have been violated.

I stress the first point—namely, that people generally cannot violate their own privacy—because it answers a question that was broached in section 1. Recall that I presented two cases: in the first, a couple is loudly arguing about their sex life and neighbors overhear them; in the second, a couple is arguing about their sex life but does not want to be overheard, so they move to the basement to do it. Someone else is using a device to listen to their conversation from afar. In the first case, their privacy is not violated; in the second case, it is. The distinction between the two cases is that in the second case, some reasonable steps are taken to protect privacy. Which steps need to be taken and which are reasonable vary with the context, but they also change the context itself. If I do not take reasonable steps to protect my privacy, then I may lose my privacy, without violation of anything that I am morally entitled to. Alternatively, when the couple is arguing about their sex life, if the man whispers in order to avoid being overheard, but the woman yells details about the man, we might think that the woman is violating the man's privacy. The rules of distribution are being violated.

*The Washingtonienne* blog case is old, but it has the outlines of more recent and familiar cases. Think about when a celebrity's phone is hacked and photos taken of them while naked circulate. These are generally cases in which the celebrity's privacy is violated, since their phones or the servers that store the photos are sufficiently well-protected. In these cases, we blame the hacker for penetrating strong defenses. There are times, however, when we come to learn that the servers are *not* well-protected: if Apple, Google, or some other company *says* to the celebrities that their images and photos are well-protected and that turns out not to be the case, then we might blame the company for failing to protect the celebrities' media adequately. If it turns out that the celebrities took no steps to protect their media, then we might not believe that a violation of privacy has occurred at all.

Lastly, this also explains the wrongness of **doxxing**—the practice in which a person's personal information—especially home address, phone number, and email address—is leaked online. Doxxing is wrong for many reasons, including the fact that it takes place most often as a way of intimidating someone; it can lead to the loss of feeling safe and even to physical harm. It is also a violation of a person's privacy because no rule governing the flow of the information permits revealing online a person's home address.

# 3. Conclusion

In section 1, we learned about different ways to justify the right to privacy. First, there is the fact that revealing someone else's personal information can lead to harm. Second, the right to privacy follows from our *autonomy*: our control over the flow of personal information allows us to manage a variety of social relationships. Third, there is the *simplifying hypothesis*: there is no right to privacy itself, but this right nevertheless exists as a cluster of other, simpler rights, such as the right for me to hide the property in my house from other people's view.

In section 2, we discussed three different approaches to respect for privacy. The first, the non-intrusion model, holds that respecting someone's privacy is a matter of leaving them alone. The second, the restricted access/limited control (RALC) model, holds that respecting someone's privacy is a matter of restricting access to some personal information and giving someone *limited* control over it. Finally, the contextual-integrity (CI) model holds that there are no universally applicable rules for respecting privacy, but the two kinds of rules that we ought to follow, which are the rules of appropriateness and rules of distribution, are different in different contexts. The RALC model captures the important idea that privacy requires control over the flow of information. The CI model captures the equally important idea that privacy is about managing different relationships.

In the course of this chapter, we discussed a variety of issues and technologies that we encounter online: doxxing, hacking, data mining, cookies, the poverty of the terms and conditions of use, and the fact that we are often lied to about what is happening with our personal information. I urge readers to consult the Discussion

Cases section, which examines specific scandals and examples, such as the Cambridge Analytica scandal, which I briefly mentioned a few times in this chapter.

# Key Terms

**Autonomy**: our capacity to determine the course of our lives. It is the capacity for self-determination. I can choose to become a football player, even though I know that doing so is bad for my health. If I am an adult with autonomy, then even though other people in my life might disapprove of my plan, they ought to respect it as *mine*. There are some conditions, usually illnesses, that can compromise our autonomy. This places decision-makers in a dilemma about how to treat someone who lacks autonomy, but these dilemmas tend to be the province of medical ethics, not the ethics of social media.

**CI model**: the contextual-integrity model of privacy articulates respect for privacy in terms of complying with rules that vary in accordance with features of the context, or a specific situation. The CI model denies that there are universally applicable rules that hold without reference to any context.

**Cookies**: packets of information, usually small text files, that are sent from a server (perhaps belonging to a website that you are on) to your browser, and then your browser sends it back to the server. The server is asking for information from your browser. What information it is asking for depends on the circumstance, but it usually *at least* includes your browser history. This is done so that the sender can show you tailored advertisements. Cookies are in large part responsible for the lack of anonymity on the internet, the underlying infrastructure of which is anonymous.

**Data mining**: the practice of extracting information or patterns of information from large sets of data. I might collect information from people about their age, level of education, and income level, but then I might *infer* from this set of data probabilities of political affiliation. The crucial point is that the inferred information is "new," such that even if I had people's permission to collect the first three pieces of information (which is a big "if"), it is not obvious that I am permitted to infer new information from that set.

**Doxxing**: the leaking of someone's personal information online. Usually, what is leaked is the victim's home address or some means of contacting the victim.

Doxxing is wrong for several reasons, not least of all the fact that it often leads to harm.

**Informed consent**: consent in general is the permission that we give other people to act on us. Consent has the ability to change what would be assault into tackling at a football match, to change what would be stealing into borrowing, and to change what would be rape into sex. However, the sort of consent that has this ability (and that is therefore morally relevant) is *informed consent*. How much information we need to know depends on the case, but we generally need to know at least enough to see how the thing that we are permitting fits into our plans for ourselves, such that our *autonomy* is respected.

**RALC model**: the restricted access/limited control model is an approach to privacy that respects people's privacy in terms of restricting access to personal information and gives people limited control over the flow of that information. These limited controls are *choice*, *consent*, and *correction*.

**Rules of appropriateness**: these govern the *types* of information that can be shared in a situation. For instance, medical information, but not romantic information, can be shared in medical contexts. This kind of rule is important to the CI model.

**Rules of distribution**: these govern how information should flow within and across contexts. For instance, in a medical context, it is appropriate to share medical information, but people who share a patient's information cannot leave the documents out in public spaces in the hospital; they need to be more careful with it. This kind of rule is important to the CI model.

**Simplifying hypothesis**: the view that the right to privacy itself does not exist independently of other rights. The right to privacy is a cluster of simpler rights. For instance, the reason why my right to privacy is violated when someone breaks into my house and snoops through my drawers is that I have a right to keep people who lack permission out of my house, I have a right to not have someone open my drawers without my permission, I have a right to not have people go through the contents of my drawers without my permission, and so on.

# Discussion Cases

## 1. Cambridge Analytica Scandal

In 2018, it was revealed that a political consulting firm, Cambridge Analytica, had used the This Is Your Digital Life app to build psychological profiles of internet users. The profiles were built using data collected from Facebook accounts. Hundreds of thousands of users were asked to complete an informed-consent form. The informed-consent form specified that the data being collected would be used only for academic purposes. That turned out to be untrue.

In reality, This Is Your Digital Life was collecting data from everyone who consented *and* the friends of everyone who consented, even though the friends themselves had not consented. This was facilitated by Facebook's software, which, at least at the time, allowed apps to procure information from both a user and that user's friends. In the end, while hundreds of thousands completed their informed-consent form, up to 87 million people had their data collected. Plus, the data was being sold by Cambridge Analytica to the 2016 election campaigns of both Donald Trump and Texas senator Ted Cruz. There are allegations that the firm also had a hand in the Brexit referendum campaign, but evidence concerning this point is inconclusive. The personal information was used to show people tailored political advertisements, among other things.

The revelations that people's personal information had been collected in this manner and for political purposes sparked a political firestorm in the Western world. Meta, which at the time was called Facebook, was fined in both the United States and the United Kingdom, and Cambridge Analytica declared bankruptcy.

Thinking about this case, what exactly was the wrong done to people whose data had been collected? To what extent is the wrong owed to the fact that the data was used to support various political campaigns? Are there any causes or movements that would justify or warrant the use of personal information in this way? Or is what Cambridge Analytica did wrong in all circumstances?

## 2. Plane-Tracking Information

In 2020, a nineteen-year-old user of what was then called Twitter began to track the location of Elon Musk's private plane. He would then post the location of the plane on virtually every major social-media site, including Facebook and Instagram. This practice surely shares at least some of the hallmarks of doxxing, and Elon Musk did not like this exposure of his personal information at all. He offered $5,000 to the user to stop posting it. Eventually, when Musk purchased Twitter, he banned the user before ultimately overturning the ban. He opted to change Twitter's rules, such that no one can post another person's real-time location. The user then pivoted to posting the location of the plane after a twenty-four-hour delay.

One crucial difference between this practice and doxxing is that the location of all air traffic is public. If a plane uses a transponder, anyone can discover its real-time location. Communication among air-traffic controllers is not encrypted. Musk said that the information that was being shared was "basically assassination coordinates," highlighting the perceived security risk. Another important consideration is that Musk himself was not being tracked; only the plane was. There is no way for someone to know who is in the plane, whether Musk, a family member, or someone else entirely.

Is it wrong to share information about the plane's location? What difference does it make that the information is publicly available? Is it wrong to make publicly available information even easier to access, when there are the same sorts of security risks involved as are involved in doxxing? What if someone used this information not to track Musk but to track one of his young children?

## 3. Celebrities' Phone Hack

In 2014, the private photos of nearly five hundred celebrities, most of whom were female, were leaked online. Many of these photos were sexual in nature, and none of them were intended for a public audience. The photos were obtained from Apple's iCloud service. There are competing theories about how the hackers obtained the photos, but Apple has claimed that they did so through a phishing attack. The scale of the attack was unprecedented.

Just as unprecedented was what the hackers did after: the leaked photos were widely distributed online, especially on Reddit.

What are the wrongs involved in hacking the phones of celebrities? What are the wrongs involved in posting the photos on Reddit? Is it wrong for us to look at the leaked photo of a naked celebrity, even if we were not involved in the actual hacking?

## 4. Sharenting

It seems to be a rite of passage for new parents to engage in *sharenting*. It is a way of announcing to the world that you have a new child. To sharent is to create on social-media sites a presence for your child. Usually, the term "sharenting" is associated with routine oversharing of personal information about the new bundle of joy. Sharenting can range from simply posting a lot of photos of your child to developing an entire social-media business about your child: some children on YouTube, for instance, have more than thirty million subscribers. Sharenting began to really take off during the COVID-19 pandemic, which was predictable: parents wanted to share updates and media with family and friends who could not see and play with the child in person.

That description makes sharenting sound harmless and new. Yet, sharenting has been around since the earliest days of social-media sites, and now that some of the first children to have had social-media presences have grown up, they do not agree that the practice is harmless. Many feel exploited, and many feel they have never had any privacy, even from the moment that they first came home from the hospital. For years, everything from their diapers to their eating habits was published online. When we consider the YouTube stars in particular, it is hard not to see a new kind of child actor. Perhaps these children will turn out better due to the fact that it is often their parents who run the show, rather than studio executives. Perhaps that could make it worse. Only time will tell.

Newborns cannot consent to the creation of Instagram accounts that exist to share photos of them. Usually, when someone cannot consent on account of their young age, we defer to their parents' judgments. Does this give parents the license to do whatever they please with respect to their child's privacy and social-media presence? How should parents balance the well-meant desire to keep far-flung relatives and friends involved in the child's life with the fact that some respect for the child's privacy is likely morally required? Bear in mind that it is nearly impossible to delete anything from the internet, and companies are collecting the child's data just as much as they are collecting the parents'.

## 5. Taylor Swift

In 2024, the *New York Times* published an opinion piece that argued that Taylor Swift was secretly a lesbian and had been hiding clues hinting at her true sexual orientation for years. The author was not alone in this: the internet hosts countless so-called Gaylors who maintain that, despite all outward appearances to the contrary, Swift is a lesbian. Shortly afterward, a source close to Swift reported to the media her displeasure about her sexual orientation being the object of public discussion: "there seems to be no boundary some journalists won't cross when writing about Taylor, regardless of how invasive, untrue, and inappropriate it is."[14]

Speculating about someone's sexual orientation will strike many people as a violation of privacy, but is it? If privacy is related to the flow of personal information, and to the extent that speculation does not reveal any personal information but involves mere conjecture and discussion about possible personal information, is it wrong? If Taylor Swift is right that it is inappropriate to speculate about her sexual orientation, what makes it so?

# Further Reading

Auxier, Brooke, Lee Rainie, Monica Anderson, Andrew Perrin, Madhu Kumar, and Eric Turner. 2019. "Americans and Privacy: Concerned, Confused and Feeling Lack of Control Over Their Personal Information." Pew Research Center, November 15, 2019. https://www.pewresearch.org/internet/2019/11/15/americans-and-privacy-concerned-confused-and-feeling-lack-of-control-over-their-personal-information/.

## Further Reading

This research by Pew is the source of the claims in section 1 concerning how people today feel about data: they generally report a lack of control over the collection of their information, a lack of understanding of how the information is being used, and a sense of concern regarding the collection of information. The exact percentages vary depending on whether the questions being asked are about the government or about businesses, but in either case, a majority of respondents give the same answers in both cases.

Grodzinsky, Frances, and Herman Tavani. 2010. "Applying the 'Contextual Integrity' Model of Privacy to Personal Blogs in the Blogosphere." *International Journal of Internet Research Ethics* 3: 39–47.

Grodzinsky and Tavani shine some helpful light on the CI model of privacy here, and they do so by applying it to particular cases involving blogs. (*The Washingtonienne* example, discussed in section 2.3 of this chapter, is included in their survey.)

Rachels, James. 1975. "Why Privacy Is Important." *Philosophy and Public Affairs* 4 (4): 323–33.

There is perhaps no article on privacy in the past one hundred years that has been more influential than this paper by Rachels. He defends the right to privacy on the grounds that it is essential for our maintenance of a variety of social relationships. He begins the article much like I begin this chapter: by surveying the ways that violations of privacy can lead to harm. Yet, his autonomy-based argument for privacy claims that privacy ought to be respected even when we have nothing to hide.

Spinello, Richard A. 2011. "Privacy and Social Networking Technology." *International Review of Information Ethics* 16 (12): 41–46.

Spinello applies the RALC model of privacy to cookies. That is sufficient reason alone to read this article, but he also concisely explains much about the basic technologies that privacy advocates take issue with, and he proposes some feasible solutions.

Tavani, Herman. 2007. "Philosophical Theories of Privacy: Implications for an Adequate Online Privacy Policy." *Metaphilosophy* 38 (1): 1–22.

I recommend this text for three reasons. First, Tavani does a great job surveying different theories of privacy, including some that are not discussed here. Second, he explains the RALC model, both on its terms and as a synthesis of the strengths of preceding models that also avoids the shortcomings of earlier theories. Third, he applies the RALC model to particular cases, such as data-mining practices.

Thomson, Judith Jarvis. 1975. "The Right to Privacy." *Philosophy and Public Affairs* 4 (4): 295–314.

Thomson defends the *simplifying hypothesis* with respect to privacy. She argues that it is impossible to understand what privacy is unless we understand the right to privacy as a cluster of other, simpler rights. She thinks that the right to privacy is violated by someone going through my drawers because a cluster of other rights, such as my right that no one should go through my things without my permission, is violated. These other rights are "un-grand," as she puts it, but they are the basis of the right to privacy.

Warren, Samuel, and Louis Brandeis. 1890. "The Right to Privacy." *Harvard Law Review* 4 (5): 193–220.

This nineteenth-century article, apparently written less by Warren and more by Brandeis, who later became a justice on the US Supreme Court, is deeply influential. The view, developed in the article, of the right to privacy as the right to be left (or "let") alone reverberated through the American legal scene, surely owing in large part to the fact that Brandeis used this conception of privacy when writing opinions as a justice, and through the philosophical literature, eventually transforming into what we now call the *non-intrusion* model of privacy.

Woolf, Nicky. 2016. "Documents Show AT&T Secretly Sells Customer Data to Law Enforcement," *Guardian*, October 25, 2016. https://www.theguardian.com/business/2016/oct/25/att-secretly-sells-customer-data-law-enforcement-hemisphere.

In section 2.2 of this chapter, I discussed cases in which a company keeps it secret from users how their data is collected and sold. I highlighted this case in which AT&T sold data to law-enforcement agencies and went to extraordinary means to conceal that fact, preferring to lose court cases rather than disclose the existence of these transactions. This case reveals a lot, but one aspect that I emphasize is that even people who go through extraordinary means to discover what happens to their personal information, such as by reading the terms and conditions of use, still might not discover the truth.

## Notes

1. See Johnson 2010.
2. The arguments in this section are influenced most of all by Rachels 1975 and Thomson 1975.
3. Rachels 1975 is responsible for this argument (i.e., the pro-autonomy, social-relationships view).
4. Thomson 1975 is responsible for the simplifying hypothesis.
5. See Auxier et al. 2019.
6. See Warren and Brandeis 1890.
7. I owe my presentation of the RALC model here to Tavani 2007.
8. See Cadwalladr and Graham-Harrison 2018.
9. See Spinello 2011 for more about the ethical issues surrounding cookies.
10. See Arthur 2012.
11. See Associated Press 2023.
12. See Woolf 2016.
13. I owe my presentation of the CI model here to Grodzinsky and Tavani 2010.
14. White 2024.

# Chapter Two: The Attention Economy

Virtually everyone agrees that morality demands *some* limitations on markets. Perhaps there should be limitations on the markets for sex, guns, drugs, and votes in a democracy. Even someone who denied that there should be constraints on those markets most likely would agree that there should not be an unfettered market for nuclear weapons. The harder questions are what the constraints on any given market should look like and what morally justifies those constraints. These questions form the **problem of the moral limits of markets**. When we consider this problem in terms of the ethics of social media, we talk about the buying and selling of attention: how social-media apps get our attention, retain it, and auction it off. This is what we call the **attention economy**, and it is the focus of this chapter.

There are two kinds of transactions at the heart of the attention economy. The first features users accessing a site or app in exchange for their attention. For example, I access Facebook and see the media posted there, and in exchange I give Meta my attention. The second kind of transaction features the owners of the site or app auctioning off consumers' attention to an advertiser. For instance, once Meta has secured my attention on the Facebook app, it can charge advertisers for the opportunity to present their product or service to me on the app. Meta possesses, for all intents and purposes, a billboard. Meta has made Facebook into a place where many people want to be, and the cost of our being there is that we have to look at this billboard. The more people who want to be there, the more lucrative Meta's billboard space becomes.

This gives the companies in the attention economy—whom we call **attention merchants**—an incentive to capture as much attention as possible. Many readers of this book will be familiar with the experience that I have in mind: knowing that you should sleep or get to work on some project but are instead scrolling mindlessly on TikTok, or perhaps scrolling on Instagram, closing the app, and then re-opening it a second later as if you had not just been on the app. Attention merchants produce these behaviors, and our attention is the commodity that they trade in.

This chapter is about the attention economy and its moral risks. The first section discusses the problem of the moral limits of markets, and the two sections that follow discuss addictions and distractions. Then, we discuss three possible responses to the harms of the attention economy. We shall conclude by briefly surveying some good things about the attention economy.

# 1. A Noxious Market

**Markets** are valuable social institutions, generally governing the exchange of goods and services. As was said in the brief introduction to this chapter, virtually everyone supports *some* constraints on markets. The hard question is figuring out which markets should be limited and why. Before we tackle that question, it is helpful to think about what makes markets valuable institutions in the first place.[1]

First, markets efficiently distribute goods. This is not to say that markets never fail or are always perfect. (After all, this chapter is about the limitations of markets.) Yet, markets, by and large, do a good job of distributing goods between people, even though they do not coordinate with each other. The crucial bit of information that markets are responding to is the *price* of the goods that they are trading. The price acts as a signal that reveals how high the demand is: I take my goods to where the demand is the highest because that is where I can charge the highest price. Given enough time, the price lowers because more people have responded to this signal and have flooded the market with the product being sold. The lower price is itself a signal, telling people that there is now less of a demand, proportional to the supply, for the product. Again, this is not to say that markets always do this in ways that we like, but it is hard to design a better system for getting goods where they should go.

Markets do this in a way that preserves and promotes freedom. This is the second reason why they are valuable institutions. We *could* coerce people to send goods where we think that they should go, but this system might not be terribly efficient: the number of variables that we would have to wrangle makes it almost impossible. Even if we could pull it off, the coercion itself would count against it, since markets are an alternative that allow people to make decisions freely. Markets are an important *part* of freedom because the list of liberties that we enjoy in many parts of the world includes the freedom to engage in transactions as we see fit, to work where we see fit, and to consume and produce as we see fit.

## 1. A Noxious Market

Throughout human history, ordinary people have been denied these freedoms, but markets help us hold on to them. Markets promote freedom too: they help us develop our capacities to choose. Those who live in market economies are always choosing and being prompted to reflect on how their choices align with their values. Moreover, because markets distribute goods without any centralized decision-making, there is much less opportunity for abuse of power. Imagine if one company controlled the *entire* supply chain for computers. That one company could get away with egregious behavior much more easily than if the company controlled only a sliver of the supply chain. Decentralized decision-making has real benefits.

However, markets clearly need some limits. Ethicists consider all sorts of candidates for markets that need to be constrained: markets for organs, sex, drugs, human beings, guns, and so on. Markets that should be constrained are called **noxious**. The word "noxious" reflects the fact that these markets undermine some of the values that we just stressed, such as freedom and efficiency. If these are the things that make markets valuable, and if some particular market undermines these values, then it stands to reason that the market should be constrained. Agreeing that the market should be constrained does not require thinking that it needs to be banned outright. There are debates about this sort of thing all the time: if society agrees that some drugs are bad but thinks that criminalizing them is *worse* than legalizing them, perhaps that market can be better managed with some judicious restrictions. Figuring out what regulations should be put on cigarettes is a great example. Some jurisdictions are satisfied with warnings on packages and with age restrictions, but others are debating banning cigarette sales altogether for people born after a certain date in an effort to have an entire cigarette-free generation.

Philosophers have developed multiple criteria for defining what is noxious. Here, I shall survey only three:

1. A noxious market produces extremely harmful outcomes for society.
2. A noxious market produces extremely harmful outcomes for some individuals.
3. A noxious market is characterized by a low level of knowledge.

To be noxious, a market does not have to satisfy all three of these criteria. Our assessment of a market can be mixed: it can strike us as noxious in some respects but not others. The attention economy satisfies all three of these criteria.

The first thing that can qualify a market as noxious is that it produces extremely harmful outcomes for society. Small harms produce no reaction from people or perhaps a reaction only from some people, but extreme harms produce a strong reaction from virtually everyone. An example of a market that satisfies this criterion: selling votes in a democracy. Such a market has to be constrained to protect democratic processes and institutions. Politicians ought to get elected by campaigning on and then implementing policies that the majority of voters support. A market for votes undermines this. Imagine a politician who wants to pursue an extreme agenda that only a few lobbyists support: the lobbyists could simply pay voters to vote for this politician. Such a market is a recipe for bad outcomes.

The attention economy also satisfies this criterion. Consider two examples that this book discusses at great length: echo chambers and misinformation (Chapters 4 and 5). Online echo chambers are communities in which users see only opinions that they agree with and in which opposing views are actively discredited. Attention merchants have an incentive to sort people into echo chambers and keep them there. People like being in echo chambers because it means that they are never confronted with anything that they disagree with, and they get to experience the unique kind of pleasure that comes from repeatedly having their own views confirmed. Showing people content that they like is a tried-and-true technique in the attention economy. Showing people content that they dislike is a good way to drive people to some other platform where they can see only things that they like. Social-media companies do not want to tackle the misinformation that proliferates on their sites for similar reasons: it attracts and retains the attention of users.

Both misinformation and echo chambers are explored in their own chapters, but here we can make the point briefly: they are bad for society. Democratic processes require that citizens be informed about the world so that they can assess the policies proposed by politicians appropriately and in accordance with their values. If Ria cares about the environment but believes that climate change is a hoax perpetrated by a foreign government, she will vote for politicians who do not believe in climate change and, therefore, against her own values. If I am stuck in my own echo chamber, surrounded only by people who agree with me, it will be difficult for many politicians to reach me and try to persuade me to vote for them. They will not even get to make a pitch to me about how they might improve my life. Attention merchants have a real incentive to encourage the growth of these problems because they increase their bottom-line profits, even at the expense of the health of society.

The second criterion is that a noxious market produces extreme harms for individuals. The market for cigarettes is a clear example. The many regulations on cigarettes are justified due to the harm that cigarettes do to their users. People sometimes debate whether there should be a special tax on extra-large sugary beverages for the same reason. Social-media use has the same kinds of problems. We do not need to look far to identify them: misinformation and echo chambers, which we just discussed, are two examples. Misinformation about, say, vaccinations or some health treatment can be so harmful that it leads to people dying. Other misinformation can defame the person that it is about. A pro-anorexia echo chamber might keep someone hooked and attentive to a social-media platform, but it is terrible for that person's health. Some echo chambers have such a strong grip on their members that they can cause people to become estranged from their friends and family.

As for the third criterion, the attention economy is characterized by a low level of knowledge. Imagine yourself buying a ticket to ride on the maiden voyage of the *Titanic*. You have an option to buy a ticket that comes with access to a lifeboat if it is necessary *or* you can pay less to buy a ticket without such access. As you deliberate, you are constantly reassured that the *Titanic* is unsinkable. Consequently, you are not properly informed about the product that you are considering purchasing, since the odds of the *Titanic* sinking bear directly on your decision of which ticket to purchase. Something similar happens in the attention economy, where we are not properly informed about the risks. Attention merchants have an incentive to keep us uninformed, since knowing the risks might discourage us from using their platforms as much as we do. The most obvious risk concerns violations of our privacy. I detailed some of these cases in Chapter 1: how social-media companies violate our privacy is often *completely opaque* to users, and they often outright lie about what they are doing, sometimes going to great lengths to obscure their actions. These obfuscations are particularly objectionable when the data being collected is used against us, just like when buying a lifeboat-free ticket to an allegedly unsinkable ship leads to our drowning. Still, something is wrong about this even when no harm actually occurs: it is objectionable for a market to be built on limiting our knowledge. After all, one virtue of markets is that they promote our freedom and capacity to choose. These things are frustrated by deception and obfuscation.

The violation of privacy is only one example of a risk that we are uninformed about. Different demographics face different risks. Children often have no knowledge of just how bad social-media apps are for them. In Chapter 3, I will discuss at greater length the way that Meta knowingly showed eating-disorder content to young girls on Instagram. Young girls would search for something related to health and fitness, perhaps how to do a pull-up, and find themselves sucked into pro-anorexia content. Broader society is gaining awareness of these threats, but young children often have no experience with these topics until they learn about them online. The same is true with inadvertent exposure to pornography online.

Some of these problems do not need to be resolved by banning the market. Later in this chapter, I will discuss different approaches to the noxiousness of the attention economy. One such approach is to include warnings that resemble those found on cigarette packages today.

## 2. Addictions

One popular argument against the attention economy is that it produces addictions to social media and that this is wrong.[2] I have put a helpful article on the subject of social-media addiction in the Further Reading section at the end of the chapter for readers to pursue this thorny and vexed topic. For the purposes of this section, I rely on the reader's own experience of having felt the *pull* of social-media platforms and having spent considerable time mindlessly scrolling.

These addictions are harmful. There is research showing that internet addiction in general is bad for a student's academic performance.[3] There is also research showing that it is bad for a person's performance at work.[4] Research on social-media addictions in particular illustrates that the more time someone spends on Facebook, the unhappier he or she is.[5] Another study showed that adolescents became more depressed when they spent more time on social-media apps.[6]

The more time that we spend on social-media platforms, the less time that we can spend studying, working, or doing other important things such as deepening our personal relationships. Here is the heart of the problem: the algorithms that social-media platforms use to capture more and more of our attention *adapt* dynamically to our own behavior and perceived preferences. It is not the same as movie producers making a film that they think people will like. This is a technology that discerns what people like and then changes as we use it in order to become more addictive, making it much harder to quit in the process. This adds insult to injury: the injury is all the harm that social-media addictions cause; the insult is that the companies make us part of the source of the addiction, to the extent that our own data—for instance, concerning what videos we tend to click on the most—is used to keep us addicted.[7] This insult is demeaning in the sense that it suggests that our well-being does not matter and that our preferences can be tracked and used against us.

Now combine these considerations with the fact that the internet is such an important part of twenty-first-century life that it is almost inescapable. Many of the internet's services are trying to addict us by means of our own preferences. In light of the way that we *need* the internet to function in modern society, people are vulnerable to attempts by attention merchants to hook us. This means that the behavior of the attention merchants rises to the level of what philosophers call **exploitation**. One plausible definition of exploitation is the following: "to exploit someone or something is to make use of him, her, or it for your own ends by playing on some weakness or vulnerability in the object of your exploitation."[8] Addicts are always vulnerable on account of their addiction, but even people who are able to resist the addiction are vulnerable in another sense: the internet is of the utmost importance to twenty-first-century life, and the more we use it, the more it learns how to hook us. We are always at risk of addiction. Contrast this with another addictive behavior such as gambling: it is possible to avoid putting oneself at risk of gambling addictions because gambling itself can be avoided.

The underlying business model of the attention economy is based on addicting users. If I buy a pack of cigarettes and then throw it out, the cigarette companies do not care; their revenue is not affected. Of course, in reality, addictions are an important part of their source of revenue, but in principle, at least, whether the consumers are addicted is incidental. The attention economy is different, however. If you have a Facebook account you never use, Meta does not make money from you. Meta needs you to actively *use* Facebook and use it as much as possible. The cigarette companies do not need you to use their product. Meta, therefore, has a different incentive than cigarette companies: Meta has an incentive to do whatever it takes to get you to spend as much time looking at advertisements as possible. That includes producing an addiction.

## 3. Distractions

Another objection to the attention economy is based on the idea that we have a right to our own attention.[9] The **right to attention** is our right to direct our attention as we see fit, and it implies another right: the right to be free from distractions on the grounds that distractions are attempts to direct our attention to something other than what we have chosen.[10] If these rights exist, then the attention economy is objectionable because it violates our right to not be distracted. We own our attention, and it is wrong to wrest control of it from us.

The argument for the right to attention is based on the right to mental integrity.[11] It is not particularly controversial to say that we have a right to *bodily* integrity: this means that it is wrong for other people to interfere with our bodies without our consent. The right to bodily integrity implies a right to mental integrity. This is true for a few reasons. The first is that the same considerations that speak in favor of the right to bodily integrity speak in favor of the right to mental integrity. For instance, we own ourselves. The fact that I own myself is why I have a right to my body, at least as much as I have a right to everything else I own, and if I own my body, then I certainly own my mind too.

Another reason is that recognizing the right to bodily integrity protects things that we consider important in just the same way that recognizing the right to mental integrity does. One such protected thing is *autonomy*, which I explained in Chapter 1 as the capacity to determine and plan our lives. If I want to go for a walk because that fits with my values, it is wrong for someone to pin me down to stop me from walking. Protecting people from bodily interference is a way of protecting autonomy. Along the same lines, protecting people from mental interference also protects their autonomy. After all, many of my plans for my life might involve thinking about something. If I want to think about the philosophy book that I am writing, and Sally and Maila keep distracting me, then they are interfering with my plan for my life. Both our attention and our bodies are crucial for our plans in life.

Our right to mental integrity requires that people be able to direct their attention as they see fit without interference from others. The moral problem with the attention economy is that it flagrantly violates our rights by auctioning off something that we are entitled to and own. Attention merchants, like everyone else, have a duty to not interfere with our attention. Furthermore, the attention economy harms us by actively undermining our own interests, since each one of us has access to good things in the world by attending to them. So, there is an opportunity cost as well: our attention that *could be* spent on the things that we value ends up being spent elsewhere. Then, there are *also* the harms that follow from whatever thing the attention merchants want us to focus on. For instance, if they want me to focus on negative news stories because these retain my attention efficiently, I might end up depressed about the apparent state of the world. These problems are in addition to the simple fact that one of our rights has been violated.

In plain terms, the attention economy causes us to perhaps spend whole days doing not much more than scrolling idly on our phones. Our values might lie elsewhere, but we are being distracted. This is harmful to us, but it also violates our rights.

This does not mean that every distraction is morally objectionable. When we drive down the street, we might face all sorts of distractions, but only in rare cases is any one of them morally objectionable. The difference between that case and the attention economy is that, first, almost nobody is *trying* to distract drivers. Someone might be walking a cute dog down the street, where a driver must focus on the road rather than the cuteness, but if someone is actively trying to distract drivers, it is easy to maintain that that is wrong because of the risks involved. Another difference is that attention merchants employ **supernormal stimuli**.[12] We call a stimulus supernormal when it takes advantage of instincts by providing us with things that are more attractive than what that instinct evolved for. Many ultra-processed foods do this: they bombard us with tastes that we evolved to seek but they do so at levels and in combinations that far surpass what was possible in our evolutionary history. When we are scrolling online, we are bombarded by persistent and constant supernormal stimuli, such as colors and sounds that grab our attention with a freakish level of efficiency. Anyone who has ever watched hours of video content on TikTok knows the way that the creators of such apps have designed things around our powerful attraction to novelty in short bursts.

# 4. Solutions

If we are convinced that the attention economy is a noxious market, then there are at least three approaches that we can take in response.

The first relies on **social antibodies**.[13] A social antibody is a kind of defense against harmful social behaviors and practices. Some bad behaviors can proliferate in society in ways that make us label them *social contagions*. Teachers and students have observed that when one student pulls out his or her phone in class, other students follow suit. Others see the first student do it, and it triggers the thought that perhaps there is something exciting or stimulating they could see if they checked their phone. Note that this behavior is contagious even though nobody has *forced* the other students to follow along or even applied any social pressure. A social antibody is a remedy for such social contagions.

Social antibodies make some bad behaviors taboo, such that undesirable behaviors become less common and less damaging to society. A ready example involves norms that Western societies have developed surrounding alcohol consumption. For instance, people do not generally drink alcohol early in the morning, unless there is some special circumstance such as having mimosas at brunch. There is a similar norm about not drinking alcohol when one is alone. It is important to note that these are not *laws*. They are not even enforced by anyone in particular. They are just taboos that have been created by society in response to possible problems with excess alcohol consumption. That is what makes them social antibodies. Society develops solutions spontaneously: this does not mean that the solutions come on the scene suddenly, but rather, that there is no top-down coordination.

If you believe that we should respond to the harms of the attention economy by means of social antibodies, then you believe that society will produce a solution on its own without any top-down coordination, such as by the government or by corporations. Possible solutions involve teachers developing practices that keep students off their phones, as well as parents giving social-media access to their children later in life. Fundamentally, the attention economy will remain intact but it will do less damage.

At one level, the point about social antibodies is uncontroversial. They clearly exist, and they are powerful tools for limiting certain bad behaviors. Some skepticism about their ability to handle the harms of the attention economy is warranted, however. Social-media technologies are changing rapidly, and the earlier parts of this chapter catalog the way that the attention economy is a kind of race to the bottom. Companies are competing more and more viciously for a dismally limited resource: our attention. (The next chapter of this book, on nudging, will detail the way that they are mining behavioral psychology to achieve such goals.) The social antibodies concerning alcohol consumption derive their effectiveness in large part from the fact that alcohol and its dangers have not changed much in centuries. Ten years ago, the social-media landscape and its dangers looked vastly different from how they look now. If, ten years from now, the technology has stagnated, then perhaps social antibodies will have a chance. Yet, it seems that innovation is *speeding up*, not slowing down. New social-media technologies and features are added every year. This invites much doubt about whether society can

## 4. Solutions

create social antibodies quickly enough to combat each new threat. The fact that social antibodies are not generated by top-down coordination makes it less likely that they will be dynamic enough to adapt to new threats with sufficient speed.

The second approach to the harms of the attention economy is **coercive paternalism**. This view has all the top-down coordination that the previous approach lacked. In general, the term "paternalism" refers to interventions in someone's decision-making to promote what is good for that person. Coercive paternalists believe that it is permissible to use coercive methods, such as force, to prevent people from choosing what is bad for them or to ensure that they choose what is good for them. During the COVID-19 pandemic, many jurisdictions required that residents get the COVID-19 vaccine to enter some spaces. This was an example of coercive paternalism to the extent that the state used force to intervene in people's medical decision-making for their own good. Now, sometimes such policies were justified on the grounds that it was good not only for vaccinated individuals but also for everyone else around them. This is no longer paternalism. Paternalistic justifications involve our interventions in *your* decision for *your* own good. Sometimes, the policy in question might be justified by multiple considerations, such as that it is good for you and for other people, but the justification is paternalistic only in virtue of the first consideration.

Laws that require people to wear helmets while biking or seatbelts while driving are examples of coercive paternalism. They use coercion to the extent that the government relies on the use of force to support its punishments. In the case of the attention economy, we can imagine several possible coercive-paternalist measures. One would be to ban the sorts of transactions that characterize the industry altogether: prevent companies from auctioning off users' attention. If the government decided to target only some harms of the attention economy, it could ban young people from social-media platforms. There are other measures that fall in between those examples, such as preventing people from being on social media for more than some defined amount of time.

The opposition to coercive paternalism mostly comes from concerns about coercion. It is not obviously justifiable to use force to prevent people from doing what *they* think is good for themselves, even if other people disagree. It is a hallmark of liberal democracies that people are free to pursue their own conception of a good life without much intervention.

Still, the coercive paternalist relies a lot on precedents. We ban all sorts of transactions and intervene in virtually every single market that exists: every jurisdiction bans the selling of *some* weapons, and many countries ban the selling of sex. People might well be aghast at the thought of poor people selling their own organs, even when doing so would help pull themselves out of poverty and even in light of the fact that people own their own bodies; yet, the market for organs is banned too. Coercive intervention in the attention economy would hardly be unprecedented.

For people who are unsure about the use of coercion but are persuaded by paternalistic considerations, there is the third possible response to the attention economy: **libertarian paternalism.** There will be a thorough discussion of this view in the next chapter, but libertarian paternalism is paternalistic in the same way as coercive paternalism, but libertarian paternalists balk at coercion. Instead, they believe that we are morally required to respect people's freedoms and therefore should not intervene in anyone's choices, which is what we do when we use force to ban certain markets. Rather, we should be paternalistic by changing the context in which a choice is made to make it likelier that people will choose what is good for them, while also keeping it easy to defy the changes that we make to the context. As an example, we might disable social-media notifications by default. Users can still opt in to receiving notifications from TikTok or Snapchat, but by default, notifications that grab our attention and pull us back in should be disabled.

In the next chapter, I discuss the evidence concerning just how powerful these changes to the context can be, but examples of this sort of thing are easy to provide. When you go to pay at a restaurant, you receive some tipping options on the screen: 18 percent, 20 percent, 22 percent, and a custom option. Libertarian paternalists recognize that you are being nudged to choose a tip of at least 18 percent because the device makes that the easiest, go-to option for you. It is possible to defy this nudge if you really would prefer to give a 15 percent tip, but the nudge is still there. When grocery stores put chocolates at checkout areas, a similar change is being made to the context of your purchase choices: we are nudged toward buying a candy bar because the candy bars are placed somewhere that we have to visit in the store and where we have to spend some time.

Libertarian paternalists think that it is possible to nudge someone away from social-media usage and away from being part of the attention economy. For instance, Apple has created iPhone features that users can program to limit time spent on an app: if we are on Facebook for more than, say, ten minutes, we get locked out. That is a nudge that you can easily defy if you want to disable the feature. Similarly, some video-sharing platforms will interrupt the automatic playing of the next video when they track that you have watched a certain number of videos: the interruption and the reminder that you are wasting your day is a nudge that you can defy if you really want to continue watching. These are nudges that companies have developed on their own, but there are other nudges using coercion that the government can implement if it so chooses. For instance, social-media companies might have to ensure that their products come with warnings about how unhealthy they can be, especially for young people. This is analogous to the way that cigarette packages come with warnings. The warnings are libertarian because they are nudges that we can easily defy, even if the requirements that the packages have to carry the warning are not.

Libertarian paternalism is just one possible response to the attention economy, but it is an important concept for understanding much of the social-media landscape, and for that reason, it is discussed at great length in the next chapter.

## 5. The Good of the Attention Economy

No discussion of the attention economy would be complete without a mention of the value that the attention economy provides.[14] It is helpful and convenient that social-media sites offer their services at no cost to users. The attention economy makes it possible for companies to do this because their business models rely on selling the attention that they attract. The best way for companies to attract this attention is for them to provide valuable services to users. Facebook, for instance, provides users with an unprecedented ability to stay in touch with friends and family members around the world. People reveal how much they prefer these apps by how much time they spend on them. If we think that the right to attention is something that we can waive or exchange, then it might make sense for us to declare that users waive or exchange this right for the sake of accessing their valuable social-media apps. We just need to ensure that people who are waiving their rights are fully informed and not being manipulated into doing so.

## 6. Conclusion

In this chapter, we have explored one of the most pressing and socially relevant questions in applied ethics: the problem of the moral limits of markets. When we apply the criteria of noxiousness to the attention economy that pervades social-media business models, we get a clear verdict about whether this market should be constrained in some way. The tendency of social-media apps to promote addictions and rights violations compounds the harms of this market. That does not make the nature of our response to these problems obvious. It also does not mean that the attention economy is entirely bad. However, it does mean the attention economy crosses some moral lines that many other markets do not, and the solutions broached in section 4 are morally warranted.

# Key Terms

**Attention economy**: the industry built around the trading of people's attention as a commodity. There are two kinds of transactions at the heart of the attention economy. The first kind of transaction features users accessing a site or app in exchange for their attention. For example, I access Facebook and see the media posted there, and in exchange, I give Meta my attention. The second kind of transaction features the owners of the site or app auctioning off consumers' attention to an advertiser.

**Attention merchants**: the companies that participate in the attention economy, either as the buyers or the sellers of people's attention.

**Coercive paternalism**: the term "paternalism" in general refers to interventions in someone's decision-making in order to promote what is good for that person. Coercive paternalists in particular believe that it is permissible to use coercive methods, such as force, to prevent people from choosing what is bad for them or to ensure that they choose what is good for them.

**Exploitation**: making use of someone or something for your own ends by playing on some weakness or vulnerability in the object of your exploitation.[15]

**Libertarian paternalism**: this view is paternalistic in the same way as coercive paternalism, but libertarian paternalists do not believe that coercion is permissible in these cases. We should be paternalistic by changing the context in which a choice is made to make it likelier that people will choose what is good for them, while also keeping it easy to defy the changes that we make to the context.

**Market**: institutions that govern the exchange of goods and services. They are valuable institutions to the extent that they are efficient and promote freedom.

**Noxious**: the term that philosophers use as an adjective to describe morally objectionable markets. A noxious market might be banned altogether or simply constrained by some regulation; the proper response to noxiousness varies from case to case. Philosophers use different criteria for determining noxiousness, but I highlight three in this chapter: a noxious market produces extremely harmful outcomes for society; a noxious market produces extremely harmful outcomes for some individuals; and a noxious market is characterized by a low level of knowledge.

**Problem of the moral limits of markets**: the philosophical conundrum concerning where to draw the line between morally acceptable and morally objectionable (or *noxious*) markets. People interested in this problem wonder whether drugs, sex, human organs, guns, and so on, should be sold.

**Right to attention**: our right to direct our attention as we see fit, which in turn implies another right: the right to be free from distractions on the grounds that distractions are attempts to direct our attention to something other than what we have chosen.

**Social antibody**: a social antibody is a kind of defense against harmful social behaviors and practices. Social antibodies are behaviors and practices that society develops without any top-down coordination in order to limit the harm caused by other behaviors; for example, rules we have developed concerning what time of the day it is unacceptable to drink alcohol.

**Supernormal stimuli**: stimuli are supernormal when they take advantage of instincts by providing us with things that are more attractive than what those instincts evolved for.

# Discussion Cases

## 1. Twin Rivers

The Twin Rivers school district in California was facing some serious financial challenges, to the point that schools could not even afford proper heating for classrooms. In 2011, the administrators of the district were approached by a company called Education Funding Partners (EFP). EFP promised that it could resolve the district's financial woes—at no cost to the district itself. All the district had to do was allow corporations to advertise within the schools in the district. EFP promised corporate advertisers "authentic access and deep engagement with audiences in the school environment" and "an unparalleled system for engagement in the K–12 market."[16] For example, hallways in the school might have posters for brands or they might be lined with televisions playing commercials. Other school districts have made similar concessions in exchange for money, such as a school district in Florida that put advertisements for McDonald's in the students' report cards with the promise that good grades would earn someone a free meal.[17] These deals reflect the value of people's attention—and how lucrative it can be to build brand awareness early in someone's life.

What sorts of protections do you think should be put in place to safeguard children's attention? Some people would defend the deals that the school districts have made; after all, the students are not being harmed in any visible way, and the school district gets money that can be put to good use. Do you think that the school districts have made a morally acceptable decision?

## 2. Clickbait

Clickbait headlines are some of the most glaring examples of practices introduced by the attention economy. Sites that do not rely on people's clicks tend to rely on clickbait much less (e.g., because they have a subscription service, such that their revenue is stable regardless of how many people click on their headlines). Some clickbait headlines are annoying: "You'll never guess what Toronto's best Indian restaurant is!" After all, the curators of the site could simply have named the restaurant in the headline, but then, you probably would have been less likely to click on the headline. There are also headlines that resemble "This pen will blow your mind!" (There's a 99.9 percent chance that it will not.) Clickbait might be harmless in one sense, but much clickbait is misleading, and some people might call it manipulative. Ideally, marketers get us to pay attention to their products by designing them such that they solve problems in a way that makes us prefer to give up our money, but getting us to click on a headline by promising us that a pen will blow our minds can sound deceptive.

What is your assessment of the morality of clickbait? Is it a mere nuisance, or can it ever cross a line and become morally objectionable? Is clickbait an acceptable, or even respectable, way to get people's attention?

## 3. Tiktokification of Media

TikTok has replaced all other social-media platforms for many users, and it has done so relatively quickly. Many users find it more attention-grabbing than any other app, and it is hard to deny the influence that it has had on other platforms, such as YouTube, that have rolled out features designed to imitate the short-form video content that TikTok specializes in. This is sometimes called "Tiktokification." TikTok recommends short-form videos to users based on an algorithm that is designed to show them what they are interested in; it is difficult to comment on how special this algorithm is since it is proprietary information, but it clearly is efficient because, in 2022, Pew Research found that 16 percent of US teens said that they "almost constantly" use TikTok.[18]

Assume that Tiktokification is an important development in the attention economy: the move toward short-form video content algorithmically selected for users is a way to reliably get attention. What, if any, sorts of market behaviors are unacceptable in the quest to get more of our attention? Use the arguments in this chapter as you draw the lines about what we should and should not tolerate, as (especially) young people are giving more of their attention to social-media platforms.

## Further Reading

Bhargava, Vikram R., and Manuel Velasquez. 2021. "Ethics of the Attention Economy: The Problem of Social Media Addiction." *Business Ethics Quarterly* 31 (3): 321–59.

I avoided discussing the thorny question of whether social-media addictions really exist in this chapter, but this article does a wonderful job pulling together all of the evidence for its existence and then tying its incidence to the dealings of attention merchants.

Castro, Clinton, and Adam Pham. 2020. "Is the Attention Economy Noxious?" *Philosophers' Imprint* 20 (17): 1–13.

Castro and Pham helpfully frame the ethical issues of the attention economy as an instance of the problem of the moral limits of markets, just as I do here. Their article considers much more fully the attention economy's satisfaction of various criteria of noxiousness (and they present a fourth criterion that I omitted here for the sake of brevity). They also present warnings about social-media use as a kind of remedy.

Chomanski, Bartlomiej. 2023. "Mental Integrity in the Attention Economy: In Search of the Right to Attention." *Neuroethics* 16: 8–19.

Chomanski's article explores both the good and the bad of the attention economy within a right-to-attention framework. I recommend his article to anyone interested in reading more about the right to attention as it is characterized in this chapter and to anyone interested in the argument for that right based on mental integrity. Chomanski avoids rendering a straightforward verdict, either good or bad, about the attention economy at the end of the article.

Conly, Sarah. 2013. "Coercive Paternalism in Health Care: Against Freedom of Choice." *Public Health Ethics* 6 (3): 241–45.

This article gives an important overview of one way of addressing the problem of people doing things that are bad for them. Conly does not talk about social-media use but instead argues for coercive-paternalistic measures concerning the purchase of large sugary beverages.

Eyal, Nir. 2019. *Indistractable*. Dallas, TX: BenBella Books.

Eyal did not invent the concept of social antibodies, but he did pioneer the use of this concept as part of a solution to the problems generated by the attention economy. In general, his book is about how we can resist attempts to wrest control of our attention from it. In that respect, it is worth reading alongside the work concerning the right to attention.

Satz, Debra. 2010. *Why Some Things Should Not Be for Sale: The Moral Limits of Markets*. Oxford: Oxford University Press.

Satz has written the go-to book for people interested in the moral limits of markets. Her discussion of the nature and value of markets directly influenced the discussion of these points in this chapter. Satz also discusses noxious markets and lays out the criteria of noxiousness that I discuss here, although she presents a few more that I omitted for the sake of brevity.

Tran, Jasper L. 2015. "The Right to Attention." *Indiana Law Journal* 91: 1023–64.

Tran approaches the attention economy from the perspective of its violations of the right to attention. As he sees it, attention merchants assault our attention from various angles almost constantly. The right to attention ought to be recognized in order to push back against the demands that the attention economy puts on us.

Wu, Tim. 2016. *The Attention Merchants: The Epic Scramble to Get Inside Our Heads*. New York: Vintage Books.

Wu's book is not philosophical but is a historical overview of attention economies. I presented the attention economy here as coinciding with internet and social-media technologies, but a rudimentary form of it dates back to nineteenth-century newspapers. Wu traces the history of the attention economy from its humble origins to its prominence today, paying special attention to the techniques that attention merchants have perfected over time.

## Notes

1. This section is influenced by Satz 2010 and Castro and Pham 2020.
2. This section is influenced by Chomanski 2023.
3. Fitzpatrick, Burkhalter, and Asbridge 2019.
4. Beard 2002.
5. Shakya and Christakis 2017.
6. Raudsepp and Kais 2019.
7. I borrow the phrase "adding insult to injury" directly from Bhargava and Velasquez 2021.
8. Wood 2005.
9. This section is influenced by Chomanski 2023.
10. See Tran 2015 and Puri 2021.
11. See Bublitz and Merkel 2014.
12. See especially Puri 2021, 214.
13. This approach is pioneered by Eyal 2019.
14. This comes from Chomanski 2023.
15. Wood 2005.
16. These quotations are from Wu 2016, 4.
17. See Wu 2016, 3–5, for details on all these cases.
18. See Vogels, Gelles-Watnick, and Massarat 2022.

# Chapter Three: Nudging

Austria and Germany have similar demographics, but they have wildly different consent rates for organ donation. Austria has a near-universal level of consent: 99 percent. Germany, meanwhile, has only a 12 percent consent rate. What explains this difference is that Austria's system is *opt-out*. People who do not want to be donors have to opt out of donating. Germany's system is the opposite: the default is that people are not donors, but they can *opt in* if they are willing. Germany and Austria designed the context in which people make their organ-donation choice in a way that promotes certain outcomes without coercing anyone. Social-media apps are designed in similar ways, and this chapter is about the ethics of that kind of design decision.

Many spaces that we enter offline are designed to make certain outcomes likelier without coercion. For instance, imagine a cafeteria where healthy food is placed at eye level and at the front of the room, where it is most visible and accessible. Unhealthy food is accessible, but cafeteria-goers must reach down to get it. In this case, people are being nudged toward eating healthily, but someone who prefers to eat unhealthily is hardly inconvenienced at all. To *nudge* is to change the context in which a choice is made in order to promote the likelihood of a certain outcome. **Nudges** are intended to be a gentle form of influencing someone's decision, so gentle, in fact, that it is consistent with the nudged person's freedom, unlike coercion. The internet—especially e-commerce sites and social-media sites—is filled with nudges, usually ones that make it likelier that we will spend our money, reveal information about ourselves for data-collection purposes, watch more advertisements, or, at least, spend more time on any given website or app.

Here is a simple nudge to illustrate the point: you are signing up for a website, and when you enter your email address, you see a sentence that reads "Click here to opt out of emails from us." This is analogous to Austria's opt-out system for organ donation.

Nudges are the tools of libertarian paternalists. In the previous chapter, we learned about coercive paternalism, which was *paternalistic* in the sense that it advocates for interference with people's decision-making in order to promote their own good (or at least prevent some harm) and is *coercive* in the sense that it permits the use of force to accomplish this. Think about a law that requires bikers to wear helmets to protect their heads: the state is using coercion to get people to do what is good for them, even if the citizens do not want to wear helmets. It is coercive because there is some penalty, such as a fine, attached to defiance. There are other species of paternalism, however. Another species is **libertarian paternalism**, which might, at first, sound like an oxymoron. Libertarian paternalists aim to promote good outcomes for others, a mission that is associated with conventional paternalists, but they do so with an eye to preserving freedom of choice, a consideration that we typically associate with libertarians rather than paternalists.

Libertarian paternalists want to accomplish their goal not with *coercion* but with *nudges*.[1] They talk about the context in which a choice is made as the **choice architecture**, and the one who designs the choice architecture to nudge people is called the **choice architect**. The focus of this chapter is the way that social-media companies, such as Facebook, TikTok, Instagram, X, and YouTube, nudge users to spend more time on their platforms and nudge users toward certain kinds of content, mostly with the aim of ensuring that users enjoy the content and then spend more time on their platforms. Social-media companies nudge users for the sake of increasing their revenue from advertising. For instance, if YouTube can nudge users to watch more videos, then they see more advertisements. Along similar lines, users might be nudged to reveal more information about themselves, which the company can then use to show them more appropriate advertisements, thus increasing the probability that users will click on those advertisements. The result is that the company can charge more lucrative fees for advertising space.

Libertarian paternalists prefer their approach to coercive paternalism because they believe that they can achieve the same desirable outcomes but without resorting to coercion. They prefer nudges because they are sufficiently gentle forms of influence. If you disagree with the choice architect about whether your life and decisions are being improved, you can easily defy them. There is no penalty attached to defiance. However, some nudges appear to be manipulative, and this is a claim we shall investigate. Generally, the focus of this chapter is on understanding the way that the internet and social-media apps are designed around nudges and the way that philosophers think about this design choice.

# 1. Nudges

We shall begin by illustrating nudges in offline contexts. One form of nudging is to make whatever the choice architect wants as the outcome the default choice. A powerful example that we already discussed is making organ donation opt-*out* instead of opt-*in*. This small change has profound effects on how many people donate their organs. Another form of nudging is to change the environment. The cafeteria example from the start of the chapter illustrates this: the healthy food is positioned most visibly; the unhealthy food is almost as accessible, but those who want it must reach down to get it.

Merely informing people may also be a form of nudging. Consider an experiment done by the state of Montana as it tried to get undergraduate students to drink less.[2] Behavioral psychologists have done research showing that the amount of alcohol people tend to consume is a function of how much alcohol they think other people consume. Montana rolled out an education program, informing undergraduate students of how much their peers, in fact, drink. Since the amount was lower than what many had previously thought, the amount that they drank decreased accordingly.

It is crucial for the libertarian paternalist that people are being nudged toward what they already think is good for them, at least by and large. Those who disagree can easily opt out, for instance, of organ donation. Much research has been done on people's preferences to donate their organs; this research indicates that people have struggled to live in accordance with their preferences.[3] Similarly, there is no plausible way to construe that undergraduate students in Montana were treated objectionably by being informed of something true.

When it comes to the ease of opting out, it is hard to specify a threshold. If a cafeteria places unhealthy food just a few steps away, then people are being nudged away from it; perhaps the same goes if the unhealthy food is in a different room altogether. But making people walk ten kilometers to get unhealthy food is far more than a nudge. Along the same lines, we might think that it is still merely a nudge if someone makes us bend down to reach the food, but bending down might be tremendously onerous for someone with a disability. We should take this sort of thing on a case-by-case basis, as opposed to specifying a universal threshold of ease of defiance that nudges need to meet.

The example of the cafeteria illustrates something profound about nudging: specifically, that it is often unavoidable. The choice architecture of the cafeteria must be designed in *some* way. The food must be arranged, and whatever arrangement there is will nudge hungry people toward this or that option. The nudge might be toward what is healthy for them or what is most profitable for the cafeteria owners, but, either way, some nudging must occur.

However, this is not the case with every instance of nudging. The Montana state government did not have to offer any information about alcohol consumption, and it could hardly be said that by withholding this information, it was nudging people to drink more. Nudges influence people; and they are *positive contributions* in the sense that people must do something in order for the action to count as a nudge. We might say that someone's ignorance of alcohol-consumption statistics contributed to their decision to drink a certain amount, but if Montana not informing someone about these statistics counts as a nudge, then, by the same token, parents and neighbors similarly nudged students to drink by not informing them. In cases where nudges are not unavoidable, the libertarian paternalist thinks that they are justified on the grounds that they promote a person's already-existing values. Even if they do not promote those values, the nudges can be defied at no meaningful cost.

Nudging is a familiar part of the online landscape. One whistleblower informed us that Facebook changed the color of its notification that a user ought to check out some new post or comment from blue to red, because red is much more effective at ensuring that users click on the notification.[4] Colors are a powerful feature of the choice architecture in online life. We know that if we change the display on our smartphone screens from color to black-and-white, we spend less time on them because we are more attracted to multicolored displays.[5] Users are being nudged to see new content that Facebook suspects they will like. Notifications themselves are nudges, in the same sense that simply being informed about something true can count as a nudge.[6] The way that a social-media company recommends content also counts as a nudge. The promotion of some content as popular or *trending* nudges us toward that content, analogously to the way that doctors might nudge a patient toward accepting the course of treatment that they list first.

We might also think of the way that social-media sites such as Reddit, X, and TikTok are designed these days with the so-called *endless scroll* in mind. Reddit, for instance, was not always this way. It used to be that one scrolled to the bottom of a page and then had to manually click to move to the next page. Nowadays, users never experience that feeling of running out of content on any given page, because they can scroll down endlessly as the Reddit app or site loads more and more content.

The goal is to have users spend as much time on a platform as possible without violating their freedom of choice. When Netflix began its streaming service, the term "binge-watch" did not exist, for all intents and purposes, in English. When a user finished watching a series episode or movie, the default option was that the user would not continue watching; he or she had to *opt in* to watching another episode or movie. However, in 2012, Netflix changed the choice architecture such that the default option was that the user would watch more content; this is Netflix's *autoloading* feature, called *post-play*. The term "binge-watch" sprung into existence not long after.[7] Such was the power of the choice architecture.

This strategy is replicated on social-media sites. For instance, on YouTube, the default option is for videos to play when one is completed, and YouTube has amassed an endless supply of videos for users to move through. YouTube, unlike Netflix, has a much more immediate financial incentive for this: YouTube wants users to watch as many videos as possible because the more videos we watch, the more advertisements we see. Generally, the same reason explains why many non-social-media sites prefer to create their content as videos or slideshows instead of the written word: videos and slideshows take longer to get through than a written page that readers can quickly skim; the longer we are on a page, the more time that we are exposed to advertisements. Plus, the slideshow format itself allows for new advertisements on each slide.

The use of the default-option nudge is powerful, as we can observe from the behavior of Netflix users. We encounter this type of nudge most frequently on the internet when we are signing up for an account on some site, and we are asked whether we would like to receive advertisements and promotional information from that site. Sometimes we are asked to *opt in* to these emails, whereas other times we are asked to opt out of these emails, as I said earlier. Sometimes we are asked to opt in to them by clicking on a box, or the box is already automatically filled and we instead must click to un-fill the box. One might wonder how it could be otherwise: there might not seem to be an alternative to either approach; either we opt in or opt out of such emails. However, sites could, and sometimes do, implement the mandated-choice nudge. Here, users are *required* to make a choice. There is no default option. One cannot move on from that stage of account creation until one has selected yes or no in response to the question about receiving emails from the site.

When signing up for an account on a site that features an online store, opting to receive emails allows the site to nudge us regularly. There is another incentive for such e-commerce sites to do the same thing, too: they want to leverage the so-called *buy-in effect* of signing up for a site. The clearest illustration of this effect is when we sign up for an account in order to receive some discount at the site. The site could simply apply the discount automatically at checkout instead. One might think that it amounts to the same thing, but it does not. Marketers are aware that consumers are more likely to *do more* once they have already done *a little*. This is the buy-in effect: once we have already bought into something, we are more likely to buy into more. Once we have signed up for an account, we are more likely to spend money at that store.

A similar idea is that people are likely to value something more when they own it. For instance, if Dropbox gives you two gigabytes of extra space for free, but then three months later starts charging you for it, you are more likely to spend the money to retain the two gigabytes than you would be to have paid for them in the first place. You will pay more money to retain something than to obtain it because the mere ownership makes it more valuable in your eyes. This can be used handily to nudge someone: give them something for free with the intention of charging them later on to keep it.

Another example from e-commerce: seven-day free trials that do not end after seven days but renew and automatically become paid memberships. Since users are free to end their membership before it becomes paid, freedom of choice is preserved, but e-commerce businesses know that users are more likely to become paying customers this way than if their memberships automatically ended after the seven-day free trial.

These are some of the clearest examples of nudging in online life. Most of these examples specifically concern social-media platforms, but others are more general, relating to the way that we shop online.

## 2. Are These Nudges Morally Permissible?

The ethical question is whether there is something wrong with designing the choice architecture this way. In other words, the question is whether it is wrong to nudge. In what follows, we shall discuss some possible objections to nudges and see that, for the most part, these objections fail—but only *for the most part*. There are some exceptions, and it is important not to paint with a broad brush. We then have to disentangle the fact that there might be nothing wrong with these nudges in principle from the fact that the problem could consist in what we are being nudged toward.

## 2. Are These Nudges Morally Permissible?

There are a couple of central constraints on what a choice architect is morally permitted to do, according to libertarian paternalists. The first of these constraints is that the nudge must comply with the **publicity principle**.[8] This principle requires that choice architects do only what they are willing to defend publicly to those nudged. First, this principle has practical value: it saves the choice architect from possible embarrassment, for instance. Second, it embodies the respect that people are meant to have for their fellow citizens; we ought to avoid using people as tools and manipulating them.

*Most* nudges in online contexts comply with this principle. There are a couple of exceptions that are better discussed later on. For the most part, few people, I suspect, would find themselves put off by learning that Facebook's notifications are meant to nudge them to spend more time on the platform. In fact, these nudges are generally so transparent that it is almost as if social-media companies have already successfully defended them to the public: they have engineered the choice architecture right in front of our eyes, not in secrecy. We might find it annoying when a site opts us in to receiving emails by default, but it is implausible that this is so egregious that the choice architect would be unwilling to defend it publicly; indeed, what is going on here is already transparent.

The second constraint is that nudges must be sufficiently libertarian. Specifically, they need to preserve freedom of choice. There are, in most cases, *some* costs to defying the choice architect and to saying no to the outcome that one is being nudged toward. Perhaps the only exception to this is the mandated-choice nudge, where one is required to make a choice: here, either decision has the same cost. With respect to other nudges, it is important that the cost of defying a nudge is as small as possible in order for the nudge to be considered *libertarian*. In other words, a cafeteria where healthy foods are at eye level and unhealthy foods are just below eye level is designed unobjectionably. However, increasing the price of the unhealthy foods by ten dollars is less libertarian and more coercive. As I explained earlier, it is hard to specify the exact point at which a nudge stops being gentle and starts being coercive.

Nevertheless, there is no need to pursue this line of thinking with respect to many nudges online. That is because none of the nudges that we have surveyed so far have an obviously high cost of defiance. It is easy to *not* click on a Facebook notification. It is easy, even if annoying for one instant, to opt out of receiving emails. It might be a more pleasant online experience to have YouTube give us more time between finishing a video and the automated start of the next one, but it is not difficult to defy this nudge, and it is rather easy to disable this feature altogether.

There are times when social-media sites seem to make things objectionably difficult. Much has made been of how difficult it is to delete your Facebook account, for instance: specifically, the fact that Facebook makes users wait weeks before the account can be deleted and makes it hard to ensure that *all* of your data is deleted (e.g., including conversations with friends). Deleting your account correctly is unwieldy enough to warrant the creation of sites dedicated to guiding you through it; consider Deletefacebook.com. This is a kind of nudge, a desperate nudge to keep us on the site. I encountered something like this firsthand while researching for this book. I had to subscribe to the *Wall Street Journal* to read some reporting about Instagram's effects on young girls, and I discovered that I could not cancel my subscription by any means other than calling the *Wall Street Journal* (unless I lived in one of four states that require them to provide some other means). This phone service was available only during limited parts of the week. During the phone call, the customer-service agent tried to keep me as a paying customer. This might not be outright coercion, but it is not sufficiently easy to defy the choice architecture that this counts as an acceptable nudge. It is equivalent to requiring a citizen to fill out a pile of paperwork to opt out of an organ-donation program: the cost of saying no might be considered objectionably high. Certainly, some nudges can and often do cross the line and cease being libertarian. However, this is not the case with most nudges online, where our freedom of choice is preserved.

Nudging is often perceived to be manipulative. This is probably the single most widespread objection to nudges. In 2014, when David Cameron, prime minister of the United Kingdom at the time, protected the British behavioral-insights team of psychologists and economists from scrutiny, the *Guardian* ran the headline "Nudge Nudge, Say No More. Brits' Minds Will Be Controlled without Us Knowing It," reflecting this fear.[9] The intuition that nudges are manipulative is powerful, and this intuition might be strengthened when we consider how effective, say, Netflix has been at getting viewers to watch more content by redesigning the choice architecture of its site.

However, there is reason to think that this intuition is not trustworthy. An interesting 2017 psychological study researching people's attitudes toward nudges in political contexts revealed how one's acceptance of a nudge depends on whether the nudge is explained using a policy that one supports or does not support.[10] For instance, conservatives disapproved of nudges when their usefulness was illustrated

## 2. Are These Nudges Morally Permissible? 65

with a liberal policy objective, such as encouraging eligible people to enroll in food-stamp programs; liberals disapproved when nudges were illustrated with a conservative policy objective, such as encouraging eligible rich people to take advantage of some relief from the capital gains tax. The same effect was observed when the participants were not voters but sitting mayors of US cities. This might explain why, whereas the left-leaning *Guardian* ran a headline worrying about nudging when a Conservative prime minister was in charge, the right-leaning *Daily Caller* ran a similarly mistrustful headline when Barack Obama was president: "President Obama Orders Behavioral Experiments on American Public." This is some evidence that our intuitions about nudging are not reliable and can easily change with how nudges are framed.

Even though whether nudges strike us as manipulative depends on how they are presented, they might really *be* manipulative. One immediate problem is the difficulty of clarifying what **manipulation** is. For instance, philosopher Joseph Raz says that instead of interfering with a person's options, manipulation undermines someone's decision-making or goal-setting processes.[11] Coercion, in contrast, eliminates some options altogether. The basic aim of manipulation is interference with our reasoning, and this interference appears to be gentler than coercion but also objectionable in ways that persuasion usually is not.

It does not seem that the sorts of nudges that we see online meet this characterization. First, many of the nudges that we see online and offline are simply inevitable in a morally relevant sense. Consider the cafeteria case. Cafeterias need to be organized in *some* way; this kind of nudge is *unavoidable*, as I explained earlier. The healthy foods need to be put somewhere: maybe at eye level; maybe not. If the choice architect puts them at eye level, then the cafeteria-goers are being nudged toward them; if they are put elsewhere, then the cafeteria-goers are being nudged toward whatever is most visible and accessible. There is no escaping a nudge like this, to the extent that cafeterias need to be designed at all. (Even if they were designed *randomly*, people would be nudged toward what is randomly chosen; the choice architect would be whoever is responsible for the random ordering.)

Something similar is going on with at least some online nudges: for instance, the interface surrounding notifications needs to be designed in *some* way. If Facebook wants to nudge people away from using their site, then it is open to them to design notifications such that we are not prompted to engage with them. Nevertheless, we are still being nudged. If Facebook wants to nudge people toward using their site more, then they can display notifications prominently and in attention-grabbing colors. There are all sorts of options in between too: notifications displayed in boring and drab colors, notifications that one opts in to, notifications about only those posts made by preselected users, and so on.

The same goes for some other nudges too. If sites want to send emails to users, then they have to ask users for permission. How they ask is part of the choice architecture: the option on the account-creation screen can have "Yes, I would like to receive emails" already selected or not selected, or users might have to choose between a yes and a no option, or perhaps the question could be phrased in another way.

However, we can see that there are some cases in which a decision to nudge is optional and avoidable. Yet, it does not seem that these other cases meet any of the definitions of manipulation presented earlier. For instance, it does not obviously pervert decision-making processes or promote irrationality to load a YouTube video automatically after a person has finished one. Neither does informing users that their comments have been liked and that the users should click to see who liked their comments. The latter might, in fact, promote rationality and good decision-making by informing the user of something true. Something similar occurs when a platform recommends content that users might like: users are being informed of the existence of something; it might feel like a relentless insistence from, for example, YouTube or Instagram, but being informed is hardly the promotion of irrationality. The same goes for the endless-scroll nudge: it is just more content or information made more accessible.

## 3. Nudges toward the Bad

If the analysis ended at this point, it would seem as though the use of nudges on social-media sites is unobjectionable. The truth is more complicated. The canonical objections to nudging—which usually revolve around manipulativeness or the promotion of irrationality—do not succeed in these cases, but the problem is far deeper: social-media companies nudge us toward what is bad for us.

One way that they do this is by nudging us to return to their platform while we are spending time away from it. The most obvious such nudge is the notification regarding some content on their platform when we are not currently using it. For instance, the Facebook app on our smartphone might notify us of something happening on the platform while we are checking our email. A second way is

## 3. Nudges toward the Bad

by prompting continued engagement with their site, such as nudging people by promoting content that the software designers of the site have predicted they might like, or by automatically loading more content after people have finished consuming content. The difference lies in whether we are not on the platform at the moment and are being nudged to return to it or we are on the platform and being nudged to not leave it. Morally, there is no difference, since spending more time on social-media sites is bad for us, and that is the outcome of both kinds of nudges.

That more time spent on these sites is bad for our well-being is borne out by a good deal of recent psychological research.[12] I have provided brief summaries of these studies in the Further Reading section at the end of the chapter; we shall discuss them again in Chapter 8 on quitting social media. Right now, we need to recognize that the negative effects are especially felt by the demographic most likely to use social-media sites, namely, teenagers and young adults. One striking feature of this research is that it shows that the more time we spend on social-media sites, the more pronounced the effects on our subjective and objective well-being become. The difference between subjective and objective well-being in this context reflects methodological differences: sometimes, researchers will ask users to report their own well-being (i.e., by asking how the respondents feel), which measures subjective well-being; sometimes, researchers will objectively measure the effects on users, such as by tracking the amount of sleep lost. Generally, research studies do both.

The implication is that there is much less harm involved in spending little time on social-media sites. That is, *social-media sites are not bad for us when we spend only a little bit of time on them*. There are many possible reasons for this. Perhaps when we spend little time on them daily, we tend to use them purposively during that time, maybe by speaking to far-flung friends. Maybe by spending little time on them daily, we are not so exposed to images from other people's lives that invite unflattering comparisons with our own lives. No matter the reason, although more research on new technologies is always welcome, it seems warranted to say that our well-being is negatively affected by spending more time on these platforms; the more time, the greater the negative effect.

The moral problem with this is that spending more time on these platforms is exactly what the nudges are designed to get us to do. We are nudged to spend more time on them when we are on them and to return to them when we are not. This is a major ethical problem for the choice architects of these sites because nudging is intended as a libertarian-paternalist tool to promote what is good for us. Richard Thaler and Cass Sunstein say, for instance, that "the golden rule of libertarian paternalism [is to . . .] offer nudges that are most likely to help and least likely to inflict harm."[13]

An important nudge that we ought to consider in this context: the promotion of content. Social-media companies often promote content to users on the basis that the content is popular or *trending* at the moment or because the user's history on the site (or off the site) makes it likely in the eyes of the software designers that the user will engage with the content. At bottom, this is another kind of nudge to spend more time on the platform. The idea is that users prefer to spend more time on a site when they are engaging with content that others have liked or that the site has predicted they will like. What is different about these nudges is that they can promote content that is bad for us independently of how much time we spend on the site. The *Wall Street Journal*'s 2021 exposé of Facebook and Instagram's effects on the mental health of teenage girls showcases some powerful examples of this design, such as promoting eating-disorder content to girls who had initially searched for content related to health and exercise.[14] Promoting content is a form of nudging, and nudging girls toward eating disorders is morally wrong.

We might also think of the way that social-media companies nudge users toward conspiracy theories such as QAnon. Leaked Facebook documents revealed that QAnon content was recommended to users who showed an interest in conservative content (e.g., Donald Trump and Fox News) within two days of their joining Facebook. In late 2021, a whistleblower, Frances Haugen, who had worked for Facebook as a product manager and had been hired to protect against election interference, disclosed that the company promoted obviously harmful eating-disorder content because of how successful it was according to their engagement-based metrics. In other words, nudges are used because they are effective at getting us to spend more time on the platforms.

By the same token, some of these social-media sites know that we are being nudged toward what is bad for us. For years, Meta has conducted research internally on the effects of the services of Instagram and Facebook on users' health. The *Wall Street Journal* published the documents released by the Meta whistleblower, and we can use them to learn what Meta itself has known about the damage that time on its platforms does to its users.[15] The research showed that as far as Meta is aware, among teenagers, 63.37 percent report sleep issues, 60.10 percent report work stress, 57.56 percent report social-comparison issues, and 55.59 percent

## 3. Nudges toward the Bad 69

report body-image issues. Among adults, 57.77 percent report sleep issues, 57.54 percent report financial stress, and 52.54 percent report body-image issues. There are other problems too: among teenagers, reports of sadness, anxiety, laziness, and fear or feeling of missing out (FOMO) were all above 50 percent; among adults, reports of sadness, anxiety, FOMO, eating issues, loneliness, work stress, and social-comparison issues were all above 40 percent. One might wonder whether this internal research is as evidentially solid as peer-reviewed research, but the point is that Meta cannot defend its use of nudging by saying that it believes that its platforms are good for its users.

When we speak specifically of teenage girls on Instagram, Meta's internal research discovered that 66 percent experienced negative social comparison (as opposed to 40 percent for boys); 52 percent said that these feelings were caused by images related to beauty; and 32 percent said that when they felt bad about their bodies, *Instagram made them feel worse*. This last part is crucial: nearly a third of girls report that Instagram worsens pre-existing problems. The pre-existing problems, of course, might have been caused by previous exposure to social-media content, too. Yet, Meta nudges them to spend more time on the platform. A nudge toward what is bad for us should be condemned on the same consequentialist grounds used to justify other nudges. The fact that Meta has evidence that they are nudging users toward something bad is even more damning.

Some of these nudges do not pass the publicity-principle test. I said earlier that most nudges on social-media platforms do comply with this principle: after all, most of the time, the companies in question are being transparent in the first place, and few people would see something wrong in principle with a company nudging you to use their free product. However, I think that the promotion of eating-disorder content and other content that harms young girls' sense of themselves *are* nudges that Facebook would be reluctant to publicly defend. We can conclude this from the fact that Facebook *is* reluctant to publicly defend these nudges when confronted with them. Even though spending increasing amounts of time on Facebook is bad for us, I do not think that Facebook would be reluctant to defend its use of nudges in general, since there is nothing particularly embarrassing or shameful about, say, notifying users about a post that was recently made by a friend. However, the public outrage—which was sparked by these leaked internal documents, which prompted the whistleblower to testify in the US Senate, and which was in large part a response to the revealed damage to teenaged girls' mental health—and Facebook's own response, which centered around denying the allegations and then also pledging to develop new so-called safety features for teenagers, reveal that there was something especially egregious about this aspect of their platforms.

## 4. The Same Technologies Can Be Used for Good

It is important that we recognize the moral permissibility of nudges in principle on social-media platforms. The problem with currently existing nudges online is that they nudge us toward what is bad. However, as long as we affirm that nudging in principle is morally permissible, we can use the same choice-architecture designs to nudge people toward what is good, namely, spending less time on these sites. For instance, when someone watches more than, say, five or six YouTube videos in a row, perhaps there ought to be a message that informs them of how much time they have spent, and they must look at this message for, say, ten or fifteen seconds before dismissing it. Other examples include making notifications opt-in, such that they are by default disabled; perhaps notifications should be automatically disabled after a user has spent more than twenty or thirty minutes on the platform that day. At a minimum, social-media companies ought to not promote content that leads to mental-health problems, such as eating disorders. It might be best for them not to promote content at all and simply let users engage with whatever they happen upon. This might help solve other often-discussed philosophical problems with the design of the internet generally, such as the rise of echo chambers, as we discuss in Chapter 4.

It is not clear whether it is too much to ask social-media platforms to change themselves. Whether the government ought to get involved and force social-media companies to change their choice architecture is a separate question. Meta's vice president of global affairs said that "we have no commercial incentive to do anything other than try and make sure that the experience is positive."[16] This is surely true in one sense but false in the sense that he meant it. He said this to dismiss the allegations that Meta had contributed to mental-health issues, and in this sense, it was false: there is psychological research showing that people overwhelmingly tend to be attracted to negative content.[17] The claim that Meta has no commercial incentive to promote negative content, therefore, is baseless. Any social-media site can easily leverage this feature of human psychology to increase user engagement. In another sense, the claim is true: the great public backlash, sparked as the effects of social-media sites are felt, noticed, and decried, gives the platforms a considerable commercial incentive to *not* harm users' mental health, even if doing so would be (and often is) in their immediate financial interests.

Further evidence that it is not unreasonable to be optimistic about social-media companies reforming themselves is that some already do nudge users in the right direction. TikTok, for instance, implemented a nudge of just this sort: notifying users when they have spent a certain amount of time on the platform. TikTok, not uniquely, also gives users the ability to set (or entirely disable) daily screen-time limits, such that interested users will need to enter their password again if they want to exceed their limit. This illustrates nudging well: helpful, yet easy to defy. Moreover, Facebook's response to the immense public backlash in light of the whistleblower's US Senate testimony included saying that they will develop a feature on Instagram to nudge people away from the site after spending a certain amount of time on it. The backlash might be sufficient to persuade these private companies to change their choice architecture.

It is not obvious that these nudges will be powerful enough to mitigate or prevent the damage done by social-media platforms to users' mental health. If nudging people away from these platforms does not appreciably improve the situation, we might consider more aggressive action, such as coercion, but nudges are convenient tools since they preserve would-be users' freedom of choice. Having social-media companies reform themselves in a way that preserves freedom of choice and that protects mental health would be a happy alternative to both the status quo and the possible world in which the government uses coercion, for both moral reasons and due to pragmatic considerations about the efficacy of government regulation of the internet. At a minimum, by transforming nudges *toward* social-media sites into nudges *away* from those sites, we improve the moral status of the choice architecture of these sites and of the internet generally.

# 5. Conclusion

In this chapter, we explored the ethics of the design of social-media apps. While the apps employ nudges that can sometimes strike us as morally wrong and manipulative, it is harder, upon reflection, to object to many of them. The problem is not with the nudges themselves but with the things that we are being nudged toward. The good news is that we can, therefore, employ the same kind of technology and user-interface designs to nudge us toward the good. The bad news is that it is not obvious how likely it is that nudges toward what is good for us will be implemented or how effective they might be against such dynamic and ever-evolving technologies.

## Key Terms

**Choice architect**: the person who designs choice architecture to nudge people toward something.

**Choice architecture**: the context in which a choice is made.

**Libertarian paternalism**: the school of thought that says that we should intervene in people's decision-making for their own good not by coercing them but by nudging them toward what is good. The nudges should be easy to defy in case people disagree about what is good for them.

**Manipulation**: manipulation does not interfere with a person's options, as opposed to coercion, which eliminates some options altogether. Instead, manipulation undermines someone's decision-making or goal-setting processes. The basic idea is interference with our reasoning, and this interference appears to be gentler than coercion but is also objectionable in ways that persuasion usually or always is not.

**Nudge**: to nudge is to change the context in which a choice is made in order to promote the likelihood of a certain outcome. Nudges are intended to be a gentle form of influencing someone's decision, so gentle, in fact, that it is consistent with the nudged person's freedom, unlike coercion.

**Publicity principle**: the principle that requires choice architects to do only what they are willing to defend publicly to the people they nudge. First, this principle has practical value: for instance, it saves the choice architect from possible embarrassment. Second, it embodies the respect that people are meant to have for their fellow citizens; we ought to avoid using people as tools and manipulating them.

# Discussion Cases

## 1. Meta's Nudges

In this chapter, we discussed Meta's nudging young girls toward eating-disorder content in the name of promoting engagement metrics. When girls searched for content even tangentially related to health (e.g., how to do your first pull-up), they would be recommended content that promoted anorexia. This is part of a larger pattern of promoting content that makes specifically (but not only) girls feel worse about their bodies. Reflect on these nudges.

**What do you think of these nudges? What are the moral problems with this sort of behavior? Companies often have products that are unhealthy for children (and adults): think about the entire fast-food industry, for instance. How do these nudges compare to marketing unhealthy products to young people?**

## 2. Notifications

Smartphone notifications are among the most powerful nudges. Part of their power lies in how habit-forming they are. Many of us know what it is like to frequently and habitually check our phone in the hopes of seeing a notification, even in the absence of any evidence that a notification will be waiting for us. Fundamentally, notifications alert us to something true: for example, an Amazon product discount. They are designed, however, to be much more than mere carriers of information: they are designed as habit-forming nudges to get us back on whatever app that notification is related to.

**In light of the content of this chapter, what do you think of the ethics of notifications? Are they invasive? Annoying? Harmless inconveniences that we can disable if we are sufficiently bothered by them? Helpful and informative alerts that something is true? Where should we draw the line on which sorts of notifications are part of acceptable business practices and which are invasive, habit-forming marketing tools that are trying to distract us?**

## 3. TikTok and Nudges

> TikTok employs the same kinds of nudges as many other social-media platforms, but in 2023, TikTok rolled out a trial for a new feature called "Nudge." As of the writing of this book, Nudge is not available to all users, but the central idea is that you can send a *nudge* to a TikTok content creator or influencer whom you have chosen. By nudging, you sign up for notifications about when that creator/influencer has posted or is broadcasting live, and you also send that person a message indicating that you want them to post or go live. In other words, you nudge that person to create more content (and you also sign up for a nudge from TikTok when new content is posted).

**Is this kind of nudge any different from the other nudges that social-media platforms employ? Consider that it has the same goal as many other nudges (e.g., it keeps your attention on TikTok), but it also seems different in some respects, such as the fact that one user is nudging another user, whereas nudges are conventionally generated by the platform itself. Also, the influencers being nudged might value the knowledge that users are looking for more content, but it could also promote burnout among influencers; evaluate this nudge from the perspective of the influencers being nudged.**

# Further Reading

Alter, Adam. 2017. *Irresistible: The Rise of Addictive Technology.* New York: Penguin Press.

> *Irresistible* does not articulate social-media technologies in terms of nudges but instead as a matter of behavioral addiction. (The distinction between behavioral and substance addictions is best illustrated by thinking about the difference between being addicted to a behavior, such as gambling, and to a substance, such as heroin.) However, many of the features that give rise to behavioral addictions, such as autoloading of videos, which Alter discusses, are nudges. I also credit him with the observation that Netflix's autoloading feature basically spawned the term "binge-watch."

## Further Reading

Cohen, Shlomo. 2013. "Nudging and Informed Consent," *American Journal of Bioethics* 13 (6): 3–11.

Cohen defends nudging in medical contexts against a wide range of criticisms, especially the view that nudging promotes irrationality and exploits cognitive weaknesses. I recommend this article to anyone who is interested in reading more about defending the use of nudges and the intersection of nudging and other important ethical concepts, such as informed consent.

Dunt, Ian. 2014. "Nudge Nudge, Say No More. Brits' Minds Will Be Controlled without Us Knowing It." *Guardian*, February 5, 2014. https://www.theguardian.com/commentisfree/2014/feb/05/nudge-say-no-more-behavioural-insights-team.

Dunt's article illustrates some of the ways that nudges are framed as manipulative in the public sphere.

Holte, Alex J., and F. Richard Ferraro. 2020. "True Colors: Grayscale Setting Reduces Screen Time in College Students." *Social Science Journal* 60 (2): 274–90. https://doi.org/10.1080/03623319.2020.1737461.

Holte and Ferraro's research confirms that the popular technique of changing the color of one's screen to grayscale significantly reduces time spent on social media and internet browsing, though not time spent watching videos. A similarly interesting 2021 study by Holte, Giesen, and Ferraro in *Current Psychology*, "Color Me Calm," found that the same technique also reduced anxiety and the kind of problematic smartphone use that is correlated with a decline in productivity, sleep difficulties, risky driving, and more.

Horwitz, Jeff. 2021. "The Facebook Whistleblower, Frances Haugen, Says She Wants to Fix the Company, Not Harm It." *Wall Street Journal*, October 3, 2021. https://www.wsj.com/articles/facebook-whistleblower-frances-haugen-says-she-wants-to-fix-the-company-not-harm-it-11633304122.

This article reports on the testimony of Frances Haugen, who blew the whistle on Facebook's practice of nudging people toward what is bad, both for the user and for the integrity of democratic institutions. Haugen's testimony provides an interesting glimpse into the company's decision-making process, according to which user-engagement metrics were seen as the most important thing. Of course, this speaks to the power of the company's nudges.

Kurtz, Sheldon F., and Michael J. Saks. 1996. "The Transplant Paradox: Overwhelming Public Support for Organ Donation vs. Under-Supply of Organs: The Iowa Organ Procurement Study." *Journal of Corporation Law* 21: 767–806.

Kurtz and Saks uncover that people do not live in a way that is consistent with their values specifically in the following way: people support organ donation but do not opt into organ-donation programs. The authors found that despite overwhelming support for organ donation in Iowa, not many people had, in fact, signed their driver's licenses to indicate that they would donate their organs: 97 percent of participants supported organ donation, but of that 97 percent, not even half had signed. Participants were also asked how strongly they wanted to be organ donors; of those who responded favorably in the strongest possible terms, only 64 percent had signed their driver's license; only about one-third had signed the organ-donation card that is required for making an anatomical gift in Iowa. Nudges are designed to bring people's behavior in line with their values, while also being sufficiently easy to defy that those who do not want to donate their organs can opt out: this is why libertarian paternalists are so keen on making organ-donation programs *opt-out*.

Lewis, Paul, 2017. "'Our Minds Can Be Hijacked': The Tech Insiders Who Fear a Smartphone Dystopia," *Guardian*, October 6, 2017. https://www.theguardian.com/technology/2017/oct/05/smartphone-addiction-silicon-valley-dystopia.

This article contains testimony from Tristan Harris, who worked in the industry as a so-called design ethicist before leaving and drawing attention to the harms that he perceived in the social-media landscape. Some of the behind-the-scenes information in this chapter comes from Harris, such as the fact that Facebook designed the color of its notifications with the click rate in mind.

Paul, Kari, and Dani Anguiano. 2021. "Facebook Crisis Grows as New Whistleblower and Leaked Documents Emerge." *Guardian*, October 23, 2021. https://www.theguardian.com/technology/2021/oct/22/facebook-whistleblower-hate-speech-illegal-report.

This article reports on some of the discoveries of Facebook's leaked internal documents, including the finding, discussed earlier, that people who showed an interest in conservative things (e.g., Donald Trump and Fox News) were being shown conspiracy-theory content (e.g., QAnon) within only two days of joining the platform.

Raz, Joseph. 1986. *The Morality of Freedom*. Oxford: Clarendon Press.

I credit Raz with the understanding of manipulation that pervades this chapter. His approach to manipulation has been influential among philosophers, and the basic outlines of it as interference not with a person's options but with their decision-making processes are generally accepted.

Soroka, Stuart, Patrick Fournier, and Lilach Nir. 2019. "Cross-National Evidence of a Negativity Bias in Psychophysiological Reactions to News." *PNAS* 116 (38): 18888–92.

The researchers study the question of whether negative content gets more attention than positive content, but it is hard to prove (not least of all because so many of the relevant metrics are proprietary information). Yet, we can study this indirectly. For instance, the researchers here explain that negative biases "in human cognition are well documented" and further discovered that their effects on news coverage (and news production) are profound and exist because negative content causes more engagement from consumers (which is surely the same effect that is leading Facebook to prioritize negative content for the promotion of user engagement, as per the whistleblower's testimony). The researchers did find that individuals tended to vary in their responsiveness to negative content and that this might lead to more positive content in the future.

Tannenbaum, David, Craig R. Fox, and Todd Rogers. 2017. "On the Misplaced Politics of Behavioural Policy Interventions." *Nature Human Behavior* 1. https://doi.org/10.1038/s41562-017-0130.

The researchers discovered that people's beliefs about whether nudging is objectionable changed depending on which examples were used to illustrate the concept of a nudge. Tannenbaum and Fox also summarized their findings in the accessible *New York Times* piece "The Curious Politics of the 'Nudge'" (September 26, 2015).

Thaler, R., and Cass R. Sunstein. 2008. *Nudge: Improving Decisions about Health, Wealth, and Happiness*. New Haven, CT: Yale University Press.

*Nudge* is perhaps the single most important book about libertarian paternalism that exists, and virtually all of the main ideas about the conceptual background of this chapter are contained in this book. However, Thaler and Sunstein do not discuss much about social media, which is, really, a consequence only of the publication date. More objectionably, they do not seem nearly as concerned about the objection that nudges are manipulative as later philosophers. (This is probably because they insist, as I do in this chapter, that since much of the time, one *must* nudge, considerations of manipulativeness are not terribly apt.) That being said, they do borrow the idea of the *publicity principle* as a standard from John Rawls.

Twenge, Jean M., and Keith Campbell. 2019. "Media Use Is Linked to Lower Psychological Well-Being: Evidence from Three Datasets." *Psychiatric Quarterly* 90: 311–31.

Twenge and Campbell found that adolescents who used social media lightly (i.e., less than one hour a day) reported substantially higher psychological well-being than those who used it heavily (i.e., more than five hours a day); specifically, "heavy users (vs. light) of digital media were 48 percent to 171 percent more likely to be unhappy, to be low in well-being, or to have suicide risk factors such as depression, suicidal ideation, or past suicide attempts." They also found that the greatest drop in well-being occurred as one moves from moderate use to heavy use.

*Wall Street Journal*. 2021a. "Teens & Young Adults on IG and FB." September 29, 2021. https://s.wsj.net/public/resources/documents/teens-young-adults-on-ig-and-facebook.pdf.

and

*Wall Street Journal*. 2021b. "Teen Girls [sic] Body Image and Social Comparison on Instagram—An Exploratory Study in the US." September 29, 2021. https://s.wsj.net/public/resources/documents/teen-girls-body-image-and-social-comparison-on-instagram.pdf.

I strongly recommend that readers check out these leaked internal documents. They do an excellent job of cataloging Facebook and Instagram's effects on users. Here is a glimpse of some of the methodology used: respondents were asked, "In the last 30 days, have you experienced . . . ?" It seems that Facebook then listed such options as "FOMO," "anxiety," etc. There were 22,410 respondents across multiple countries including the United States and Japan. I do not know how the respondents were chosen. It could well be that there is some self-selection bias among respondents who completed the survey; that is, it might be that the people with pronounced negative effects were more likely to respond to the survey, whereas people with generally positive or indifferent experiences were more likely to decline to respond. Since the research was released by a whistleblower, we lack the full context required to interpret the data. I do not use this research to conclude that the use of Facebook's platforms has all of the effects that are reported in the documents and summarized earlier because it is not obvious that this research is as evidentially solid as peer-reviewed research; instead, I use it to conclude that Facebook cannot defend itself by saying that it believes that time on its platforms is good for users. When we take the peer-reviewed research that is available and combine it with the data that Facebook has collected internally, we see that there is no way for the company to plead ignorance. *As far as they know, they are nudging people toward what is bad for them.*

Wechsler, Henry, Jae Eun Lee, Meicun Kuo, and Hang Lee. 2000. "College Binge Drinking in the 1990s: A Continuing Problem. Results of the Harvard School of Public Health 1999 Alcohol Study." *Journal of the American College of Health* 48: 199–210.

The gist is that Harvard School of Public Health found that 44 percent of college students engaged in binge drinking in the two-week period before the study. Lurking behind this behavior is the belief that alcohol abuse is common, more common than it really is. Montana tried to solve this problem by alerting students to the reality that people drink alcohol far less than the undergraduate students perceived. The educational campaign also included information about the popularity of smoking (e.g., "most (70 percent) of Montana teens are tobacco free"). By informing people, Montana successfully nudged many away from smoking and drinking.

Wells, Georgia, Jeff Horwitz, and Deepa Seetharaman. 2021. "Facebook Knows Instagram Is Toxic for Teen Girls, Company Documents Show." *Wall Street Journal*, September 14, 2021. https://www.wsj.com/articles/facebook-knows-instagram-is-toxic-for-teen-girls-company-documents-show-11631620739?mod=hp_lead_pos7&mod=article_inline.

This article reports on the leaked internal research that was conducted to ascertain Instagram's effects on the mental health of its users. It is important evidence that the company cannot defend its use of nudging on the grounds that it was ignorant of the bad outcomes it was promoting.

## Notes

1. I owe this understanding of libertarian paternalism above all else to Thaler and Sunstein 2008.
2. See Wechsler et al. 2000.
3. See Kurtz and Saks 1996.
4. See Lewis 2017.
5. See Holte and Ferraro 2020.
6. Could being informed about something *untrue* count as a nudge? That would probably be closer to manipulation than nudging, but there is nothing about the definition of "nudge" that rules out this possibility.
7. See Alter 2017.
8. Thaler and Sunstein 2008 employ the publicity principle, which they in turn got from John Rawls.
9. Dunt 2014.
10. See Tannenbaum, Fox, and Rogers 2017.
11. See Raz 1986.
12. E.g., Riehm et al. 2019; Twenge and Campbell 2019; and Hunt et al. 2018.
13. Thaler and Sunstein 2008, 72.
14. See Wells, Horwitz, and Seetharaman 2021; *Wall Street Journal* 2021a, 2021b; and Kari and Anguiano 2021.
15. See *Wall Street Journal* 2021a, 2021b.
16. See Tharoor 2021.
17. Soroka et al. 2019.

# Chapter Four: Echo Chambers and Polarization

**Echo chambers** are one of the most pernicious features of social-media life today. By "echo chamber," philosophers mean a community where opposing views are actively discredited. Echo chambers are closely related to **filter bubbles**, which are communities in which opposing views have merely been left out or excluded, perhaps deliberately or just accidentally. The active discrediting that happens in echo chambers is important because it primes people to dismiss evidence before it even comes to light. People in an echo chamber might believe that the media is conspiring to push a dangerous medical procedure, but when more scientific research reveals that the procedure is safe, they double down on their beliefs because they believe that the community of scientists is part of the conspiracy. There does not appear to be any way for evidence to disabuse these people of their beliefs.

Some of the most well-known echo chambers involve the denial of a consensus among scientists, especially concerning climate change, vaccines, medical conditions such as anorexia, and whether the Earth is flat. There are also echo chambers that arise regarding what one might call social issues. For instance, there are so-called incel, or involuntarily celibate, communities, in which men blame women for not having sex with them. Throughout this chapter, we will discuss other examples, although it is encouraged for readers to think of their own examples. It is likely that many readers will have spent some time in echo chambers or filter bubbles. Since this is a book on the ethics of social-media technologies, the focus is almost always on *online* echo chambers, but there is no reason to exclude offline groups, such as religions and cults, from consideration as echo chambers.

In the first section of this chapter, we discuss some technological and psychological factors that give rise to online echo chambers. The second section focuses on two different software design principles. Then, we consider the harms that individual members of echo chambers suffer. Next, we discuss the harms that echo chambers inflict on democratic societies. In the last section, rather controversially, we go through some of the benefits and upsides of echo chambers.

## 1. Why Echo Chambers Arise

Two kinds of factors conspire to give rise to echo chambers: *technological factors* and *psychological factors*.

One technological factor is the cost-free expulsion that is possible online. It has always been possible to expel people who disagree with you from a group. If someone is at a meeting of a city's Marxist-Leninist group and expresses doubts about Marxism-Leninism, it is possible to expel that person, but it is costly. There are practical questions about how to expel him or her, and there are also difficult social costs attached to forcibly removing someone. Not least of all, it tarnishes a group's image for someone who disagrees with the group to be expelled from a get-together. It is easier to simply talk to that dissident. Even hardcore members of the group might naturally moderate their opinions if they know that dissidents are around. In contrast, none of these considerations apply to a Marxist-Leninist group on Reddit, Discord, Facebook, or any other social-media app.

On social media, it is easy to remove someone who fails to toe the party line. Echo chambers readily arise online because technology makes it so easy to police orthodoxies. Banning someone from a Reddit community is far easier than keeping dissidents out of an in-person gathering. There are even tools that have no comparable in-person analog: for instance, we can downvote some undesirable post online so thoroughly that most users never see it and so it never elicits any kind of discussion.

Another important technological factor is filtering. Filtering is the act of curating or limiting the kinds and quantity of content that we see online. There are two kinds of filtering that we see online: **manual filtering** and **algorithmic filtering**. To manually filter content that we see online is to deliberately populate our news feeds, home pages, and so on, with content that we ourselves have chosen. For instance, I can log on to Facebook and see something that my aunt has posted because I chose to be her friend on Facebook. In contrast, algorithmic filtering is not something that users do; instead, developers design ways of predicting what sorts of content should populate our social-media apps, and the apps themselves then recommend content to us. For instance, if I watch ten videos on YouTube concerning philosophy, YouTube is more likely to recommend to me similar viewing options in the future because one of the tracked metrics is the time that we spend watching videos with certain tags or themes. In practice, most social-media sites combine algorithmic and manual filtering. YouTube is a good example: users

# 1. Why Echo Chambers Arise

can subscribe to channels that they want to follow, but YouTube also recommends videos to users.

These technological factors conspire with a few different psychological factors. The first is the deindividuation of people on social-media apps.[1] Deindividuation is the process by which a person is perceived not as an individual but instead as merely a representative of a group or worldview. The larger psychological model here is called the social identity model of deindividuation effects, or SIDE model. The idea is that when we are deprived of visual cues, such as someone's body language and facial cues, we naturally tend to view that person as less of an individual. If I encounter someone in a Republican Facebook group, I am more likely to view that person as merely another Republican, not as a full human being. This means, among other things, that I am more likely to attribute similarity to the people I meet online: I will view them all as people with the same beliefs and motivations just because, in my mind, they are representatives of some particular worldview or ideology. People I encounter in a libertarian Reddit community are much more likely to strike me as *just more libertarians*, rather than full-fledged people who disagree and have nuanced differences between their views, which is how they might strike me in an in-person setting. This is analogous to the way that drivers are more likely to treat other people badly on the road because they are rarely able to see each other's faces, so they attribute unflattering motivations to every behavior they encounter. It is also analogous to the way that cyberbullying is easier and sometimes more cruel than in-person bullying.

Another psychological factor is the tendency that humans have to congregate with people with whom they agree and to avoid people with whom they disagree.[2] People tend to seek out evidence that they agree with and avoid evidence against their own views, which is called *confirmation bias*. Confirmation biases can be combined with the pleasure we get from talking to people we agree with. Consider how fraught the dynamics are at a Thanksgiving dinner with relatives with whom we have deep political and religious disagreements. Dealing with people we disagree with is a demanding task. It is no wonder that many people avoid it, and it is no surprise that many people take advantage of the ability to create their own news feeds and home pages on social-media apps in order to ensure that they do not see content that they disagree with.

The third psychological factor is a consequence of the second. When people who agree with each other talk about their agreement, they reinforce each other's views, which leads to **polarization**. Like-minded people polarize each other—they make each other's beliefs or attitudes stronger than they were initially. If a group of moderates get together, they will walk out of a discussion with more-polarized beliefs than before, even if none of them held their beliefs particularly intensely beforehand. This goes for both online and offline contexts. In-group discussions tend to polarize participants. As one group of researchers put it, "The major effect of deliberation [among like-minded people] was to make group members more extreme than they were when they started to talk. Liberals became more liberal [...]; conservatives became more conservative."[3] Interestingly, conversations with people with whom we disagree have the opposite effect: they tend to moderate us. Agreements polarize; disagreements moderate.

It is not difficult to see how these forces work together to generate echo chambers. We tend to gravitate toward people we agree with, and those agreements polarize us. People are reduced to identities based on their beliefs, and those beliefs tend to become more extreme over time because there is no mechanism by which they can moderate themselves. Given normal human psychology, disagreements moderate our beliefs and attitudes. However, thanks to the important technologies that make cost-free expulsion and filtering possible, people online might never encounter views that they disagree with—and communities can easily expel people who do disagree.

This process of polarization is not always an irrational phenomenon. In fact, one reason why it occurs is perfectly rational. Imagine a group of Flat-Earthers whose beliefs polarize each other. They meet on Reddit and heavily gatekeep their community so that those of us who believe the Earth is round cannot join. Since they all believe that the Earth is flat, they present arguments and evidence that support their conclusion. Due to an entrenched confirmation bias, they omit all of the evidence that counters their view. Each person in the group responds in a perfectly rational and intelligible way to the evidence that circulates about the flatness of the Earth, and their attitudes naturally get stronger. The problem is not whether their response is rational. The problem is that the pool of evidence that they are responding to is terribly slanted in one direction and is, therefore, incomplete.

Another reason why groups polarize is due to reputational considerations. People want to fit in. Imagine an anti-vaxxer community. In that community, people spread the myth that vaccines cause autism in young children and that, accordingly, parents who vaccinate their children are bad and reckless. When parents encounter that community, they might not be full-fledged anti-vaxxers, but they do not want to be thought of as bad parents. So, some do not vaccinate their children. In other cases, some might vaccinate their children but then self-censor in the presence of the group. Reputational considerations cause people with minority positions to either silence themselves or leave. Either way, the discussions in the group become much more extreme as a result.

Filtering is understandable, too. There is a lot of information available online, and thoroughly researching any vexed political, scientific, or religious subject is difficult and time-consuming even for someone paid to do research. Filtering out information is an understandable reaction to the sheer quantity of information out there, and it is perhaps the only feasible way to avoid being overwhelmed. The problem is not with filtering itself but with the fact that filtering, when combined with basic human psychology, may give rise to echo chambers and filter bubbles.

## 2. Design Principles

Philosophers have discussed two major design principles in relation to echo chambers. The first is **consumer sovereignty**. When we design technologies that show users only what they want to see (or what we predict they will want to see), this is the principle guiding us. Consumer sovereignty foregrounds the consumer's values and preferences. Filtering out content that would show users something they would prefer to not see is another application of this design principle. Examples abound on social-media apps so thoroughly that virtually everything about them reflects this principle. These apps are designed to show us content on so-called For You pages or Recommended pages and are built around users' decisions to follow certain accounts.

Both algorithmic and manual filtering illustrate the dominance of consumer sovereignty as a design principle. In each case, it is understood as a good thing that users are shown only things that they wish to see or that the software predicts that they wish to see. In 1995, Bill Gates outlined this vision:

> Customized information is a natural extension. [...] For your own daily dose of news, you might subscribe to several review services and let a software agent or a human one pick and choose from them to compile your completely customized "newspaper." These subscription services, whether human or electronic, will gather information that conforms to a particular philosophy and set of interests.[4]

In the same spirit, Mark Zuckerberg has said: "A squirrel dying in front of your house may be more relevant to your interests than people dying in Africa."[5] *The consumer is sovereign*, and that is reflected in what content we see when we open social-media apps.

It is not difficult to see how this design principle can generate echo chambers and filter bubbles. Today's technology can sort us into echo chambers just by showing us what we want to see, or what developers think that we want to see, and they believe that they are doing nothing more than delivering a commodity to a consumer. Apps can do this better than any other technology in human history: better than billboards, newspapers, televisions, radios, and movies. When we combine the technological ability to deliver on this potential, and insights gleaned from behavioral psychology about how to determine preferences and nudge us to spend more time on an app, it is easy for echo chambers to come about. If I am an incel, I am going to see incel content online. I might be stuck in a pro-anorexia bubble because Instagram can detect that such content grabs my attention more than anything else. Whether I am a Republican or Democrat, YouTube knows to avoid showing me content that I disagree with. Every time I go on YouTube, I see only things that I agree with, and so my opinion gets stronger because my views keep being confirmed by everything that I see.

The opposing design principle is **serendipity**. When we design technologies with serendipity in mind, we build into them the tendency to show users things that they might not have thought about previously or wished to see. For instance, imagine that Apple Music recommended country music to you when there is no evidence that you even like country music. A bit of reflection reveals why serendipity is valuable. We often stumble upon things that we have no reason to think that we would like, and then discover, serendipitously, that we like them after all. Such discoveries do not happen in a world where we are shown only things that align with our current preferences. In social-media contexts, we might imagine people who see only content that they already agree with, in line with consumer sovereignty, but who would benefit tremendously from having their worldview expanded, just as someone who has never listened to country music has their musical tastes expanded by Apple Music's suggestion to try country.

Older technologies did not need to be built with serendipity in mind. It was just so difficult to tailor content to an individual viewer's preferences that serendipitous encounters happened naturally. A commercial on television and an advertisement in a newspaper are good examples. Today, the problem is that although we can reflect on the value of serendipitous encounters, it is altogether a better business model to rely on consumer sovereignty. The value of consumer sovereignty lies in the idea that it is good to satisfy people's preferences and bad to show them things that they would prefer not to see. Even if we agree that this idea is not always correct, it remains true that businesses have a good reason to act this way: a major part of a business's success relies on satisfying people's preferences. If I am selling a product that does *not* satisfy preferences because I think that serendipity is good, whereas you are selling a product that shows consumers only what they want to see, it is no surprise that you win the competition.

Serendipity is sometimes presented as an antidote to echo chambers. Causing people to see content that they disagree with online, or simply content that they would have not wished to see (perhaps because they did not know it existed), could be a powerful way to impede the growth of echo chambers and polarization. The same features that polarize, such as recommendations on YouTube or X for certain content, could be used to expand worldviews and break down echo chambers: by showing people content they disagree with.

As I wrap up this look at the two design principles and transition to a discussion of the harms of echo chambers, think about the way that individual users might benefit from seeing things that they might not have wished to see. Think also about the way that *society* overall benefits from its members seeing more than just things they agree with. These points lead to two major discussions about echo chambers: the way that members of some echo chambers are harmed by their membership, and the way that society overall is hurt by the fragmentation of citizens into insulated online communities.

# 3. Individual Harms

Echo chambers are bad for the people inside them. There are a few different costs that members pay.

The first cost is harm in the most straightforward sense: bodily harm. People in echo chambers often put their lives and health at risk. Some of the most prominent echo chambers are based on the active discrediting of medical science, including the science of vaccines. People in these communities are jeopardizing their own health. The situation is just as bleak when we turn to echo chambers that discredit psychiatry. Pro-anorexia groups, sometimes called "pro-ana communities," thrive on every major social-media platform. There are plenty of less well-known ones, such as pro-apotemnophilia groups. Apotemnophilia is a condition in which a person's conception of themselves has fewer limbs than their body actually has, and so they want an amputation to correct the discrepancy. Online echo chambers for apotemnophiliacs exist in which members are insulated from the advice of mental-health experts and in which those experts are actively discredited. Instead of seeking out proper medical care, people with this condition might perform the amputations themselves. There are real risks to our well-being when we actively discredit opposing views.

Of course, there are plenty of apparently harmless echo chambers. Many are about low-stakes topics, such as which movie or sports team is the best. These echo chambers do not endanger members of their communities in anything like the way that pro-anorexia communities endanger their members. This is not to say, however, that there is not a more expansive sense of "harm" that we can apply to these cases. First, many echo chambers result in estrangement from family, friends, and romantic partners. If the beliefs in question become sufficiently extreme, this estrangement can be severe and destructive. Think about a man who watched so many TikTok incel videos that he has done lasting damage to his relationships with every woman in his life. Membership in the incel echo chamber heightened his frustrations with women who will not have sex with him. That might not be *harmful* in the same sense that anti-vaxxers might harm themselves, but there is clearly a steep price to pay for membership in that echo chamber. Along the same lines, just as we can imagine some Flat-Earthers not suffering any cost from their beliefs, we can also imagine other Flat-Earthers who have become so deluded that they have pushed away families and friends outside of the echo chamber.

If we expand the meaning of "harm" even further, we can say that it is harmful to have false beliefs and to have our reasoning systemically distorted by our environment. Even the Flat-Earthers who continue to enjoy healthy relationships with friends and family are being *harmed* in this sense: they are badly confused about the nature of the planet they live on. We have intuitions about these people that speak to this point. For instance, few outside of these echo chambers would ever wish to be a Flat-Earther, and it does strike us that something has gone badly wrong with someone who sincerely believes that the Earth is flat. Again, this sort of harm might not be as obvious or straightforward as the sort of harm that comes with our health being on the line, but to the extent that our lives going well depends on having true beliefs, and having access to as full a range of views as is realistic when we are forming those beliefs, it does seem that Flat-Earthers, and others, are being harmed by their membership in echo chambers.

However, it is possible to take this too far. It seems excessive to say that membership in an echo chamber that esteems some truly terrible sports team is harmful, even if it is inculcating false beliefs in members and distorting their reasoning processes. Some echo chambers do not really seem objectionable at all. In fact, at the end of this chapter, we shall survey respects in which some echo chambers are *good* for their members.

The important thing to note as we end this section is that membership in some echo chambers comes with costs. We can escape these costs by leaving the echo chamber, since it was our membership that was generating the problems for us.

## 4. Social Harms

In contrast, the harms that echo chambers do to society are felt by more people than just the members of those echo chambers, and even when a member leaves the echo chamber, some harms remain. Everyone in society suffers the social harms of echo chambers.

Democratic institutions require that citizens have a shared or common set of beliefs. Echo chambers and, in general, the fragmentation of society pose a threat to the common set of beliefs. Cass Sunstein, an important American legal scholar, sums up the problem this way:

> Consider a few examples. Many Americans fear that certain environmental problems—abandoned hazardous waste sites, genetic engineering of food, climate change—are extremely serious and require immediate government action. But others believe that the same problems are imaginative fictions, generated by zealots and self-serving politicians. Many Americans think that most welfare recipients are indolent and content to live off the work of others. On this view, "welfare reform," to be worthy of the name, consists of reduced handouts—a step necessary to encourage people to fend for themselves. But many other Americans believe that welfare recipients generally face severe disadvantages and would be entirely willing to work if decent jobs were available. On this view, welfare reform, understood as reductions in benefits, is an act of official cruelty. Many people believe that the largest threat to American security remains terrorism, and that if terrorism is not a top priority, catastrophic attacks are likely to ensue. Many others believe that while terrorism presents serious risks, the threat has

been overblown, and that other problems, including climate change, deserve at least equal attention.[6]

The root of the problem is the apparently intractable disagreements that pervade democratic conversations in the twenty-first century. When people disagree so vehemently and so deeply, it is hard to imagine how they could make progress.

Instead of making progress on important questions and persuading our fellow citizens, political parties will merely trade power. Now, one party will gain control of the legislature, and that party will do what it wants. Then, another party will come to power, undo what the previous party did, and will then do what *it* wants. The government will function, but always at the expense of the wishes of the other half of the nation.

Thanks to this sort of pervasive and intractable disagreement, the important norm of **public reason** in democratic decision-making is abandoned. Public reason is the idea that the rules that govern political processes and the reasons that governments respond to should be, in some sense, acceptable or justifiable in the eyes of all citizens. For instance, if a Western government passed a law that banned some behavior because the Bible said that the behavior was sinful, that would violate the idea of public reason. Western countries have many citizens who do not recognize the Bible as authoritative. Public reason is an important idea in the liberal political tradition, and it is one reason why governments that act on the basis of religious reasons are considered illiberal.

In contrast, liberal governments can cite the *constitution* of their government when explaining their actions. Imagine the American government passing some legislation that protected some part of the American Constitution and citing the Constitution in their reasoning. It might seem at first that there is not much of a difference between citing the US Constitution and the Bible as the reason for some legislation. Public reason explains to us what the difference really is: the US Constitution has widespread endorsement among Americans. Even when they do not like it very much, citizens recognize its legitimacy as a basis for government action. That is why liberal governments act in accordance with their constitutions.

Plato, in the *Laws*, discusses a disagreement between three quarreling brothers.[7] Surely, the worst result is that the quarrel does not get resolved in any way. Another possibility is that a judge resolves the disagreement by simply putting one brother in charge of the others and so uses force to end the matter. Yet, the best imaginable result is for the three brothers to be reconciled. Public reason captures this sentiment because it requires that we do not rely exclusively on coercion but that we instead engage with our fellow citizens' personhood.[8] In practice, this might involve citizens accepting that even if they disagree with the outcome of some political process, they accept the legitimacy of the process, and so they accept the result itself.

Imagine a hiring committee in a philosophy department deciding which applicant should fill a job opening. Four out of five members agree on one applicant, but one member disagrees. The fifth member might not like the outcome but has nevertheless agreed to the process: if a majority of the committee chooses an applicant, then that is the one they go with. Everyone recognizes that the majority's consensus is a good *reason* for acting, even though there is still one dissident. I doubt that I have to remind anyone that in the United States today, there are echo chambers in which members deny the legitimacy of some elections altogether. The disagreements in twenty-first-century political life are so extreme that even the integrity of basic processes is doubted.

In this sense, echo chambers undermine the basis of public reason. Fellow citizens stop seeing the same things as good reasons for acting. In fact, as the quotation from Cass Sunstein earlier illustrates, fellow citizens do not even accept the same description of whatever action is being proposed. Again, governments can function in this condition, but the norms that underlie democratic institutions are frustrated by widespread, intractable disagreement. This is like the situation from Plato's *Laws* where the judge has not reconciled the brothers but has ended the disagreement simply by putting one brother in charge. That is better than unchecked anarchy, but it is not the political community that we want and have enjoyed for decades. It has to be noted that some echo chambers are built *around* conspiracy theories that deny the very basis of liberal governments. The Sovereign Citizen movement is one example that has thrived in the United States, Canada, Australia, and elsewhere: people in these echo chambers believe that laws apply only to those who have explicitly consented to them and that filling out some paperwork can cause a person to be exempt from paying bills or even from the law itself. Some echo chambers, such as those that deny the reality of human-caused climate change, impede progress in particular conversations. Others, such as the Sovereign Citizen movement, undermine the shared basis of democratic political life altogether.

I will briefly add that democratic legislatures, such as the US Congress or the Canadian House of Commons, are bad at resolving the sorts of disagreements that Sunstein cataloged earlier. Consider just one example: environmental problems. If we believe that human-caused climate change is real, then the question becomes what we ought to do about it. Perhaps a cap-and-trade system. Perhaps an outright ban on some emissions. Perhaps new subsidies for sustainable technology. Perhaps nothing at all. These are possible outcomes of a conversation in which all the participants accept the reality of anthropogenic climate change, and we can imagine all of these as outcomes of a legislative session. Now imagine that a large subset of the legislators believe that climate change is a hoax perpetrated by a foreign government. The conversation will likely go nowhere, or, if it goes anywhere at all, it will be like the situation lamented by Plato, in which there was no true reconciliation between the brothers. *Congress is not a place where the reality of climate change can be profitably debated* because Congress lacks the appropriate institutional guardrails. Academics and scientists debate human-caused climate change, and their debates are profitable because the venues of academic debate are different. Institutions, such as the peer-review process, shape the debate differently. Democratic institutions are bad at settling the sorts of questions that echo chambers cause politicians to debate because there is nothing about them that is sensitive to the truth in the way that, say, peer-review processes are. Appropriate debates occur when everyone is on the same page, but echo chambers make that difficult. This is a major cost of echo chambers even for non-members: we all suffer from dysfunctional political communities.

One reason why echo chambers have this effect is that the cost of reaching people dramatically increases due to both algorithmic and manual filtering. This is true of filter bubbles and echo chambers, although the cost is even higher in echo chambers. In order for productive and healthy conversations to happen, people who disagree with each other need to be able to reach and talk to each other. Candidates from one party need to be able to reach voters who lean toward the other party in order to try to speak to their needs and preferences, and citizens need to know what the other party is offering in order to make an informed choice. The cost of reaching people who disagree with you was once much lower. For instance, there was a time when there were a small number of television channels, and the majority of citizens watched the same television channels. Today, it is possible to get news solely from a niche Reddit community or online publication and ignore what everyone else is saying. Filtering gives us the opportunity to avoid starting a conversation. In fact, we might not even know that there is another conversation happening at all. When politicians cannot reach, talk to, and listen to increasingly large subsets of the population, fewer voters will recognize their values reflected in elected officials. Politicians also have less incentive to graciously invite people who disagree with them into their movement because those people cannot hear them to begin with.

Unfortunately, there is an incentive for politicians to maintain this situation. That is not to say that they all like it or that they all benefit from it, but there is an incentive. Specifically, politicians do not have to worry as much about losing their base of support to a political opponent. They *know* that their base will not flock to their opponent because their base will not even listen to their opponent. Their base listens only to each other. This means that politicians have one fewer thing to worry about in a campaign. They will very likely have to make some maneuvers to win over the shrinking group of undecided voters, but they can count on their maneuvers not causing a loss of support among the base because it just is not plausible that their base will abandon them.

We might liken this point to *brand loyalty*. Companies try to build brand loyalty because it makes it more likely that their products will survive competition even against objectively better products. In theory, a company will lose a competition against someone selling a superior product. For that reason, companies have an incentive to create a better product and always innovate. In reality, companies have ways to survive competition against better products, and cultivating a fiercely loyal base of consumers is one such strategy. Politicians do the same thing when they create echo chambers and filter bubbles around them. A filter bubble provides strong protection because opponents' messages do not get through the filtering. An echo chamber is even better for the politician because opponents' messages are actively discredited; if one gets through, it is lampooned.

This might be good for the career of an individual politician, but democratic societies suffer. These are harms that nobody can escape. My opting out of social media altogether does not mean that I avoid these harms. Society itself is a victim of dysfunctional democratic institutions.

## 5. In Defense of Some Echo Chambers

We conclude this chapter by making a somewhat controversial point: some echo chambers and filter bubbles are *good* things.[9]

There are times when people *reasonably* prefer to be insulated from those who disagree with them. Echo chambers do not merely insulate us from opposing views, they also actively and intentionally discredit those views, and sometimes this is good. The clearest example of how an echo chamber can support a reasonable preference for insulation concerns marginalized people. Technologies that often get maligned in traditional discussions of echo chambers are useful and valuable here. For instance, consider cost-free expulsion: it is much easier to expel someone from a Reddit community than it is to expel someone from an in-person community, and this fact makes it easier for online administrators and moderators to expel someone who is not toeing the party line in a given community. This is something to be thankful for when we are talking about protecting marginalized people.

We can illustrate this point with an example. Consider a person who has some minority status and who lives in a small rural town. This person might not know anyone with the same minority status offline, and it might not be reasonably easy or even at all possible for this person to get in touch with such a person offline. In this case, the features of social-media platforms that allow for similar people to find each other come in handy. In fact, the possibility that someone with hateful or mean-spirited intentions might enter the community is easily avoided by the fact that expelling and banning this other person is much easier online than it is offline.

This insight turns the usual discourse around echo chambers on its head. Usually, we hear that the like-minded people who are congregating on social-media platforms are themselves hateful and mean-spirited, and every attempt to discourage their behavior gets a person expelled and banned from these communities. Think of racist echo chambers, for example. We might also observe that, in the past, there was virtually no chance that a Flat-Earther could meet someone else with the same delusions and reinforce each other's false beliefs, but it is lamentable that today this occurs so easily online. Sometimes this is true, but in other cases, echo chambers are valuable: it is good that marginalized people can meet and discuss their experience, with an almost entirely cost-free way of banning people from their community; it is similarly good that these communities allow people to overcome large geographical distances when their demographic is so small.

Along the same lines, cost-free expulsion can help when there is no reasonable expectation that a person should have to engage with some subset of views. Consider a group of Holocaust survivors. It is unreasonable that Holocaust survivors

## 5. In Defense of Some Echo Chambers

should have to let Holocaust-deniers into their community. Consequently, the survivors might know very little about the pseudo-historical arguments presented by the deniers and know even less about how to refute them. They most likely actively discredit the deniers by thinking that their positions are entirely baseless and are nothing more than dressed-up gibberish. The survivors' community conforms to the formal definition of an echo chamber, but nobody could call it unreasonable or objectionable. If an in-person meeting of Holocaust survivors were disrupted by some deniers, we would not object to the deniers being thrown out of the meeting, and we might even be indignant at the fact that the survivors had to go through the trouble of expelling the deniers. Online communities make this easier, and when some privacy settings are enabled such that deniers cannot even *find* the group, expelling someone is no longer even necessary. These are the same formal features of echo chambers that are often found alarming, but they are unobjectionable in our example of the Holocaust survivors.

It is also helpful that online communities allow participants to escape social pressures. This statement is not universally true, of course: some communities might enforce stringent rules that mirror in-person social pressures, but others do not. In some cases, this is unfortunate. There is no doubt that sexist communities flourish online because the participants are made anonymous by default. Being a sexist offline generally, though not always, comes at a cost. Being a sexist online does not, especially in those communities that allow sexism to flourish. By the same token, there is sometimes a disapproval of marginalized lifestyles and identities offline. The absence of this disapproval on some social-media platforms is a *good* thing because it means that these marginalized lifestyles can flourish. Again, we are noting the same formal features: the absence of disapproval means that the disapproved-of thing can flourish online; just as this is a bad thing in some cases, it is a good thing in others.

One last point worth making in this section is a reminder: echo chambers often come into being because people distrust institutions, professionals, and elites. This is true of virtually every prominent echo chamber: anti-vaccination communities are against the medical establishment; pro-anorexia communities are against the psychiatric establishment; QAnon communities are against the political establishment; and Flat-Earthers are against NASA. We can easily imagine more examples. The dangers of this distrust are clear: there are serious costs incurred, and violence may not be far behind. The technology that makes expulsion and banning virtually cost-free is used to disastrous effect when, for example, medical doctors are expelled from a community that is denying the legitimacy of life-saving treatment.

However, we ought to remember that these communities often have good reason to be wary of certain institutions. The distrust did not come out of nowhere and nothing. The pro-anorexia online community is an example of a harmful echo chamber, and it seems right that everyone in the community would do well to listen to their health-care providers. It also seems important to sympathize with members of the pro-anorexia community and to hear why they distrust the medical establishment. Their echo chamber is not a good or worthwhile one, all things considered, but to this extent, it *is* good: namely, to the extent to which people with anorexia can find support among people who understand what they are going through, without having to engage with a medical establishment that they believe has failed them or made them feel crazy. They might be worried, specifically, about the possibility of compulsory treatment. We can say the same thing for other echo chambers. We might find, for instance, that communities which vigorously deny some scientific discovery were failed by the scientific establishment at some point in their education; perhaps they were made to feel like they had no place learning about science.

Earlier in this chapter, I explained that one important feature of echo chambers is that they actively undermine opposing views. So far in this section, I have merely argued that being *insulated* is a good and unobjectionable thing in some cases. This is a weaker notion than what we find in echo chambers, in which views are actively discredited, but it does not take far to get there from here. Let us return to the example of people with anorexia. We want such people to be insulated from pro-anorexia views; it is, all things considered, good to be so insulated. Moreover, it would be *even better* if they believed that pro-anorexia communities had nothing to offer or even that such communities were toxic, unhealthy, and predatorial. In many (and perhaps all) cases, this is true. It would be better for people who are recovering from eating disorders to think that there is simply no evidence for the beliefs of pro-anorexia communities. We ought to heap epistemic discredit upon such beliefs. We would probably achieve better health outcomes more reliably if we primed the patients in question to be such that *if they do encounter pro-anorexia communities*, then they immediately dismiss them, instead of trying to take their views seriously and ending up engaging regularly with these communities.

Virtually all of us live in communities in which Flat-Earther beliefs are seen as baseless, and it is hard to see what is wrong with actively discrediting the beliefs of Flat-Earthers. What is remarkable about the anorexia example is that it shows that there are not only cases where it is permissible to actively undermine opposing views but also cases where it is *better* to do so, to the extent that it more reliably promotes better health outcomes. The same could be said for other cases, too, such as anti-vaccination communities: we might want parents of young children to be insulated from people who say their children should not be vaccinated against polio; we would be even more satisfied if parents believed that the anti-vaccination communities were completely foolish and worthless. However, it is important to remember that if these echo chambers became bad, they would lack any mechanism for correction.

It is also unclear whether adopting serendipity as a design principle would be a good thing. In some cases, serendipity clearly leads to bad outcomes. We already saw this earlier: there are some cases in which it is reasonable and unobjectionable for communities to be insulated. If we can avoid having Holocaust survivors see Holocaust-denying content unless they prefer to see that content, then it does not seem that there is any reason to expose them to this content. Yet, just as Holocaust survivors might serendipitously stumble upon an interesting documentary that they had never heard of, they might also serendipitously stumble upon some Holocaust-denying content. Those who defend the value of serendipity overlook the fact that some people have a reasonable and unobjectionable preference to not see some content. Serendipity seems like a poor pretext for recommending bigoted content to a marginalized person.

It also seems like a poor pretext for showing someone with an eating disorder pro-anorexia content because it would have been better to let someone recovering from anorexia not see that content. Serendipity appears valuable when we consider the way that people often have unreasonable preferences to not see some content, such as when someone prefers not to see opera music suggested to them on their streaming app solely on the grounds that he or she has never listened to it before, never really considered it, and does not really know what opera music is like. It seems to us that this person would benefit from having their worldview expanded, but it is helpful not to generalize from such cases because there are other cases in which the preference for being insulated is reasonable and unobjectionable.

# 6. Conclusion

In this chapter, we explored the ethics of echo chambers and polarization. In section 5, we saw that not all echo chambers are bad, and sometimes it is good to be insulated from opposing views and even to actively discredit those views. That argument should not take away from the fact that, as discussed in the earlier sections, echo chambers generate many different kinds of harms. Some of these harms are felt only by the members of the echo chambers, but others are felt by everyone in society. As more people flock to social-media platforms and as the platforms become more efficient at sorting people into echo chambers, both sorts of harms worsen, and the need to rethink our commitment to some of the design values discussed in section 2 grows more pressing.

## Key Terms

**Algorithmic filtering**: a kind of online filtering done by an app itself, not by the app's users. The app infers from the behavior of users what sorts of content that they engage with and would prefer to see more of. For instance, when we load TikTok's For You page or Instagram's Explore page, we see content from users that we are not necessarily following but that the app predicts we would like to see. Content that it predicts we would *not* like to see is excluded. Note that many apps combine algorithmic and manual filtering.

**Consumer sovereignty**: a principle that governs the design of, among other things, software platforms such as social-media apps. This principle states that consumers should be shown only what they wish to be shown (or what the developers predict that they wish to be shown). This principle explains why virtually all social-media sites are built around *filtering*.

**Echo chambers**: communities in which people are insulated from opposing views and in which those opposing views are actively discredited. Another viable definition is that echo chambers are rigidly closed-off communities that amplify the voices of their members and insulate them from rebuttals.

**Filter bubbles**: communities in which opposing views have been left out, and it is possible that this has happened merely accidentally. They do not actively discredit opposing views, and they are not *rigidly* closed-off communities. They are sometimes called "epistemic bubbles."

**Manual filtering**: one of the two kinds of online filtering. To manually filter content is to decide for yourself what content should populate your social-media apps when you open them. The exact mechanism varies from site to site: we *follow* someone on X; we *friend* them on Facebook; we *subscribe* to someone on YouTube; and so on.

**Polarization:** the process by which beliefs and attitudes become more extreme and are held more strongly.

**Public reason:** a norm of decision-making in liberal democratic theory. The idea is that the reasons for government action should be acceptable to or justifiable in the eyes of everyone in society. Public reason, therefore, excludes acting on the basis of religious beliefs because not everyone in society would find religion compelling or authoritative. In contrast, acting on the basis of the nation's constitution would be acceptable. Echo chambers undermine the idea of public reason because they make it hard for everyone to get on the same page.

**Serendipity:** the design principle that users should at least sometimes see content that they would not have wished to see in advance. Serendipity is regarded as an anti-echo-chamber design principle because following it involves showing users content that challenges their beliefs. Of course, there is no guarantee that users will change their minds based on what they see.

# Discussion Cases

## 1. r/The_Donald

In June 2020, Reddit banned the r/The_Donald community that was dedicated to supporting Donald Trump and that the platform had hosted for years. Reddit did this on the grounds that the community failed to meet the site's most basic expectations. It was alleged that r/The_Donald spread conspiracy theories and was racist, sexist, and Islamophobic. The community also happened to be one of the most prominent and popular communities on Reddit.

Was Reddit right to ban r/The_Donald? Some people worry that in cases like this, banning is simply ineffective: users will flock to some other site and set up shop there (and, to some extent, r/The_Donald did re-form on its own site). Should this consideration weigh heavily on a platform's decision to kick a community off? What is the right way to dismantle an echo chamber?

## 2. Pro-anorexia Communities

The internet has many pro-anorexia communities. They flourish in particular on Instagram and TikTok. These echo chambers and filter bubbles are tough to break through because many users who join them in the first place distrust and resent the medical establishment. If we sent medical professionals into these online communities to try to dispel some of the myths around weight loss and dieting, there is a good chance that only the least enthusiastic members, if anyone, would be persuaded. Many people with anorexia are women, and women often feel unheard by doctors; telling members of pro-anorexia communities that their beliefs are false and that they are in an echo chamber might not help the situation. However, the situation does need to be helped: anorexia is the most lethal mental illness.

**What should we do to reach and help people in echo chambers who are at risk of serious harm? What are some effective ways to communicate with them?**

## 3. Good Polarization

Polarization and echo chambers are often thought of as bad things, but it is possible that there are some upsides. Consider slavery, which was once widespread throughout the Western world (and supported by various philosophers, such as Aristotle). Now there is virtually no one in the Western world who is pro-slavery. In the United States in particular, it was not so long ago that many people *practiced* slavery. This is a remarkable about-face and is an example of polarization: our attitudes and beliefs about slavery became extreme, relatively quickly, as a society.

**How can polarization be used as a tool for making progress toward a more moral society? Are there any problems that we might encounter? What are some other examples of polarization being a force for good?**

# Further Reading

Campbell, Douglas R. 2023. "In Defense of (Some) Online Echo Chambers." *Ethics and Information Technology* 25 (3): 1–11.

> This article picks up on the idea from the last section of this chapter, namely, that there is something good about being insulated from opposing views. The article uses the same sort of argumentative moves as the anti-echo-chamber position: for instance, just as echo chambers can produce bad health outcomes (e.g., in the case of pro-anorexia communities), they can also produce good health outcomes (e.g., when someone is insulated against pro-anorexia content). It can be even better when the members of the echo chamber are not merely insulated against some views but when the opposing views are actively discredited as well.

Larmore, Charles. 1999. "The Moral Basis of Political Liberalism." *Journal of Philosophy*, 96 (12): 599–625. https://doi.org/10.2307/2564695.

> I recommend Larmore's article for its justification of public reason that appeals to respect for other people. He argues that we ought to respect our fellow citizens as more than mere means to our desired political ends, and this respect requires acting on principles or reasons that are justifiable to our fellow citizens.

Nguyen, C. Thi. 2020. "Echo Chambers and Epistemic Bubbles." *Episteme* 17 (2): 141–61.

> Nguyen's article was certainly not the first one on echo chambers, but it is foundational in the field. That is because it provides the conceptual foundations of many of the ideas in this chapter. Most of all, he introduces the now-standard meanings of the terms "echo chambers" and "epistemic bubbles" (which are sometimes called "filter bubbles," as is the case in this chapter). I recommend this article to anyone who wants to read more about the basic concepts at work in this chapter.

Parsell, Mitch. 2008. "Pernicious Virtual Communities: Identity, Polarisation, and the Web 2.0." *Ethics and Information Technology* 10: 41–56.

> Parsell's article was written early enough in the history of the ethics of social media that he does not even use the term "echo chamber." Instead, he prefers the term "pernicious virtual community." His article provided for this chapter, among other things, the illustrative (and vivid) example of apotemnophiliacs as well as much of the discussion concerning the harms that echo chambers cause for individuals. I also recommend his article to those who are interested in thinking about the way that online echo chambers reduce people to individual identity markers (e.g., Democrat, libertarian, and so on).

Reviglio, Urbano. 2019. "Serendipity as an Emerging Design Principle of the Infosphere: Challenges and Opportunities." *Ethics and Information Technology*, 21 (2): 151–66.

> Reviglio's article is a wide-ranging survey of the benefits, limitations, and possible unintended consequences of adopting serendipity as a design principle. Of particular importance is his idea that serendipity can be used to promote what he calls "media pluralism," which is when users consume a more well-rounded online media diet online and which is the opposite of the single-mindedness of the content seen in filter bubbles and echo chambers. Reviglio specifically discusses the power of serendipity to weaken filter bubbles and echo chambers.

Sunstein, Cass. 2017. *#republic: Divided Democracy in the Age of Social Media*. Princeton, NJ: Princeton University Press.

> For anyone interested in the harms that echo chambers inflict on society, Sunstein's book is the go-to resource. The third chapter, entitled "Polarization," in particular develops many of the core ideas of this chapter. Sunstein also presents much of the research concerning *why* polarization happens, and he discusses the two design principles that I highlight here: consumer sovereignty and serendipity. In his view, reliance on serendipity is our best bet for reversing much of the damage caused by echo chambers.

# Chapter Four: Echo Chambers and Polarization

## Notes

1. For a discussion of the SIDE model with respect specifically to echo chambers, see Parsell 2008. For the psychological research concerning the SIDE model in computer-mediated communication, see Spears, Postmes, and Lea 2002 and Postmes, Spears, and Lea 1998.
2. There are decades of replicated research showing this; see Byrne 1971. See Parsell 2008 and Sunstein 2017 (esp. 59–97) for discussions with respect to online echo chambers.
3. I quote Schkade, Sunstein, and Hastie 2007. See Sunstein 2017, 68–71, for a great job interpreting this important and illustrative experiment (that he himself co-ran) in Colorado that demonstrated this effect.
4. Gates 1995, 167–68.
5. Quoted in Pariser 2011, 1.
6. Sunstein 2017, 67.
7. *Laws* I 627c–628a, in Cooper 1999.
8. Larmore 1999 is a good example. See, for instance, Larmore 1999, 607–8: "if we try to bring about conformity to a rule of conduct solely by the threat of force, we shall be treating persons merely as means, as objects of coercion, and not also as ends, engaging with their distinctive capacity as persons [... and] to respect another person as an end is to require that coercive or political principles be as justifiable to that person as they presumably are to us."
9. This section is adapted from Campbell 2023.

# Chapter Five: Misinformation

In 2021, a prominent anti-vaccine activist, Sherri Tenpenny, claimed that the COVID-19 vaccine would magnetize people—that anyone who got the vaccine would soon attract fridge magnets and other household items. This was somehow linked, Tenpenny said, to 5G phone towers and microchips that Bill Gates had put into the vaccine. That was not the most unfortunate part. Even more dire was her prediction, made early in 2022, that "by the end of 2022, every fully vaccinated person over the age of 30 may have the equivalent of full-blown vaccine-induced immune suppressed AIDS."[1] At this point, her predictions became less silly and simply unintelligible. For instance, she asserted that the vaccines would create a kind of quantum entanglement between every vaccinated person that would interact with our Google credit scores.

Sherri Tenpenny was one of the most prolific purveyors of misinformation on the internet. She and eleven other users comprised a group, called the Disinformation Dozen, that was responsible for 65 percent of all anti-vaccine misinformation online.[2] She achieved such notoriety that she even testified in front of the Ohio House of Representatives health committee during the pandemic, saying that household objects such as keys would be magnetically attracted to vaccinated individuals.

Eventually, YouTube and what was then called Twitter removed her accounts because she violated their policies concerning misinformation. Some other social-media platforms, such as Rumble, have no policy against misinformation and, accordingly, never removed her.

Highlighting Tenpenny's story brings to the foreground something that all of us who have used social media know well: **misinformation** is an ever-present aspect of online life, and it spreads like wildfire. The pandemic shone a bright light on it because so many people were at home, listening intently for new recommendations and witnessing the vast disagreements in society. Misinformation was coming from everywhere, even from the president of the United States of America, and to such a degree that our critical-thinking skills were constantly being outstripped by the anxiety and uniqueness of that historical moment. Even apart from the pandemic, misinformation exists about virtually every subject that is important to human life. There is misinformation about our health and bodies, every major political issue (and the integrity of important political processes, such as elections), and scientific theories, such as the shape of the Earth and whether human-caused climate change is real. This, of course, predates the pandemic: for instance, misinformation about various fad diets has long been a staple of popular online (and offline) culture.

In the first section of this chapter, we identify what misinformation is and what the harms are. Then, we look at *cybercascades*, which explain why misinformation spreads like wildfire online. Afterward, we consider some of the philosophical issues surrounding the context in which misinformation is spread. We conclude the chapter by discussing whether social-media sites have a duty to remove misinformation from their platforms.

Sometimes people use the word **disinformation** to refer to false information that is spread by someone who knows that it is false. Such a person might want to sow discord or make some money by spreading the false information. "Misinformation," then, would be reserved for cases of false information spread by someone who does not know that it is false. That distinction gets at an important nuance, but it does not really bear on the specific questions that we ask in this chapter, so we shall use "misinformation" to refer to both kinds of false information. Further, misinformation includes statements and other media that are misleading, even though not outright false. For instance, a deepfake video of a politician being racist is misleading in a way that causes it to count as misinformation, even though it might not contain any explicitly false statements.

## 1. Harms

Misinformation is responsible for three kinds of harms. The first involves *personal harms*. The second involves *harms to democracy*. The third involves *harms to our information environment*. Popular discourse has tended to foreground the first two kinds of harms, whereas philosophical attention has been focused much more on the last kind.

It is not hard for us to think of examples of how misinformation can harm us personally. Health misinformation can, in obvious and visible ways, harm our health. In 2019, for instance, there were about 100,000 cases of measles recorded in Europe. In New York City alone, there were hundreds of measles cases between 2018 and 2019. The vast majority of these cases were in unvaccinated people.[3]

# 1. Harms

What underlies these cases is the misinformation that the measles, mumps, and rubella (MMR) vaccine causes autism. This misinformation led to these outbreaks. In the first half of 2024, the Canadian province of Ontario recorded its first death from measles in decades, in the tragic case of an unvaccinated child younger than five years old.[4]

In other cases, misinformation scams us out of money or merely inconveniences us. Sometimes misinformation is used to defame high-profile people. One of the most important thinkers in the ethics of social media is Cass Sunstein, and his work in the Obama administration from 2009 to 2012 sparked conspiracy theories about him: some people said he was stealing people's organs, while others thought that he was secretly behind WikiLeaks.[5] These harms affect a person in direct and measurable ways. If we put in charge someone who believes this misinformation, it can have terrible consequences on other people too. For instance, in the early days of the internet, the president of South Africa, Thabo Mbeki, picked up from the internet the false belief that there was no link between HIV and AIDS. His public statements on the matter led to many South Africans being badly misinformed and to an unknowable amount of infections.

The second kind of harm is suffered by our democratic institutions. The threat that misinformation poses to democracy was highlighted by Barack Obama a few years after leaving the presidency:

> If we do not have the capacity to distinguish what's true from what's false, then by definition the marketplace of ideas doesn't work. And by definition our democracy doesn't work. We are entering into an epistemological crisis.[6]

Obama here highlights the way that democracies require an informed citizenry. I identify certain policies that make sense in light of my values, and then I vote for politicians who champion those policies and can implement them in the legislature. If I am not informed, then this system does not work well.

Climate-change policies illustrate this conundrum. Let's say that my values include living and raising my children in a hospitable environment. It makes sense then that my values entail supporting policies which mitigate the effects of climate change. The problem is that I have been duped by people online into believing that climate change is a hoax perpetrated by foreign governments. There is no way that I am going to vote for someone who represents my values: even though my values are pro-environment, I am misinformed about the nature of climate science. When enough people agree with me, we voters will begin to elect politicians who mirror my false beliefs. In fact, this has already happened: one US president has said that climate change is a hoax perpetrated by the Chinese government.[7] The resulting policies might be bad but, even if not, this situation represents a failure of the democratic process because now I and others like me are voting against our own values and interests on account of the misinformation.

Other political institutions can be threatened too. For instance, the integrity of elections and the basis of peaceful transitions of power rely on people respecting the outcome of political processes even if they disagree with them, on the grounds that they respect the electoral process. I might not like the person who was just elected, but I like fair elections and think that they are a good way to establish the legitimacy of representatives. However, if misinformation online has convinced me that the election was not fair, then I will not respect the outcome. This is a difficult place for a democracy to find itself in.

The first and second kinds of harm are not entirely distinct. Individuals are hurt in direct and measurable ways when democracies are in sorry states, but it is important to remember that the harms suffered by individuals are not the *only* harms that misinformation can cause.

The third kind of misinformation concerns the damage that is done to our **information environments**.[8] There are different phrases here that capture the same thing: our information environment becomes more hostile or less friendly; our information diet worsens; we live in the midst of an infodemic. The term "infodemic" was coined in 2003 but became popular among journalists and philosophers during the COVID-19 pandemic to capture the way that misinformation spreads like an epidemic from one person to the next.[9] While it is hard to know people's motivations with certainty, it does seem that the worsening of our information environments was done deliberately, at least to some extent. Consider the words of Steve Bannon, a former counselor to the US president and editor of *Breitbart*: "The Democrats don't matter. The real opposition is the media. And the way to deal with them is to flood the zone with shit."[10] He is crudely getting at the worsening of our information environments.

Flooding our information environments with misinformation worsens them in measurable ways. The more misinformation there is, the more likely it is that we encounter false reports about something happening when it is not. We have to be more vigilant about what we trust, too, because the average quality of available information is decreasing. More fact-checking is necessary. The quality of even reliable sources of information can be impacted as more misinformation slips through the cracks. Some of our true beliefs can be undermined when the sources of those beliefs are slandered by misinformation, causing us to lose trust in them. For instance, imagine that I learned from the *New York Times* that a bombing happened somewhere, and then I learn from some misinformation that the *New York Times* is biased and untrustworthy, and so I abandon the initial belief. Even if the initial reporting was true, misinformation has caused me to lose my belief in its truth. In this way, misinformation is responsible for more than just false beliefs. It also can cause me to lose my true beliefs.

Social-media sites can exacerbate these problems because we now have access to **misinformation conduits**. A misinformation conduit is someone who, while not the *source of the misinformation*, spreads it. The most visible conduits are influencers. We do not always encounter the sources of misinformation, but there are people who use their platforms, knowingly or unknowingly, to amplify the misinformation. Joe Rogan is a good example of this. In 2020, he apologized for incorrectly claiming that wildfires were being started by left-wing activists and that traditional media platforms were not reporting on the arrests of these activists.[11] Misinformation conduits cause us to encounter misinformation more often, thus polluting our information environment to a greater extent than the initial source of the misinformation.

## 2. Cybercascades

One of the most philosophically interesting questions concerning misinformation is why it spreads online like wildfire. Some thinkers have said that the spread is due to a social dynamic known as a **cybercascade**.[12]

Cybercascades are dynamics in which vast numbers of users rely on other users for information. Put this way, cybercascades seem like they are mundane, understandable phenomena—and indeed, they sometimes are. Misinformation spreads like wildfire online because normal people do not have any easy way of verifying for themselves how many millions of years ago dinosaurs existed or how many battles Napoleon won. Each of us generally relies on **testimony** as a source of justification for our beliefs. By "testimony," we mean something like the way that someone or something tells us that something is true, on account of which we come to base our belief that it is true without verifying it ourselves. We rely on testimony even for many of our beliefs concerning things that we could verify for ourselves: for instance, we might rely on an app on our phone to tell us whether it is warm outside even though we could verify that ourselves.

Cybercascades arise precisely because we rely on other people's testimony. Further, it is entirely sensible that we rely on this testimony. It would be terribly cumbersome to verify everything ourselves, especially when we often want to know something so that we can do something with that knowledge. If we spent all of our time researching, we would never get around to doing the thing that we wanted to use the research for. Reliance on what a scientist says about the efficacy of a vaccine is virtually a necessity, as opposed to our digging through the research ourselves, especially since it would probably take a long time to be skilled enough to properly interpret research. Many of us want to get the vaccine in question and move on with our lives.

This is the first thing about misinformation that we should highlight: it spreads for perfectly understandable reasons, not unlike other forms of information.

Second, there are two kinds of cybercascades that help fill out our account here. The first is **informational cybercascades**, which happen when we form our beliefs in accordance with signals from our peers. In particular, we look to our peers for a sense of what the *consensus* is on some issue, and then we believe that. This makes sense as a general practice because consensuses are typically reliable guides concerning what we should believe. For instance, if I speak to five of my friends and each of them has done the drive between Lansing and Chicago, and they all agree on which way is fastest, it makes sense for me to believe that their way is the fastest. Of course, it is not a guarantee, but their information is reliable. If they each disagreed, the question would get trickier, but the consensus is reflective of some reliability. Notice what is important about this case: *each of them* has done the drive from Lansing to Chicago. What makes the consensus a powerful source of justification is that it has been reached by many independent processes of verification. Other people have verified a hypothesis independently and reached a certain result, such that I am warranted to believe it.

However, the problem that we often encounter online is that people *believe others who have never independently verified whatever claim is being thrown around*. Psychologically, the experience of being in an informational cybercascade is that users perceive a consensus of independent thinkers—but, in reality, it might well be (and frequently is) the case that everyone believes the claim because someone else believes the claim, and the first person to believe it *could* be right, could be deluded, or could even be a bot that was designed to muddy the waters of some community's beliefs.

## 2. Cybercascades 113

A prominent example is the QAnon conspiracy theory. In 2017, it started on 4Chan, a social-media site, with someone, posting as Q Clearance Patriot, predicting the arrest of Hillary Clinton and eventually transitioning into predictions that featured the arrest of allegedly cannibalistic and pedophiliac politicians. Q might well have been joking around, but other people believed Q. As the QAnon movement grew, it became easier to sway other people. Each person could think to him or herself, "Wow, look how many people believe Q! If they all believe it, there has to be something to it, doesn't there?" In some cases, this sort of reasoning makes sense. However, it does not make sense when each person believes it only because someone else does. In that case, the belief is only as strong as the first person's belief. In an informational cybercascade, we believe, for all intents and purposes, that something is true only because one other person believes it. It feels to us like the consensus is genuine, but it is manufactured. Worryingly, the consensus becomes more persuasive each and every time someone else joins in because the consensus has grown larger, but this increase in persuasiveness is not tied to any improvement in the reliability of the consensus.

The essence of informational cybercascades is the quick and unimpeded spread of information within the group. The key bit of information that gets spread is who is on board with some theory or claim, as well as how many other people are similarly on board. On social-media sites, this is particularly easy. It is obscenely common for people to judge the quality of a health influencer's information, for example, by how many followers he or she has. The more followers, the more credible he or she must be. The effect compounds because each increase in the number of followers attracts *more* followers because the influencer's priority in the site's recommendations increases. The thought behind the attraction to a popular influencer's content is simple: "Wow, look at all of the followers! That many people can't be wrong, can they?" Of course, many users are unaware of the fact that *other* users said the same thing when *they* started following the influencer; they, too, were responding to the number of followers, not the quality of information. The fact that the influencer might have purchased their first large influx of followers, or that the influencer might not exist at all but is a bot propped up by nefarious forces, looms in the background here—an all-too-frequent and devious reality on social-media sites.

A final observation about informational cybercascades is that, here again, they are understandable social dynamics. They occur offline all the time. Consider doctors who are general practitioners and are therefore not specialists in kidney health. They might have no free time to read the latest research on kidneys for themselves. If they do read the latest nephrological research, then that squeezes out their time for reading pancreatic research. The result is that doctors might rely on what other doctors are saying around the clinic—but the other doctors might be in the same position. So, the doctors are relying on a consensus that might not be made of people who are independently verifying their claims.[13] The hope, of course, is that the *ultimate* source of the information is peer-reviewed research, but still, this is a kind of informational cybercascade.

The other kind of cybercascade is a **reputational cybercascade**. This kind of cybercascade happens when the people in the dynamic respond not to the way that a consensus makes some view seem plausible or likely but because they feel pressured by groups of people into agreeing for the sake of their reputation. I might not sincerely agree with Rachel and Julia when they tell me that climate change is a hoax, but I act as though I do agree because I do not want anything to come between us and I certainly do not want to come across as ignorant or naïve. So, I share posts and memes on Facebook about the great hoax of climate change that give the impression that I do agree with Rachel and Julia. Ria might see the posts and feel the same pressure as I did, initially. She, too, might not sincerely agree but posts anyway. Misinformation spreads like wildfire in such circumstances. The interesting thing is that Rachel and Julia might not have sincerely believed climate change is a hoax, either. Perhaps they were responding to similar pressures from other quarters of their social-media community. The term "spiral of silence" is sometimes used to capture what is going on here: people are pressured into staying silent. The pressure grows as more people remain silent, since fewer people are modeling behaviors that call out misinformation.

Nothing prevents the two kinds of cybercascades from coinciding. Scott, Jolene, and I might be responding to peer pressure when we post about climate-change denialism, but we do not sincerely believe what we are posting. Frank, in contrast, sees the posts but is remarkably immune to reputational pressures. He is, however, impressed by the consensus that appears to be emerging among his Facebook friends. He is conscious of how little he has researched climate-change science, but he concludes that Scott, Jolene, and I have independently looked into it since we are confidently and smugly posting memes about it. So, he concludes that he, too, should not believe in climate change. Frank is participating in an informational cybercascade, but Scott, Jolene, and I are part of a reputational cybercascade. Both are feeding each other here, since people who are responding to the reputational cybercascade contribute to the same appearance of a consensus that the informational cybercascade is based on.

## 3. Language-Games

The goal of this section is to further illuminate the context in which misinformation spreads online.[14] One important observation that we should make is that social-media sites' *sharing* features play an important role in the spread of misinformation. People can, for instance, repost other people's messages. This allows people to repost a lie about climate change but deny responsibility for it because the initial post was not theirs. They might say that "reposts are not endorsements" or that they reposted it because it was funny or interesting, not because they agreed with it. This is sometimes called **bent testimony**. Bent testimony is the sort of testimony that someone gives and is happy to accept credit for when it turns out to be right but that the same person denies responsibility for when it is wrong. People who give bent testimony distance themselves from their assertions in all sorts of ways. Imagine Jolene reposting a meme about vaccines causing autism but then getting in trouble for it among her family. She assures her family that she was only reposting it to draw attention to the foolishness of the anti-vaccine community on X. Her friends, however, praise her for the repost because they agree with her, and she happily accepts their praise. That is bent testimony.

Bent testimony reveals something important about the nature of misinformation online: it is not clear what someone means by any given post (or shared post). The context is too unclear. In offline life, if I tell you that vaccines cause autism, you will attribute that belief to me and hold me responsible for it. Only in very rare circumstances could I convince you later that I was merely joking. In online life, nothing in particular tells us how to interpret what someone is saying.

In the first place, this is due to the absence of visual and auditory cues. Without access to someone's body language and tone of voice, it is hard to tell that someone is joking. In addition, we sometimes know virtually nothing about the sources of online information. Even influencers who tell us that they have medical degrees might be lying. This observation leads to an important insight: online, there are *institutional* reasons for the spread of misinformation. If I encounter a doctor in a hospital who tells me about the safety of some vaccine, it is possible that she is lying, but there are all sorts of institutional reasons for me to trust her: I can be reasonably sure that she earned her degrees, since hospitals have good security systems to prevent impostors from masquerading as doctors, and they do competent background checks on new employees. I can trust that she is not whimsically giving me misinformation because if she were, she would be opening herself and the hospital up to various liabilities.

When it comes to the institutions of social-media sites, in contrast, we have to distinguish between *purposeful* and *general* sites.

**Purposeful social-media sites** have a clear focus that unifies the behaviors of users. LinkedIn is a clear example: people use it for professional purposes. Wikipedia, Quora, and StackExchange are purposeful social-media sites. Most purposeful sites have only one unifying purpose, but dating apps, such as Tinder and Bumble, have more than one since they allow people to meet both romantic partners and friends. (Someone could plausibly argue that there is still only one purpose: meeting other people.) Purposeful sites benefit tremendously from the clarity of their purpose since it allows them to easily object to certain behaviors and content. For instance, if someone uses LinkedIn to date, it is easy for us to call that use objectionable. If someone uses Tinder or Bumble but never intends to meet someone offline through the app, we have good reason to get annoyed or frustrated with that person.

Most of all, purposeful sites usually have an infrastructure in place to remove misinformation promptly—because their purpose gives them an obvious obligation to remove the content. If I post a negative Yelp review that is totally misleading and false because I want to damage the finances of the restaurant owner, everyone recognizes that Yelp should remove my review. Yelp should make it easy for other people to report the review as false, and users generally act as moderators for the community by reporting and flagging inappropriate content. The same goes with dating apps: if Jolene uses AI-generated photos to pretend to be someone that she is not, people will find that obviously objectionable. They can reason in accordance with the stated purpose of the site that the misinformation is incompatible with that purpose.

Certainly, there are purposeful social-media sites whose purpose is compatible with posts containing misinformation. Reddit communities that are devoted to satire are a clear example. The purpose of such communities is not aimed at the truth, but that is not a problem because their purpose is evident. They are not at all like the reposts I mentioned earlier. We do not know how to reliably interpret those climate-change reposts. However, we can interpret the Reddit posts in a satirical community because the purpose has *fixed* the context for us.

**General social-media sites** are different. These sites have no unifying purpose at all, and people are encouraged to use the site for a variety of purposes. When people hear the phrase "social-media site," they mainly think of these general sites. The most prominent examples are Facebook, Instagram, X, TikTok, and similar apps. We can use these sites to talk with friends and family, find information on our former romantic partners, learn about what is happening geopolitically, speak with strangers about our favorite sports teams, find people to play video games with, and so on.

When someone posts their employment history on LinkedIn, the site itself provides us with the context required to interpret that post. That is because LinkedIn is a purposeful site. This is not so with Facebook: the same kind of contextual information is not available when someone posts something on Facebook, because Facebook *has no unifying purpose*. Misinformation can spread on Facebook and other general sites with remarkable ease because they do not have the same sorts of norms or standards that allow everyone to find a false Yelp review objectionable.

For this reason, we need to introduce the concept of a **language-game**.

The concept of a language-game was invented by Ludwig Wittgenstein, an important twentieth-century philosopher. Language-games are part of an approach to the meaning of our language that stresses speaking as an activity which is guided by rules. The meanings of our words are determined by their interaction with these rules. Thus, speaking a language is like playing a game. Consider an example that Wittgenstein gives:

> The language is meant to serve for communication between a builder A and an assistant B. A is building with building stones: there are blocks, pillars, slabs and beams. B has to pass the stones, and that in the order in which A needs them. For this purpose they use a language consisting of the words "block," "pillar," "slab," "beam." A calls them out;—B brings the stone which he has learnt to bring at such-and-such a call.—Conceive this as a complete primitive language.[15]

Consider the way that saying "block!" could mean different things in different contexts. I might be asking someone to pass me a block, as in Wittgenstein's example, or I could be telling someone *to* block. My interlocutor would know only based on the context. That is a key part of language-games. We *do* things with words, and what we do with any given utterance changes in accordance with the context's rules.

One important observation is that, just as in a game, there *are* rules, but there are also ambiguous cases and grey areas. For instance, if I am playing a game of tennis, I know that one rule is that I have to get the ball above the net. However, it violates the whole spirit of the game and its rules if the ball goes 10,000 feet over the net. At some point, the ball obviously goes out of bounds. Yet, it is incredibly difficult to pinpoint the *exact* cutoff point. If we say 10,000 feet over the net is out of bounds, and a player hits the ball 999.99 feet over the net, someone could plausibly argue that we should round up. Something similar happens in language. We might agree that it is wrong to say mean things to someone, but friends routinely tease each other. It is unclear where to draw the line with that teasing. It might be permissible for me to mock my friend Ria for her weird ear, but if I have another friend Scott, who is self-conscious about his ear, saying the same thing to him might be wrong, even though it was fine for me to say to Ria. It goes without saying that different language is acceptable on a playground than in a job interview. There are different rules.

A game is different from free-form *play*. Games, by definition, have structure and rules. There are always some ambiguities and grey areas, but we try to keep these to a minimum. Purposeful social-media sites succeed at that, by and large. We mostly have an intuitive grasp of what is appropriate to say on LinkedIn and what content should be removed. However, with general sites, the story is different. The rules of the language-game are not immediately obvious. Imagine a Reddit community that is dedicated to creating memes satirizing people who think that the 2020 US presidential election was stolen. Users might post something along the lines of "Soon it will be revealed that the election was rigged and stolen by extra-dimensional aliens!" Now, imagine reporters from CNN stumbling upon this community. There might be no obvious sign that the users are *making fun* of conspiracy theories, not producing them. CNN might well report that "far-right Reddit users turn to extra-dimensional aliens!" On LinkedIn, we know that the language-game is such that when I post about a new job, I am not kidding around. On Reddit, that is not so obvious.

Philosophers wonder how we can make sense of the language-games on general social-media sites. Thankfully, we have empirical research that shines some light on the situation. When we consider the habits that users have regarding the sharing of information, since we are mostly interested in misinformation in this chapter, we find that people are often motivated by considerations unrelated to the quality or accuracy of the information. For instance, psychologists have discovered that the central motivational categories when it comes to posting and consuming content online are entertainment, socializing, information-seeking, self-expression, and status-seeking.[16] Other researchers boil motivations down to just two: the need to belong and the need for self-presentation.[17] When researchers study specifically the motivations of people who share misinformation online, they find that "respondents share misinformation often for non-informational reasons."[18] As some researchers put it: "catchiness rather than truthfulness often drives information (and misinformation) diffusion on social media."[19] In other words, *it sounds good*—or, perhaps, *it helps me fit in* or *it signals my allegiance to some group*. Perhaps the reason was even simpler: *it was just for fun*.

An analogy: imagine kids gossiping or spreading rumors on a playground. They spread these rumors to promote group cohesion, to signal who is an outsider and who is an insider, or to signal that someone has a trait that the group approves of. Spreading some conspiracy theory about a rigged election is *not* an act motivated by a desire to *inform* people: it is a way of signaling something, such as allegiance to a group, just as spreading a rumor is not a way to *inform* people.

This shines a real light on the language-games of general social-media sites. People are doing the equivalent of spreading rumors and gossiping. They want to belong to a group and present themselves as people with certain kinds of values and attitudes. This tells us a lot about the spread of misinformation online when we combine it with one more datum. About half of all Americans get news from general social-media sites, such as Reddit, X, and Facebook.[20] It is not just news, either. Think about the people in your life who get health information from TikTok influencers or who got all of their information regarding COVID-19 from YouTube during the pandemic. There is a mismatch here that resembles my earlier example of the CNN report. People post online for reasons unrelated to informational quality, but we consume content as if our Facebook news feed were a newspaper or an academic journal. *We are wrong about what the language-game is.*

This is a crucial reason for the spread of misinformation online: people post things because they want to fit in or show what sort of person they are, but people believe the posts as if they were made by journalists or researchers. We need to remember that this is a language-game that does not have the institution of peer review. That is the first thing that we can do: stop treating general social-media sites as sources of news or health information. Another thing that we can do: clarify the meanings of our posts. If you are trying to make a serious point and share some research that you have done, be upfront about that. It is tricky with comedy or satire because a note that something is satirical or comedic can take away from its value, but specifying in an account's profile that it is a satirical account can be beneficial without many costs. Our vigilance and changes to the way that we get our information might be the most secure bets, since they do not depend on other people's behaviors changing.

## 4. A Duty to Remove?

One remedy to the problem of misinformation might be to require social-media companies to police and remove misinformation from their platforms. It is not difficult to imagine how this could be done, especially with the emergence of AI technology that can make this task logistically simple, and there is no doubt that the major companies could afford to deploy this technology. The philosophical question is whether there is such a duty. There are roughly three positions on this question.

The first position is that social-media companies have no responsibilities at all when it comes to misinformation. Someone who wants to defend this view might start by observing that these companies are privately owned businesses and, to that extent, can do whatever they want with the content on their site. If I owned a restaurant in my town and wanted to host a night every week where people come to discuss why doctors should not be trusted, some people would say that this is my right and that I should be allowed to do that.

The opposition to this view might cite the tremendous amount of harm that misinformation poses to individuals, society, and democratic institutions. I discussed the different kinds of harm in the first section of this chapter. The moral duty that companies have might simply follow from a larger responsibility to mitigate and avoid harm. One common analogy that is often used to circumvent this duty is to liken social-media companies to telephone service providers, rather than editors of a magazine. If Ria and I conspire on the phone to murder someone, the phone company does not get blamed for this, even though they provided a service that two conspirators used. Meanwhile, if a magazine published Jolene's instructions to kill someone, we *would* hold the magazine and Jolene responsible. That is because magazines are edited, and so editorial and curatorial decisions were made that we can object to. In other words, magazines are hands-on, whereas telephone companies are hands-off. The allegation is that social-media companies are hands-off and so resemble the telephone companies.

## 4. A Duty to Remove?

As we reply to this objection, it is almost impossible to avoid painting with a broad brush. Different social-media companies have different levels of involvement in the content on their platforms. The more involved they are, the more blameworthy they are for the harmful misinformation that gets spread. Some platforms directly weigh in on debates: X, for instance, provides context for misleading tweets, thus changing the way that users interpret the content. If X tried to argue that it was hands-off, it would not come across as plausible. Many platforms, such as YouTube and Facebook, have explicit policies concerning the removal of misinformation. Specific details will change over time. Again, it would not be plausible for them to claim that they were hands-off and had no involvement in limiting the spread of misinformation. This is not to say that they should walk back these policies, but it *is* to say that it is hard to believe that these companies are as hands-off as they suggest. In contrast, 4Chan has no policy concerning misinformation, as far as I can tell. 4Chan might plausibly claim that it really is more like a telephone service provider than a company with responsibility for the content on the platform.

Nevertheless, someone might still object that even the most hands-off platform is required to remove misinformation. If you hold this view, then you think that 4Chan being hands-off is simply a dereliction of the duty to *be more involved* for the sake of limiting harms. There is something to say in support of this stance: after all, if we were not talking about the removal of misinformation but instead about the removal of child pornography, we would think that 4Chan and every other site has to double down on removing it.

At this point in the debate, the opposition to the duty to remove misinformation changes its tactics. Instead of saying that there is simply no duty to remove misinformation, they say that *platforms have a duty to not remove misinformation because doing so violates the free speech of those who posted it*. Someone who takes this view would say that child pornography uncontroversially should be removed because it violates rights and is not protected speech, but someone posting about vaccines is merely exercising free-speech rights, and companies should not intervene to remove that speech.

This view gains its initial appeal from the fact that social-media companies, when they remove posts, are censoring people, and Western countries have generally had a strong opposition to censorship. The problem with this simple anti-censorship position is that it overlooks that we regularly tell people to stop talking, and we are justified in doing so especially when stopping that person from talking avoids or mitigates harms. This is pertinent since the avoidance or mitigation of harms is precisely the goal when we remove misinformation. The right to free speech can be characterized in many different ways, but it usually protects our speech from censorship by the government. Mothers do not violate the rights of their children when they tell them to stop talking, and conference venues do not violate the free-speech rights of patrons when they tell them that they will not host an anti-vaccination conference. It is not clear that anything different is going on when social-media companies remove misinformation.

There is a possible difference, though. The difference could be that social-media platforms have such a crucial role in twenty-first-century civic life that removing certain views from these platforms is, for all intents and purposes, removing them from the public sphere. Views that can be spread on social media have a tremendous advantage over views that cannot. X provides a reach that is virtually impossible to match. We might lament that we have allowed these companies such an important role in our democratic society, but if true, then we might very well be required to let some pernicious views stick around so that they are not eliminated from public consideration.

A staunch defender of the duty to remove misinformation will always point to the same consideration: the harm of misinformation. In this case, we might say that if social-media companies are so important to twenty-first-century civic life, then that is all the *more* reason to think that they should intervene to remove misinformation. Reflect on one of the harms that I presented earlier: the direct threat to the integrity of our democratic institutions. If social-media platforms are so integral to the health and well-being of those institutions, then it stands to reason that their special importance gives them a special responsibility, and that could include removing misinformation.

Overall, this is a vexed question, with multiple arguments on each side of the debate. There are more considerations than just those that I have put forward here. Someone else, for instance, might point out the difficulty of identifying some claim as misinformation. That is no doubt a good point, but we should not overlook all the uncontroversial and easy cases. Once we acknowledge the harms of misinformation and the way it spreads, the debate about the duty to remove it becomes more urgent than ever. We also should wonder whether it is terribly important that misinformation can sometimes be hard to identify. If we have a duty to, say, shelter the needy, it might sometimes be hard to identify who is needy and who is not, and we might occasionally fail at carrying out the duty because of some misidentifications, but nobody would conclude on that basis that the duty does not exist at all. It might be misleading to stress the difficulty of identifying misinformation, as a result. Instead, the difficulty should make us more urgently inquire into the question of whether some content indeed counts as misinformation so that we can respond appropriately.

# 5. Conclusion

In this chapter, we explored the ethical issues surrounding misinformation. As harmful as misinformation is, a careful look at the kinds of cybercascades that promote its spread reveals that it can sometimes spread for understandable reasons that follow from the difficulties of navigating our complicated information environment. Unfortunately, the proliferation of misinformation has badly polluted this environment, and understanding the nature of this pollution calls us to think more about Wittgenstein's idea of a language-game and to settle the thorny debate concerning the possible duty to remove misinformation.

# Key Terms

**Bent testimony**: the sort of testimony that someone is happy to accept credit for when it turns out to be right but that the speaker denies responsibility for when it is wrong.

**Cybercascade**: online dynamics in which vast amounts of users rely on other users for information.

**Disinformation**: false information spread by someone who knows that it is false (perhaps for profit or other reasons). In this book, the category of *misinformation* includes disinformation.

**General social-media sites**: sites that have no unifying purpose, and people are encouraged to use them for a variety of purposes. When people hear the phrase "social-media site," they primarily think about these general sites. The most prominent examples are Facebook, Instagram, X, TikTok, and similar apps.

**Information environment**: the environment in which we find ourselves as knowers and in which the sources of our information are found. This environment gets polluted by misinformation.

**Informational cybercascade**: cybercascades that happen when we form our beliefs in accordance with signals from our peers. In particular, we look to our peers for a sense of what the consensus is on some issue, and then we believe that.

**Language-game**: this concept is part of an approach to the meaning of our language that stresses speaking as an activity guided by rules. The meanings of our words are determined by their interaction with these rules. Thus, speaking a language is like playing a game. The meaning of an utterance and which utterances are acceptable vary between language-games.

**Misinformation**: information that is false or misleading. Misinformation is sometimes distinguished from disinformation, which is false information spread by someone who knows that it is false. In this book, the category of *misinformation* includes disinformation.

**Misinformation conduits**: people who, while not the sources of misinformation, transmit misinformation to us. Influencers are some of the most prominent misinformation conduits online, and the sheer number of them means that we are more likely to encounter misinformation than we would otherwise.

**Purposeful social-media sites**: sites that have a clear focus that unifies the behaviors of users. LinkedIn is a clear example: people use it for professional purposes.

**Reputational cybercascade**: cybercascades that happen when the people in the dynamic respond not to the way that a consensus makes some view seem plausible or likely but because they feel pressured by groups of people into agreeing for the sake of their reputation.

**Testimony**: a source of justification of beliefs that involves being told that something is true.

# Discussion Cases

## 1. The President

Earlier in this chapter, I discussed misinformation that politicians spread, such as US president Donald Trump's claims that climate change is a hoax perpetrated by the Chinese government through various tweets: "the concept of global warming was created by and for the Chinese in order to make US manufacturing non-competitive" and "ice storm rolls from Texas to Tennessee—I'm in Los Angeles and it's freezing. Global warming is a total, and very expensive, hoax!"[21] At times, he and his representatives have tried to walk back these claims, saying either that they were jokes or that they were never said at all.

How do you think that we should handle such misinformation? It is important for democratic countries to debate freely about how to respond to climate change, but are there any instances of such obvious lies that we should not tolerate? Moreover, does the fact that these are the words of the US president change how we should feel about the case? Lastly, what do you make of claims that Trump was merely joking? In social-media contexts, we hardly ever have access to knowledge of whether someone is joking or being sarcastic, but this can change how we interpret the person's posts; sometimes, claims that someone is joking or that something is just a prank can feel disingenuous, even if true.

## 2. High-Stakes Scenarios

During the COVID-19 pandemic, some misinformation was ridiculous, such as the claims that the vaccine would magnetize everyone who got it. However, especially early on in the pandemic, there were legitimate questions about whether masking and social distancing were effective and whether asymptomatic transmission was likely or even possible. The landscape changed quickly as new evidence emerged, and as the virus mutated, key facts about transmission and severity changed as well. The evidence might support one hypothesis on one day, but then a few days later, a competing hypothesis would emerge. A well-supported theory at one point in time could plausibly be regarded as misinformation not long later.

How do you think that we should handle cases when the information landscape is rapidly changing? Consider that during the pandemic, labeling something as misinformation could have life-or-death implications. That is a reason to not make mistakes: you do not want to remove something from a social-media site if it is true, but you also do not want to leave it up if it is false and could lead to medical harm. What do you think should be done about misinformation in high-stakes scenarios when it is just not clear what is true or false?

## 3. TikTok and Misinformation

The spread of misinformation looks different on each social-media platform, but there are broad and general truths about misinformation-spreading trends that this chapter has documented. However, TikTok seems unique in a few respects. First, TikTok's bent toward short-form video content means that there are visual cues that misinformation conduits can exploit in the spread of misinformation. Second, TikTok's demographic skews much younger than other platforms: 63 percent of all US teens (ages thirteen to seventeen) say that they use TikTok.[22]

What sorts of challenges do young people in particular face as they use apps riddled with misinformation? As companies popularize new ways of spreading information (e.g., in short-form video content), what sorts of challenges does society face in combating misinformation? Does TikTok really pose any new threats to our information environment?

# Further Reading

Carey, Brandon. 2023. "Misinformation and Epistemic Harm." *Social Philosophy Today* 39: 89–100.

Carey argues that misinformation is harmful to us as knowers. He spends most of the article pushing back on the idea that misinformation is merely false or misleading information. He provides a much more in-depth analysis of the question of what misinformation is than I do in this chapter. The last section of his article also investigates misinformation's pollution of our information environment.

De Ridder, Jeroen. 2021. "What's So Bad about Misinformation?" *Inquiry* 67 (9): 2956–78. https://doi.org/10.1080/0020174X.2021.2002187.

This article investigates the third kind of harm that I identified in the first section of this chapter: the worsening of our information environment. De Ridder distinguishes between different kinds of effects that misinformation can have on our environment: direct effects, indirect effects on individuals, and indirect systemic effects.

Lewandowsky, Stephan, Ullrich K. H. Ecker, John Cook, Sander van der Linden, Jon Roozenbeek, and Naomi Oreskes. 2023. "Misinformation and the Epistemic Integrity of Democracy." *Current Opinion in Psychology* 54: 101711. https://doi.org/10.1016/j.copsyc.2023.101711.

This brief article discusses the pervasiveness of misinformation in current American politics. The article is light on philosophizing about misinformation and much more focused on highlighting the urgent threat that misinformation poses to American democratic institutions.

Marin, Lavinia. 2021a. "Sharing (Mis) Information on Social Networking Sites. An Exploration of the Norms for Distributing Content Authored by Others." *Ethics and Information Technology* 23 (3): 363–72.

Marin's article is important in the way that she introduces Wittgenstein's notion of language-games to explain why misinformation spreads online. The chief idea is that online contexts are not primarily informational contexts, even though we treat them as such when we consume media. She also introduces the distinction between general and purposeful social-media sites.

Marin, Lavinia. 2021b. "Three Contextual Dimensions of Information on Social Media: Lessons Learned from the COVID-19 Infodemic." *Ethics and Information Technology* 23: 79–86.

This article does a good job of further exploring the context in which misinformation is spread and the importance of language-games. She identifies three contexts: emotional, epistemic, and normative. In the emotional context, people spread misinformation to create a kind of solidarity. In the epistemic context, normal people take on the role of an expert to create a kind of control. In the normative context, the aspect of misinformation that tells us what to do and value is stressed: for instance, much misinformation was spread during the pandemic that supported shaming some people baselessly.

Sunstein, Cass. 2017. *#republic: Divided Democracy in the Age of Social Media*. Princeton, NJ: Princeton University Press.

Sunstein's book is a ground-breaking text in the ethics of social media, and I also recommend it in the chapter on echo chambers. Here, I point readers specifically to the fourth chapter, entitled "Cybercascades," because that is where he tackles the question of why misinformation spreads like wildfire online and where he distinguishes between reputational and informational cybercascades.

## Notes

1. Gage 2022.
2. Srikanth 2021.
3. See Ferreira Caceres et al. 2022.
4. See Pelley 2024.
5. Sunstein 2017, 109.
6. Goldberg 2020.
7. Emery 2016.
8. See Carey 2023; de Ridder 2021; and Marin 2021b.
9. E.g., Marin 2021b uses and discusses this term.
10. See Illing 2020.
11. See Flynn 2020.
12. I owe this concept particularly to Sunstein 2017, whose work has influenced virtually this whole section of the chapter.
13. The idea of *medical fashion* is explored by Burnham 1987.
14. This section is inspired by Marin 2021.
15. Wittgenstein §2.
16. See Chen et al. 2015; Diddi and LaRose 2006; and Lee and Ma 2012.
17. Nadkarni and Hofman 2012.
18. Chen et al. 2015, 113–14.
19. Chen et al. 2015, 111.
20. Walker and Matsa 2021.
21. Emery 2016.
22. See Eddy 2024.

# Chapter Six: Cancel Culture: Online Shaming and Caring

In 2013, Justine Sacco, a woman with 170 followers on what was then called Twitter, boarded a flight from London to Cape Town. Before she boarded, she tweeted, "Going to Africa. Hope I don't get AIDS. Just kidding. I'm white!" She then turned off her phone for the flight. During the eleven-hour-long flight to South Africa, her tweet went unexpectedly viral. Her employers were notified about her tweet before she had even landed. Needless to say, people on Twitter felt a unique kind of thrill as they waited for her to land. The hashtag #HasJustineLandedYet trended, and people went to the airport to take her photograph. One tweet captured the sentiment well: "The Internet has spoken." Sacco lost her job before her flight even landed, and the harassment that ensued led to mental-health problems.[1]

The story of Justine Sacco illustrates the theme of this chapter: the kind of shaming that today is routinely called "canceling." The technical definition of "to cancel" that we will work with here is that **canceling** someone is a matter of withdrawing "any kind of support (viewership, social-media follows, purchases of products endorsed by the person, etc.) for those who are assessed to have said or done something unacceptable or highly problematic, generally from a social-justice perspective especially alert to sexism, heterosexism, homophobia, racism, bullying, and related issues."[2] Let's highlight a few things in order to make this discussion as profitable as possible. First, canceling someone involves *public shame*. Taking someone aside and chiding him or her for saying something racist does not count as canceling, even if it otherwise meets the definition just presented. Second, in order for someone to *actually* be canceled, he or she needs to have met with appreciable consequences. Sacco was canceled. On the other hand, Dave Chappelle was not really canceled: he was criticized for jokes about trans people, but he has since received ultra-lucrative contracts. A harder case is someone like J. K. Rowling: she really has lost at least *some* professional opportunities for her comments about sex, gender, and trans issues, but whether the losses are appreciable for someone as wealthy as her is hard to say.

Cancel culture is an aspect of life on social media that is both widely discussed in popular discourse and deeply divisive. Many people deny the existence of cancel culture altogether. One 2023 study found that in postindustrial societies with liberal social environments, such as Sweden, the United States, and the United Kingdom, right-wing scholars were most likely to perceive the existence of cancel culture, whereas, in countries with traditional moral cultures, such as Nigeria, left-wing scholars were the ones most likely to believe in cancel culture.[3] This study was done on scholars, so perhaps we cannot generalize the results to the rest of the population, but the point, however limited, is a powerful one: cancel culture is a heavily politicized phenomenon, and whether we notice it might depend on our own values. A motif in the discussion throughout this chapter is that the effects of being shamed are felt acutely by the one shamed, often tremendously out of proportion with the intentions and beliefs of the shamers.

While most of this chapter concerns online shaming and its moral implications, cancel culture is far from entirely bad. Shame is a valuable human emotion, and it can be used for good: it can prompt us to be better people, for instance. However, we shall explore the possibility that some things about cancel culture need to change in order for the shaming to be effective. As we discuss later, it needs to be less about punishment and more about growth.

Moreover, cancel culture is not all that there is to social-media life. There is the possibility for a radical kind of empathy online. Later, we shall discuss the ethics of care and the possibility of a *caring culture* online.

This chapter is intended as an introduction to these issues and as the start of a discussion, not the final word. This is true of this entire book, but especially this chapter and its deeply divisive subject matter.

# 1. Cancel Culture, Disproportionality, and Shame

There is a crucial difference between public and private shaming.[4] Taking someone aside to gently chide them for a racist joke can be unpleasant and awkward for both parties, but beyond these negative feelings, there are not many costs. The hope is that the discretion of doing the shaming privately will not negatively damage our relationship with that person and that he or she will grow as a result of the experience. Public shaming can be much more costly for the person shamed. John Stuart Mill, an important nineteenth-century philosopher, explained that society "practises a social tyranny more formidable than many kinds of political oppression, since, though not usually upheld by such extreme penalties, it leaves fewer means of escape, penetrating much more deeply into the details of life, and enslaving the soul itself."[5] These considerations lead Mill to lament "the tyranny of the prevailing opinion and feeling."[6] Twenty-first-century philosophers join Mill in this criticism: Martha Nussbaum, for instance, argued that this sort of public shaming is analogous to "justice by the mob," and this so-called justice is not "deliberative, impartial, or neutral."[7] The severity of the consequences when a person is publicly shamed is illustrated by Justine Sacco's case. The combination of these extreme outcomes with the lack of any opportunity for appeal and any due-process rights is particularly unfortunate.

Public shaming happens all the time in online spaces, with multiple psychological phenomena coinciding to give rise to this culture. One is **self-licensing**. When we self-license, we give ourselves permission to do something because we are good people; priming ourselves with the belief that we are good allows us to do something that we would otherwise consider bad. We experience less inhibition and less guilt when it comes to this behavior.[8] The self-licensing effect might be even more powerful in social-justice contexts because our shaming actions are accompanied not only by the feeling that we are good but also by the thought that the people whom we shame are bad. Consider again what happened to Justine Sacco. It is hard to see what sort of thing could *justify* going to the airport to take a photograph of a stranger as part of an online harassment campaign, but perhaps those who did go did not think of themselves as needing special justification due to the self-licensing effect. They had primed themselves with the belief that they were good people.

Two more psychological forces are the distance from the victim and the uncertainty we have concerning the identity of the people we are harassing. These two go hand in hand. The fact that we are deprived of the visual, especially facial, cues concerning the person we are shaming allows us to be crueler and more vicious without any increase in cost to us. We can bully someone with fewer feelings of guilt because we never *see* them. In fact, we might be so distant from the target of the shaming that we will never meet them. If we combine this with the fact that many social-media platforms are text-based in a way that never lets us get a sense of who this person is, the problem is compounded. Someone on Reddit is nothing but a username to most of us, which is an easier target than someone whom we all know as a real-life human being.

The last psychological factor we should call attention to is called a **magnitude gap**.[9] A magnitude gap is the difference between the importance of the experience for the victim and for the person committing the action. We could also frame it this way: the interaction between the perpetrator and the victim is much more casual for the perpetrator than it is for the victim. Explorations of cases of online shaming have revealed that shamers often believe that the victim is fine and that they have not really been harmed or affected in a long-term way.[10] The perpetrators feel they have done nothing but post a sarcastic tweet or Reddit comment, but the victims experience something much more serious: actual professional, social, and mental-health impacts. There is often a striking magnitude gap between what the shamers think that they are accomplishing and what the victims experience.

It is interesting that, if the shamers do not think that their actions are having any real effect and that they might even go unnoticed by the shamed person, then much of the righteousness that underlies the actions of shaming seems insincere. We cannot say that we are shaming *because* the shamed deserve to be punished—but then also hold that our actions are not having any effect and that the shamed will not really be punished by them. If our actions are justified by the consequences but then we deny that our actions *have* any consequences, something is amiss. We need to rethink why shaming happens.

An important concept here is the **imaginal relationship**. An imaginal relationship is not the same thing as an imaginary relationship. When we have imaginary relationships as children, we imagine that we are in a relationship with someone or something that does not really exist. In contrast, an imaginal relationship is a relationship with someone who is real but is distant from us in one way or another, on account of which we have to rely on our imagination to fill in the gaps for us. Consider a woman and her best friend, who later moves away and is no longer in contact with her; when she graduates from college, she wonders what he would say to her. This is an imaginal relationship because even though both parties really exist, she now relies on her imagination to fill in some of the gaps, such as what advice he would give to her as she begins a new chapter in her life. These imaginal relationships can be powerful psychological motivators.

The point is that *shamers online are in imaginal relationships with each other*. In 2016, researchers studied the behaviors and motivations of shamers on Twitter.[11] The motivations of shamers seemed to be such things as one-upmanship, displaying one's own righteousness, and getting more followers. Notice that whether the shamed victim deserves to be shamed at all is irrelevant to these motivations. The victim is altogether irrelevant because he or she is reduced to a tool by means of which the shamer can connect with fellow shamers. There is also the enjoyment of being part of a group of people who all approve of your behavior. Whether the other shamers *actually* approve or even know you exist makes no difference: the relationship is imaginal. This explains why many cancellations are aimed at high-profile people: there is the joy of taking people down a notch, and there is a thrill that comes from banding together with like-minded people. The possibility that you might walk out of this with your most reposted tweet ever is exciting as well.

What is lost in all of this is the well-being of the victim. The victim is in an imaginal relationship too: namely, with the shamer. We can advise victims of public shaming to stay away from social-media sites so that they will not encounter harassment, but this overlooks the sort of harassment that they will experience in their own minds. The shamers live there. When people from Instagram and TikTok show up at your house to harass you, you will have a hard time returning home because you will imagine them there (even if they are not really waiting there).

Recall John Stuart Mill. He called for some kind of "protection [...] against the tyranny of the prevailing opinion and feeling; against the tendency of society to impose, by other means than civil penalties, its own ideas and practices as rules of conduct on those who dissent from them [... and] a limit to the legitimate interference of collective opinion with individual independence."[12] The picture of cancel culture that I have been sketching similarly calls for such protection. This argument is sometimes called the **risk of disproportionality** because it highlights the risk that cancel culture presents. Most of all, what is disproportional about Justine Sacco's case is the way that what she suffered was much worse than her original offending action. Imagine if we fined someone a million dollars for stealing something worth ten dollars. The mismatch between the crime and the punishment would be objectionable. The idea of the magnitude gap underlines another kind of mismatch: what victims suffer is out of proportion with what the perpetrators believe the victims suffer.

# 2. Co-deliberation

Disproportionality is not the only risk that cancel culture presents; there is also the risk to co-deliberation.[13] This subject touches on the ethics of deplatforming and silencing people. **De-platforming** refers to the removal and banning of someone from a platform, such as a social-media site.

The risk to **co-deliberation** consists in the way that we undermine the pursuit of truth by canceling people. We need open discussion in order to correct faults in our reasoning. Much of the time, when we cancel someone, we silence them. Even when they are not outright silenced, they might be discouraged from participating in a conversation with us (and we might not want them in a conversation anyway). Besides, we have withdrawn attention from them, so even if they continue speaking, their voice will not be heard. This creates a *chilling effect* on speech. Even if this is not considered morally wrong, such philosophers as John Stuart Mill have thought that we worsen our own condition by removing competing opinions for our consideration. In other words, we create an echo chamber.

This position is based on the idea that moral truths are discovered through a process of co-deliberation. This means that we discover what is right and wrong not on our own but by thinking through problems in collaboration with other people. These other people have to think differently than us in order for the process to work: we correct each other's mistakes, notice blind spots in each other, and offer solutions. This process breaks down if we think that the moral truths can be dictated by one side or that the truth has already been discovered and one person simply has to listen to the other. That is no longer a conversation, and it is certainly not a process of co-deliberation.

Co-deliberation requires mutual respect. Shaming does not offer mutual respect. When one party shames another, the shamed person is accountable to the other: this might mean that, among other things, the shamed person has to apologize or even leave the discussion altogether. Mutual respect can certainly involve an apology, but it has to be a two-way street. For instance, there are certain things that the shamers owe the shamed. The specifics depend on the circumstances, but this could mean that the shamers owe the shamed an opportunity for forgiveness or reintegration into the community. It could mean that the shamed are owed an opportunity to explain themselves, or perhaps the shamers owe the shamed some kind of persuasive response that shows them where they went wrong. In either case, the idea is that we owe something to them just as they owe something to us.

Those who stress the importance of co-deliberation think that moral truths are being investigated and negotiated right now. If moral truths were already discovered and widely known, it would be harder to defend this view. In reality, it is hard to say decisively when morality has been violated or that some position is false. When someone claims that morality has been violated or that some false position has been asserted, our job is to respond with reasons and arguments. The people that we disagree with ought to, in turn, respond with reasons and arguments. This advances the process of co-deliberation.

A clarification: the view here is *not* that people need to listen to those who are abusing them or saying hurtful things about them. It is not that each individual who hears hateful things needs to put up with each abusive person or hear them out. Rather, it is about how we *as a community* respond to such people. We should not remove them from the larger conversation that the community is having.

## 3. Upsides and Revisions

If John Stuart Mill is the archnemesis of public shaming historically, then we should regard Plato as the champion of shame as an important human emotion. In this section, we shall consider the value of shame in a way that is inspired by Plato.[14] This should not be interpreted as a straightforward vindication of cancel culture because, as we shall highlight throughout what follows, Plato also guides us about how we should think through *revising* cancel culture.

Plato believed that shamelessness was a vice. He condemns shamelessness in the *Republic* when he condemns societies in which "insolence [is called] good breeding, anarchy freedom, extravagance magnificence, and shamelessness courage" (560e–561a).[15] In his dialogues, Plato often depicts his teacher, Socrates, shaming his fellow citizens: he shames them to improve them, and shameless people would be even more resistant to this powerful tool for self-improvement.

To see how shame might improve someone, consider a culture in which people say that they do not care what other people think of them. At first, they might seem to be liberated, even enlightened, but in reality this insensitivity is disguising a problem. People who worry about their health but feel insufficiently self-motivated to be more active might hire a personal trainer, knowing that being accountable to someone else and being ashamed of skipping workouts would improve their consistency. Someone who wants to study ancient Greek philosophy but is similarly insufficiently self-motivated to read on their own might join a reading group with friends: any of them who fail to read the assigned texts will feel ashamed. These are people who have perceived a flaw in their character that they want to fix, and being shameless would be detrimental in these cases. It is important for us to avoid the vice of shamelessness because shame is such a powerful and important emotion.

Socrates, in Plato's dialogues, relies on shame in precisely this way. He describes his own life's mission in the *Apology* in these very terms. Consider the following passage:

> Good sir, you are an Athenian, a citizen of the greatest city with the greatest reputation for both wisdom and power; are you not ashamed of your eagerness to possess as much wealth, reputation, and honors as possible, while you do not care for nor give thought to wisdom or truth, or the best possible state of your soul? (29d–e)

His last words in the *Apology* reflect this sentiment, as he urges those listening to him to reproach his sons if they begin to fall into vice after he has died:

> When my sons grow up, avenge yourselves by causing them the same kind of grief that I caused you, if you think they care for money or anything else more than they care for virtue, or if they think they are somebody when they are nobody. Reproach them as I reproach you, that they do not care for the right things and think they are worthy when they are not worthy of anything. If you do this, I shall have been justly treated by you, and my sons also. (41e–42a)

The first passage makes it clear that Socrates believes that it is right for his audience to be ashamed of themselves and hopes that this shame will instead motivate them to care for the right things. The second passage makes it clear that reproaching someone for caring about the wrong things is morally important. Socrates thinks that it is required for his sons to be reproached, should they mistake the value of other things as more significant than the value of virtue. Unlike large parts of today's society, in which people are explicitly told not to shame other people, Socrates says that shaming can be part of treating others justly.

The most powerful kind of shame gets people to change their way of life. This kind of shame is best illustrated by another of Plato's dialogues, the *Alcibiades*. In this dialogue, Alcibiades is getting ready to present himself to the other Athenians as he begins his political career. Socrates thinks that his ambition is bottomless: "Suppose one of the gods asked you, 'Alcibiades, would you rather live with what you now have, or would you rather die on the spot if you weren't permitted to acquire anything greater?' I think you'd choose to die" (105a). Socrates's goal is to get Alcibiades to put his ambitions on hold and come study with him. In light of Socrates's correct analysis of the depths of Alcibiades's ambitions, this seems impossible, but Socrates gets Alcibiades to turn himself around by *making him feel*

## 3. Upsides and Revisions

*ashamed* that he does not know what justice is, even though he hopes to be a career politician before long. Yet, it is what Socrates does next that cancel culture ought to learn from: Socrates positions himself as someone who can *help* Alcibiades learn what justice is. Alcibiades even commits himself to Socrates as his attendant forever, with Socrates happily agreeing (135e).

There are some important things that we can learn from this story. First, it stresses that Socrates's approach to shaming someone is *positive*. When we think about people shaming others, we might imagine that people are being *cut down*. This is analogous to the way that, in contemporary settings, shaming someone involves taking them down a notch (or as many notches as possible). It is purely negative. Yet, the conversation with Alcibiades is positive: it is deliberately aimed at Alcibiades's improvement.

The fact that Alcibiades has committed himself to Socrates, with Socrates's agreement, reflects two more essential points: the first is that the process initiated by shaming is not hands-off; the shamer ought to believe in the possibility of the redemption of the shamed victim. "Believe in" might even be a bit too weak: Socrates is *invested* in Alcibiades's improvement. He *cares* for Alcibiades. It was for the sake of this improvement in the first place that Socrates started the conversation with Alcibiades. It cannot be the sort of activity in which Socrates singles out Alcibiades, makes him feel ashamed just as he was on the verge of beginning his long-awaited career, and then leaves. Socrates is thinking to himself that something is wrong with Alcibiades, that first Alcibiades needs to come to see this, and that shame is the appropriate tool to promote this outcome; *and then* Socrates commits himself to doing the follow-up work. This is what we need to appreciate about how Socrates tries to change the course of Alcibiades's life. Shame is not chiefly about cutting him down; it is about building him up. He just needs to be cut down first, as a way of getting his attention, if nothing else. He needs to go through the painful process of seeing that he *needs* to be improved. This process is the shaming.

If Socrates thought Alcibiades was morally reprobate, irredeemably evil, and not worth a second of his time, the dialogue would not be happening. Socrates's *love* for Alcibiades is a motif in the dialogue, and it explains his deep interest in Alcibiades's well-being. His love for Alcibiades is, as a matter of fact, reflected in the very first words of the dialogue: "I was the first man to fall in love with you, son of Clinias" (103a). Few people today on X, YouTube, TikTok, and so on, shame those they *love*, or love those they shame. In fact, the reverse is most likely the case;

we are more likely to let off the hook those we love, and those we hate are those we shame. Socrates offers himself to Alcibiades as a teacher, a moral exemplar, a fellow citizen, and someone who loves him. The major insights from Plato in using shame to improve someone center around the role of the shamer as a teacher who must be hands-on and involved and around the importance of believing in the shamed victim's possible redemption and improvement.

At this point, it is worth again stressing that we are not *describing* our current shaming practices and justifying them by citing themes from Plato's dialogues. In general, today's shaming practices tend to be aimless, rather than being directed toward the victim's moral improvement, and mean-spirited, rather than constructive. They might be governed by a belief that the shamed victim is incapable of redemption. It is virtually certain that the vast majority of shamers online today take no interest at all in the moral improvement of the victim, if they even believe that moral improvement is possible in the first place. To this extent, Plato urges us to improve ourselves as shamers and offers up Socrates as a model for us to follow.

Let us anticipate an objection. One problem that someone might have with the current practices surrounding shaming is that the punishments are so severe. This concern looms large in various accounts, not least John Stuart Mill's condemnation of the *tyranny of the prevailing opinion and feeling*. Many of the considerations from the previous section get at this idea too. Recall the *magnitude gap*, which is the difference between the harms suffered by the victim and what the shamers *think* the victim will suffer. For instance, the shamer believes that the shamed victim will experience nothing more than the harm of being called transphobic, whereas, in reality, the shamed victim might start to feel deeply unsafe due to death threats that result from being called out. Certainly, it is sobering to consider the catalog of harms suffered by shaming victims: significant damage to a person's well-being, career losses, friendships ended, and so on.

There are real things to be concerned about here. Yet, it is hard to imagine institutional solutions that protect against some of these threats. For instance, an institution could (or should) not prevent a person from ending a friendship because of another person's shameful views. It is perhaps slightly easier to imagine a way that job losses could be prevented: imagine contracts that stipulate a person cannot be fired over a bad reputation brought upon by the expression of shameful views, but these contracts might be undesirable for various reasons. Firms have a legitimate interest in protecting their brand, and their brand might

## 3. Upsides and Revisions            141

well be negatively affected by vicious employees with shameful views. In fact, we might even want firms to care deeply about this sort of thing and to have a stake in the moral image of their brand: an important tool of desirable social change is that firms fire associates with bad moral reputations because their bottom-line profits depend on severing those ties. Further, it does not seem right for an Asian business-owner to be contractually or legally forbidden from firing an employee with a history of anti-Asian social-media posts. Even if we are worried about job losses, it still is desirable to *not* force an Asian person to employ someone with a history of anti-Asian posts. If a person does not want to be associated with someone with shameful views, then severing those ties does not seem to be something that we could or should prevent. It would be dystopian to *force* me to associate with someone who is loudly racist only because of how damaging it might be to the racist's mental health if everyone in society cut ties with him or her.

Further, Plato's point is that the threat of these punishments is precisely what gives the shamed people some skin in the game. Making the consequences less severe only serves to make shaming less effective in the long run. Imagine again people relying on the feeling of shame to prompt them to go to the gym to work out: they are ashamed of missing workouts with their personal trainers, so they are consistent in working out. Imagine if we tried to make the punishment of missing a workout less severe, perhaps by ensuring that the trainer never verbally acknowledges a missed workout. We have spared the shamed victims some bad feelings, but we have undermined the very purpose of the shame in the first place: *the bad feelings were the point*. The severity of the punishment is the point.

However, in making this reply, we might have misrepresented those who are calling for reduced punishments. After all, they draw our attention in particular to hate mail, death threats, and angry people showing up at their houses to yell at them, making them feel deeply unsafe and afraid. These behaviors exceed how Socrates imagined the Athenians would reproach his sons for caring excessively about money and honor. To some extent, the law already provides us with the appropriate remedies, including restraining orders for people whom we do not want around us. Yet, we should grant the broader point that some shaming practices cross the line. This is clearly not the case with *all* shaming behaviors: it is hard to imagine some moral rule that prevents people from calling out racist tweets online, for instance; in fact, there might even be a moral rule that *requires* it. It is hard to specify exactly where this line is, but one helpful criterion is that shaming behaviors need to be *productive*. Showing up where people live to throw rocks at their windows or to yell at them as they go to work because of a racist tweet is, among other things, counterproductive with respect to that person's moral improvement. Someone in that position might even double down on their racist views, having seen that the most visible representative of the anti-racists is someone who does not respect boundaries.

For this reason, it is good to highlight Plato's view that moral improvement ought to be guided by moral exemplars and teachers. Socrates was there for Alcibiades. This ensures that the shamers do not engage in purely destructive behaviors but helpfully instruct the person whom they have shamed. It is important that the shamers do not take a hands-off approach or believe that the shamed victim is beyond redemption.

It is important to believe in the possibility of someone's growth and redemption. Martha Nussbaum objects to the way that public shaming results in someone's **spoiled identity**.[16] To have a spoiled identity is akin to my carrying a sign that says I am not welcome in this community and I am irredeemable. Nussbaum conceives of it as a kind of permanent stain that is not consistent with the belief that people have equal worth and dignity. Nussbaum stresses the same point as Plato: the belief in someone's possible growth is essential. We might also think of her as calling for the possibility of someone's *reintegration* into the community: people need to be able to rejoin the community.

## 4. Shaming in Public

In the previous section, we argued that shame can be usefully employed to bring about moral improvement. If that is all there is to it, then it does not seem necessary to shame people *publicly*. Perhaps there are some people who will respond to shame most effectively if shamed in front of other people, in which case we ought to shame them publicly, but in many cases, taking someone aside and gently chiding them may be sufficient. If so, then John Stuart Mill's criticism of public shaming and Plato's praise of shame can both be true at the same time. Although it is always nice to be so ecumenical, some philosophers disagree and think that public shaming has unique advantages.

Paul Billingham and Tom Parr explain this position: "Public shaming provides a way that we can express our endorsement of valuable social norms, thus

## 4. Shaming in Public

strengthening our shared sense of commitment to those norms, and the values that they promote or respect."[17] They mean that when we publicly condemn some behavior, we are doing more than hopefully initiating some change in the wrongdoer; we are sending a message about what we as a community stand for. If we expect Reddit, X, or any other platform to do anything about the hateful content they host, we might be waiting a long time. Their administrators generally prefer a hands-off approach to managing their communities, and many people agree with their preference. Public shaming allows communities to self-manage by specifically calling out some behaviors and setting examples.

Public shaming has the advantage of setting some clear precedents in a way that private shaming does not. If you post something online, and I take you aside to chide you for what you did, no one else will know, so no one else will be deterred. By making the shaming public, I send the community a message about which sorts of behaviors are off-limits. People are not only deterred from acting that way, but also informed about what sorts of behaviors are not tolerated in our community.

This is closely related to deplatforming. Earlier, we highlighted the risk that deplatforming poses to co-deliberation, but here we consider an argument that speaks in favor of deplatforming people as a way of shaming them and expressing the values of our community.

In this respect, canceling someone is not merely *moral criticism*. Canceling someone also involves directing a community's attention. This has the beneficial effect of making it known to the community what is right and wrong and, therefore, what our values are. Of course, this is also where many concerns begin. Such vulnerable people as Justine Sacco, and virtually every other ordinary person, have no real way to deal with the attention of the entire social-media-using world when it is brought to bear on them. The risks of cancel culture need to be weighed against its positives, and we addressed these risks earlier in this chapter. Some of the steps discussed in the previous section that aim at making the shaming process more constructive will go a long way to mitigate the risks.

This approach to public shaming also makes sense of the definition of "to cancel" that was concerned with the withdrawal of support, such as the loss of followers. The withdrawal of support does not really come from shaming someone in private, but it fits well with an understanding of cancellations that involves redirecting a community's attention in accordance with its values.

## 5. Online Caring

It is easy to focus on the way that life on social-media apps is dominated by shaming. The popular discourse around cancel culture makes that easy. This is part of the broader negativity of social-media usage: we often open the apps and then feel lonelier and more discontent with our lives and bodies. We discuss that research more in Chapter 8 on quitting social media, but it is worth noting here that there is a reason for the frequently given advice on YouTube and Instagram that we should not read the comments on a post. They can often be negative and cutthroat. Cyberbullying has become so common that it is hard not to wonder whether we have become less empathetic as a result of social-media usage. There is some research that shows that, in particular, American college students have become less empathetic over time, with the most pronounced drop occurring around 2000. Researchers speculate that increasing time spent online has contributed to this decline.[18] It is not obvious that this speculation is correct, but it is an important hypothesis.

These considerations have their place, but we can also develop a *caring culture* on social-media sites. There are three kinds of caring to highlight now, and all three are possible in important ways on sites such as X: caring about, caring for, and caring with. These ideas come from what philosophers think of as the **ethics of care**, which is an approach to ethics that stresses the importance of relationships between people and the moral significance of caring for each other.[19] In general, the ethics of care emerged from a kind of feminism that considered the way caring had been devalued in society and attempted to champion the significance of caring. Social-media technologies can play a crucial role in this project.

**Caring about** is a matter of recognizing someone else's needs or struggles as important. Social-media sites allow us to care about someone by giving us an unmediated and regular glimpse into other people's lives. Traditional media platforms, such as broadcast news, give us valuable information about the state of a war-torn country, but X allows people living in that country to live-tweet their stories. We can follow along and interact with the people in those countries directly in ways that have never been possible before. I can watch the news to learn about the struggles that people face when feeding their families in impoverished parts of the United States, but we can use social media to *care about* them too. Some platforms, such as X, even give users the opportunity to assign a hashtag to these accounts, sort them that way, and search through them. We can organize people's stories accordingly.

**Caring for** someone combines two things. First, it requires that we assume some responsibility for the need or struggle that we care about. This involves determining how to address the need or struggle. Second, it requires that we engage in caregiving. Caregiving involves meeting a need or resolving some struggle. We witness caring for on social-media sites all the time. Sometimes, it is a matter of donating money to a crowdfunding campaign for a worthy cause. Sometimes, it involves simply listening to each other.

**Caring with** is a matter of building a community around some need or struggle. This speaks to the way that the ethics of care conceives of care as an ongoing and collective process that involves reaching out to people and working alongside them. Consider how rare (and dangerous) it can be for marginalized people to meet each other in some parts of the world. There might not even be opportunities for such meetings outside of large urban centers. X, Reddit, Discord, TikTok, and countless other social-media sites allow us to build a community of mutual trust, respect, and empathy. It is unfortunately unlikely that marginalized groups can have a presence on a social-media site without *some* interference from malfeasants. Yet, the benefits certainly outweigh the costs of the occasional hateful message. The benefits include the ability to overcome geographical barriers (and thus overcome demographic barriers if you live somewhere remote, rural, or unaccepting) *and* the ability to remain anonymous if one so chooses. Many sites allow us to form whole communities around caring about people affected by specific tragedies and events.

## 6. Conclusion

As we said at the outset of this chapter, the reflections here are not intended to be the final word but, on the contrary, the start of a discussion about cancel culture. We have seen that cancel culture poses real dangers, both to people's well-being and the practice of co-deliberation. We have also seen that shame is an important human emotion and that shaming people publicly can be a way to reallocate attention and clarify society's values. The thought of older philosophers, such as Plato and John Stuart Mill, has guided our reflections, and their approaches have added an important historical perspective to a problem that can seem deeply contemporary. Ultimately, although much of online discourse can seem hopelessly combative and hostile, there is the opportunity for another kind of culture to arise, a culture of caring that is illuminated by the ethics of care.

## Key Terms

**Canceling**: I borrow Eve Ng's definition of "to cancel" as the withdrawal of any kind of support for those who are deemed to have done something objectionable, generally from a social-justice perspective, especially concerning sexism, heterosexism, homophobia, racism, bullying, and related issues.[20] I also add that canceling has to involve *public* shaming and appreciable consequences for the canceled person.

**Caring about**: caring about someone is a matter of recognizing that person's need or struggle as important.

**Caring for**: caring for someone combines two things. First, it requires that we assume some responsibility for the need or struggle that we care about, which involves determining how to address the need or struggle. Second, it requires that we engage in caregiving, which requires meeting a need or resolving some struggle.

**Caring with**: caring with someone is a matter of building a community around some need or struggle. This speaks to the way that the ethics of care conceives of care as an ongoing and collective process that involves reaching out to people and working alongside them.

**Co-deliberation**: the process of reasoning through something difficult alongside other people. It is possible that truths about morality are discovered through co-deliberation, in which case silencing people with dissenting views endangers the integrity of this process because we need people who disagree with us to correct our mistakes and add new perspectives.

**Deplatforming**: removing and banning someone from a platform, such as a social-media site.

**Ethics of care**: an approach to morality that stresses the importance of relationships and the value of caring.

**Imaginal relationship**: a relationship with someone who is real but is distant from us in one way or another, on account of which we have to rely on our imagination to fill in the gaps for us. We might imagine what an old friend would say to us, for instance. These are not *imaginary* relationships because both parties exist. They can be powerful psychological motivators.

**Magnitude gap**: the difference between how harmful the person committing an action thinks that the action is and how harmful it actually is for the victim. We could also frame it this way: the interaction between the perpetrator and the victim is much more casual for the perpetrator than it is for the victim.

**Risk of disproportionality**: the problem with cancel culture to the extent that the punishments are worse than the crimes that people commit; it is also related to the large difference between the quantity of suffering inflicted by the shamers, which is rather large, and the quantity of the suffering that the shamers *think* that they are inflicting, which is considerably smaller.

**Self-licensing**: the act of priming yourself with the belief that you are good, before engaging in an action that would otherwise be considered bad. Reminding yourself that you are good gives you permission to do the otherwise bad thing. This self-license causes reduced feelings of inhibition and guilt concerning the action in question.

**Spoiled identity**: according to Martha Nussbaum, to have a spoiled identity is akin to my carrying a sign that says that I am not welcome in this community and that I am irredeemable. Nussbaum conceives of it as a kind of permanent stain that is inconsistent with the belief that people have equal worth and dignity.[21]

# Discussion Cases

## 1. Sacco

Consider Justine Sacco, an ordinary woman with 170 followers on what was then called Twitter, who boarded a flight from London to Cape Town. Before she boarded, she tweeted, "Going to Africa. Hope I don't get AIDS. Just kidding. I'm white!" She then turned off her phone for the flight. By the time she landed, her tweet went viral and the hashtag #HasJustineLandedYet trended. Sacco even lost her job before landing in South Africa, and the harassment that ensued led to mental-health problems for her.

In general, what do you think of Justine Sacco's case? What do you think of the tweet that she posted? If you think that it violated morality in some sense, what would a realistic and fitting response to her tweet look like? Should the tweet be responded to in public differently than in private? How does the response you just imagined compare to the actual response?

## 2. Rowling

Since 2019, J. K. Rowling has weighed in on debates concerning gender and trans issues. Rowling positions her views as protective of the rights and well-being of women. Her critics accuse her of transphobia, since she has often denied that trans men are men and that trans women are women, preferring instead to call the latter "crossdressing men."[22] The ensuing debate about who is right is deeply divisive, and Rowling herself has often used the term "cancellation" to describe what has happened to her. There is no doubt that Rowling's legacy has been affected by this controversy, and she has lost some professional opportunities as a result (but perhaps also gained some as a social commentator). She has millions of followers on X, and she remains the world's richest author, with a net worth of more than one billion US dollars.

What do you make of Rowling's claims that she has been canceled? When a high-profile celebrity has been accused of transphobia or some other form of prejudice, what sorts of actions, if any, should we take against that person? What is the correct way to respond to Rowling?

## 3. Chick-fil-A

In 2012, Chick-fil-A experienced a lot of divisive press regarding its CEO's outspoken defense of Christian values in opposition to gay marriage. Adam Smith in Tucson, Arizona, had a brother-in-law who had faced his own opposition when coming out as gay, and Smith wanted to join a protest of Chick-fil-A. He filmed himself going to Chick-fil-A, ordering nothing but a (free) cup of water, and confronting an employee about her decision to work there: "I don't know how you live with yourself and work here. I don't understand it. This is a horrible corporation with horrible values." He posted the video, believing that it presented him in a good light and that the protest was benign. He received death threats, and his workplace received bomb threats. He lost his job, and no employer wanted to hire him for months. He contemplated suicide. His family of six was forced to go on food stamps, and ultimately, he and his family had to leave the country. The motivations of those who shamed him are not clear: it is possible that they were sticking up for Christian values or that they did not like to see someone confront a rather helpless fast-food worker, or a mix of both.

What do you think of this case? Does the fact that Adam Smith was standing up for gay rights make any difference in your assessment of the case? Was the response to his protest justified?

# Further Reading

Campbell, Douglas R. 2023. "Cancel Culture, Then and Now: A Platonic Approach to the Shaming of People and the Exclusion of Ideas." *Journal of Cyberspace Studies* 7 (2): 147–66.

This article defends cancel culture from a certain perspective. It is mostly inspired by Plato's dialogues, and many of the key themes are reflected in the section of this chapter that discussed Plato. The article also discusses how cancel culture excludes ideas from society. This part of the article argues that excluding ideas from the public sphere can be helpful to the extent that some ideas undermine democratic institutions and decision-making. The article does not defend the view that excluding ideas is altogether a good thing, though: many people are rightly reticent about excluding ideas from a liberal society.

Konrath, Sara H., Edward H. O'Brien, and Courtney Hsing. 2011. "Changes in Dispositional Empathy in American College Students Over Time: A Meta-Analysis." *Personality and Social Psychology Review* 15 (2): 180–98.

The researchers evaluated college students from seventy-two different campuses in the United States between 1979 and 2009. They found that starting around 2000, there was a sharp drop in students' ability to be empathetic: in particular, their ability to take a different person's perspective and their ability to be concerned for other people. The study did not investigate the cause of this decline, but the researchers speculated that time spent online was hindering the students' ability to engage with people offline effectively and that the nature of online life was so self-focused that it was hard for students to be empathetic as a result. (Think about the way life on social-media apps is structured around building a profile and following for oneself.)

Norris, Pippa. 2023. "Cancel Culture: Myth or Reality?" *Political Studies* 71 (1): 145–74.

Norris's study considered data from 2,500 scholars in more than a hundred different countries, who were asked whether they perceived an increasingly chilly culture around speech. Norris's aim was to discern differing attitudes toward cancel culture. As I said at the start of this chapter, Norris discovered that right-wing scholars in places with liberal social values were most likely to say that they perceived cancel culture worsening; in contrast, left-wing scholars in countries with traditional moral culture were most likely to say that cancel culture was worsening.

Norlock, Kathryn J. 2017. "Online Shaming." *Social Philosophy Today* 33: 187–97.

Much of section 1 of this chapter summarizes Norlock's main argument, which is now known among philosophers as highlighting the *risk of disproportionality* of online shaming. Norlock's central contribution, in my mind, is her argument that shamers are in an imaginal relationship with each other and that this relationship is the thing that they are trying to foster by shaming other people. They are looking for approval and social rewards. The well-being of the victim is entirely irrelevant.

Puotinen, Sara L. 2011. "Twitter Cares? Using Twitter to Care about, Care for and Care with Women Who Have Had Abortions." *International Review of Information Ethics* 16: 79–84.

Puotinen's article is responsible for the section in this chapter about caring. She does a great job applying insights from the ethics of care to life on social media, especially what was then called Twitter. Her article specifically looks at the way that women who had abortions shared their stories and cared with each other online, but, as you will be able to tell from the way I presented her ideas in section 5, her points generalize to any kind of need or struggle. I especially recommend her article as an antidote to the often-circulated message that social-media platforms are or have to be purely negative and mean-spirited.

Nussbaum, Martha. 2004. *Hiding from Humanity: Disgust, Shame, and the Law.* Princeton, NJ: Princeton University Press.

This is not a book about cancel culture, but it is a book about the place of shame in our lives and society. Many of the ideas from this chapter, such as *spoiled identity* and some of the criticisms of public shaming, come directly from Nussbaum's thorough survey of shame. Nussbaum is deeply critical of the way that shame figures in different kinds of punishments.

Ronson, Jon. 2015. *So You've Been Publicly Shamed.* New York: Riverhead Books.

Ronson is a journalist, and this book is journalistic in tone, not so much philosophical. I recommend this book to anyone interested in learning more about episodes of public shaming. Ronson interviewed many victims of public shaming, and readers who are interested in cases like Sacco's will enjoy this book. He does a great job of capturing the reemergence of public shaming as an online phenomenon in a journalistic way.

Thomason, Krista. 2021. "The Moral Risks of Online Shaming." In *The Oxford Handbook of Digital Ethics,* edited by Carissa Véliz, 145–62. Oxford: Oxford University Press.

Thomason highlights some important risks of online shaming, including disproportionality and co-deliberation. Her paper surveys some of the arguments *for* shaming that I discuss in this chapter. There is also a discussion of both what shaming is and what some of the alternatives might be. Overall, I recommend her article to readers who are looking for a wide-ranging survey about online shaming.

## Notes

1. See Ronson 2015 for a discussion of Sacco's case (and many others); Norlock 2017 also discusses Sacco's case briefly and for the same purpose that I discuss her case.
2. I credit this definition to Ng 2020, 623.
3. Norris 2023 is the study that I have in mind.
4. Much of this section is inspired by Norlock 2017, although I also bring in insights from Thomason 2021.
5. Mill 1991, 9.
6. Mill 1991, 9.
7. Nussbaum 2004, 234.
8. See Merritt, Effron, and Monin 2010 for this research.
9. This concept comes from Baumeister 1997, 18–19.
10. See Ronson 2015 and Norlock 2017 for more.
11. See Basak et al. 2016.
12. Mill 1991, 9.
13. This section draws upon Thomason 2021's discussion of these moral risks. Note that Thomason also discusses the problem of disproportionality that I developed in the previous section, even though I relied mostly on Norlock 2017 for that.
14. This section is adapted from Campbell 2023b.
15. All translations of Plato are from Cooper 1999.
16. See Nussbaum 2004, 230, 239.
17. Billingham and Parr 2019, 7.
18. See Konrath, O'Brien, and Hsing 2011.
19. In particular, see Tronto 1994, although much of what I say in this section applies Joan Tronto's ideas to social-media life in a way that follows Puotinen 2011.
20. Ng 2020, 623.
21. See Nussbaum 2004, 230, 239.
22. See Johnson 2024.

# Chapter Seven: Friendship

Of all the relationships that we have, perhaps none of them has been more impacted by social-media technologies than our friendships. Before the language of *followers* took over, mostly in parallel with the rise of influencer culture, social-media interactions were cashed out in terms of friends: we talked about our *Facebook friends*, for instance. It is natural to ask about the ethical significance of the advent of purely online friendships. As far as philosophers are concerned, friendship has always been recognized as a crucial ingredient of a good human life. Plato wrote an entire book about it, the *Lysis*, and dealt with the subject elsewhere too, in the *Laws*. In Aristotle's ethical masterpiece, the *Nicomachean Ethics*, he devotes more space to friendship than to any other subject. The tradition of philosophical reflection on friendship that Plato and Aristotle inaugurated in the West continues today with philosophical treatments of online friendships.

For the purposes of this chapter, we consider a **friendship** to be a close relationship in which there is deep mutual affection, a tendency to assist in the welfare of the other person, and a lasting desire to engage with the other person in shared activities.[1] We use this understanding of friendship because it is common in the texts of philosophers who work on the ethics of social media, but ultimately it does not matter much whether our definition is exactly right. It is sufficient for the reader to call to mind his or her friendships; these are what we are talking about. It is worth noting that the term "friendship" does not exclude other kinds of relationships: ideally, we are friends with our romantic partners (though they might not like it when we call them "friend"), parents, siblings, and cousins.

As for what counts as an online or offline friendship, this is a bit trickier. Students often report to me that they have friends with whom they at one time had in-person contact, but who moved away, so they now speak only online. Certainly, we are also familiar with the reverse: so many romantic partners today meet each other online and then get together offline. For our purposes, think of an online friendship as one in which the friends go long periods of time without seeing each other offline and in which there is no obvious end to the online phase of the friendship.

The philosophical question is whether offline friendships, all things being equal, are superior to online friendships, or vice versa. If we wanted to frame the question less competitively, we might wonder about the unique advantages offered by each kind of friendship, if there are any, as well as what the possible drawbacks are.

The question is apt. Regardless of whether we are inclined to say that online or offline friendships are superior, there is no plausible way to deny that our friendships have *changed*. Sherry Turkle, an important social scientist, reports that adolescents and young adults complain about the time that is spent engaging with friends online and about the demands on their energy that follow from being constantly tethered to each other.[2] Technologies that make talking to our friends easier might take up more of our time and energy. It is healthy for friends to be separated from each other sometimes. It might even make us better friends: separation helps us develop a stronger sense of self that we can then bring to the friendship. Separation might also prevent us from getting too fatigued.

Social scientists such as Turkle think of the underlying problem as *narcissism*. Here, we do not mean excessive self-love or self-obsession, but instead, someone with a personality so fragile that it requires constant support. Turkle catalogs the attitudes of many adolescents in her research. Here is a telling report from Julia, a sixteen-year-old girl, about how she feels when one of her friends does not reply to her messages:

> I get mad. Even if I e-mail someone, I want the response, like, right away. I want them to be, like, right there answering me. And sometimes I'm like, "Uh! Why can't you just answer me?" [...] I wait, like, depending on what it is, I wait like an hour if they don't answer me, and I'll text them again. "Are you mad? Are you there? Is everything okay?"[3]

If nobody replies to Julia fast enough, she does as follows: "I go to another friend and tell them." To some extent, this tendency predated social-media apps. After all, sociologists in the 1950s such as David Riesman were researching a shift from inner- to other-directed senses of self. People with an other-directed sense of self look to their peers for validation. What has changed in the twenty-first century is the way that smartphones and social-media technologies have come together to facilitate what Turkle calls a hyper-other-directedness. Consider what Ricki, a fifteen-year-old girl, says: "I have a lot of people on my contact list. If one friend doesn't 'get it,' I call another."[4]

This sociological research reflects the way that social-media use is unhealthy for us and causes symptoms of many mental illnesses. Some of the research

# 1. Offline Friendships Are Superior to Online Ones

on that subject is discussed in Chapter 8 on quitting social media. In the present discussion, we will make the limited observation that social-media technologies have changed our friendships and, with them, ourselves. So far, these transformations do not sound positive. Perhaps that is a point in favor of thinking that offline friendships are superior and that we ought to prefer them over online ones. That position will be the first we consider in this chapter, but the arguments for this position are not those based on the psychological or sociological research. Instead, the arguments we shall consider are philosophical.

Before we turn to those arguments, a clarification: when we argue that offline friendships are superior, we are not denying that online friendships are better than being bereft of company, and we are not arguing that they are totally devoid of value. For instance, if I were trapped in the Arctic at some philosophical research station, and the only people I could communicate with were on Reddit or a Discord server, I should be endlessly grateful for the technologies that make it possible for me to have these friendships. By the same token, I would be even more grateful if I could trade in these online friendships for offline ones.

## 1. Offline Friendships Are Superior to Online Ones

The first two reasons we consider for the superiority of offline friendships involve self-creation and self-knowledge.[5] The first such reason is simple: we can do more shared activities with our in-person friends. Online friends are able to do things such as play video games together and share in other online activities, but offline friends can do these things too. Offline friends get to do everything that online friends can do *and more*. This highlights an important dimension of friendship: friends help reveal (and create) parts of ourselves. This is because the ability to engage in activities with friends helps us explore new things about ourselves.

For example, I hate putting things together and building things. Lego toys are the opposite of *fun* for me. However, my best friend encouraged me to try sailing with her, and, as anyone who sails knows, the process of rigging the boat before one can sail is rather involved and certainly exceeds my threshold for complexity in putting things together. Yet, I tried sailing anyway because my best friend was doing it. Two things followed. The first is that I, with some help from my friend, transformed myself into someone who enjoys sailing. The second is that I came to learn about myself that I can tolerate assembly projects that are appropriately directed toward something fun with my friend.

Friendships do this sort of thing all the time. We try out ballet or Brazilian jiu-jitsu because our friends want us to. The respects in which friendship does this sort of thing are understated by any usual verb in English. If we say that our friends *encourage* us to try new hobbies, that might do disservice to the way that we would feel anxious and unsupported without our friends' presence and to the way that we clamor to visit new restaurants and parks when we *are* with our friends. We might never have an idea to try some particular thing without our friends. In fact, in general, we might just keep doing the same things until our friends disrupt our routines. That is not mere *encouragement*. We simultaneously learn new things about ourselves and create new parts of ourselves thanks to the way that friends interact with us.

To some extent, online friends can do the same thing: we can watch a new movie at the same time over Zoom, for instance, or try cooking new recipes with each other while on FaceTime. The same kind of self-creation is in principle possible online, but it is drastically limited. There is no way, for instance, that I would have tolerated rigging a boat if my best friend were in another country and we were rigging two different boats at the same time but talking about the process on Zoom.

There is another case to be made for the superiority of offline friendships along the same lines as the first, since it also involves self-knowledge, but it is far more complicated. To understand the contours of this argument, we need to return to one of the earliest and arguably the single most important philosopher who held forth on friendship: Aristotle. Aristotle develops a view of friends as *mirrors for each other*:

> Surely, it is not possible for us to study ourselves. (That it is not possible for us to study ourselves is clear from the fact that we censure other people for doing things that escape our notice when we do them; this happens on account of partiality or passion; for many of us, these things impede our ability to judge correctly.) So, just as whenever we wish to see our own faces, we look into a mirror, similarly when we wish to know ourselves, we are able to know ourselves by looking at a friend. For a friend, we say, is another self. (*Magna Moralia* 1212b8–24; translation mine)

## 1. Offline Friendships Are Superior to Online Ones 157

Aristotle's point is that friends are keys to our self-knowledge because we can use them to learn about ourselves, just as we use mirrors to learn about our appearance. Aristotle cites passion and partiality as reasons why we cannot learn about ourselves directly without the mediation of friends. The idea, to put it simply, is that we are biased in favor of ourselves, with the result that we overlook things about ourselves. My experience with undergraduate students and fellow academics is that this *bias* means we sometimes overlook positive and good things about ourselves, too, even though that does not seem to be what Aristotle has in mind.

In today's philosophical literature, Aristotle's argument is expanded and defended in ways that he could not have foreseen. Expanded versions of his argument start by observing a crucial feature of friendships: people respond to **cues** from their friends. Cues are information that is communicated verbally and non-verbally, such as through behaviors. We develop a sense of who our friends are and who we are through cues. Now, online, we have access only to a limited range of cues. For instance, when I am curating the content of my Instagram account, I might choose to post only about my dog, my luxurious holidays in Hawaii, Pokémon, and Plato's *Timaeus*. Any would-be friend would get the wrong sense of who I am. "Curation" is the name of the game on social-media sites. I might choose to downplay some parts of myself, such as an autoimmune condition that I have, not because I do not want anyone else to know but simply because it is not something I get enjoyment from discussing. If I am given a platform that I can use to post whatever I want, then I am going to post about my decadent holidays and Pokémon, not about things that might displease me. It is easy to move from this observation to the cynical claim that I am trying to deceive people or grandstand about how wonderful my life is, but that is not necessarily what I intend: I could just subconsciously filter things out.

Contrast this with what happens in offline friendships. Let's say that Rachel and Ria, two friends, are at a party together, and Ria notices that Rachel has just spotted her ex-boyfriend enter. Ria might immediately notice that something is awry on account of the way that Rachel's body language changes. Ria can respond appropriately to this important cue and move to get Rachel to leave the party with her. This response to a cue is called an **interpretation**: to interpret a cue from a friend is to recognize the significance of the cue and to integrate it into our understanding of our friend. When appropriate, we then respond to the cue in light of our interpretation. This sort of thing is part of how friendships are structured. For instance, we might tease a friend for taking a nap within a few hours of waking up: that is a cue that we respond to by teasing. We might see that our friends are uncomfortable or having a great time simply thanks to their body language, not something communicated verbally, and we can then interpret that cue appropriately.

In online friendships, we can no doubt interpret *some* cues. Perhaps I can interpret someone's long delay in replying to my text message as revealing that he or she would rather not speak with me. The problem with interpretations in online contexts is that the range of available cues is profoundly limited, and it is much easier for a cue to be insincere or entirely dishonest. Consider the following two contrasting cases, in both of which I have given a terrible lecture to undergraduate students that I really wanted to go well. In one case, Jolene, a friend, then sends me a text message to ask me how the lecture went. I reply by saying that it was fine. Jolene might immediately detect that the lecture, in fact, went disastrously and that I need to be consoled, although I do not wish to make this obvious because I do not want to be vulnerable. She might recognize that I would never have said "I'm fine" if the lecture had gone well; I would have said something far more self-assured. Jolene could then persist and ask whether I am sure that it was fine, or something to that effect. At this point, I *could* reveal the truth to Jolene after she has insightfully intuited that something is wrong, *or* I could double down on hiding how I feel: I could insist that everything went fine. In fact, if I really want to hide how things went from my friend, I could say that the lecture was great and then accompany the message with several emojis.

In contrast, if Jolene and I got together offline, and she asked me how the lecture went, I *could* try to lie and say that it went fine, but it would be much more difficult: Jolene might hear me say that the lecture went fine but she could notice features of my face and body language. Again, we are not denying that people can lie offline and that people can detect dishonest behavior from their friends online. It is simply much harder to lie offline and much harder to detect lies online. This is especially true when we are talking about our friends.

Instead of thinking about this merely in terms of deceit, hiding information, and being dishonest, we can frame the problem in terms of cues. *Our offline friends have access to a fuller range of cues.* That is the crux of the two cases concerning me and Jolene. In the online case, Jolene has access only to the self-reported information about how the lecture went. In the offline case, she is able to weigh the self-reported information against other cues, such as my body language and facial expressions. This is a clear point in favor of offline friendships: offline friends do

## 1. Offline Friendships Are Superior to Online Ones

not rely merely on self-reported cues, but instead on other cues as well. Of course, it is possible that some of the other cues might be insincere or dishonest: after all, I could try to put on a smile when I am sad, which is altering an important non-verbal cue. I emphasize that the argument here is *not* relying on the claim that the non-verbal cues always reflect reality. Instead, the argument relies on the greater range of cues that offline friends have access to *and* the fact that non-verbal cues are harder to convincingly feign.

This is called the *cues-filtered-out* argument against the value of online friendships. In addition to the cues that online friends simply lack access to, such as our body language, we also naturally filter out some cues for the reasons that I mentioned earlier when discussing my hypothetical dog-filled Instagram account: sometimes, we just prefer not to talk about something. This is what happens when I try to lead Jolene into thinking that my lecture went fine when it was a horrific failure. I simply do not want to make myself vulnerable.

However, at this point, we should consider a crucial objection: we might concede that online friends have access to a smaller range of cues by default, but this does not stop them from thoroughly disclosing every bit of information about themselves. This might involve exchanging a lot of tedious information and making ourselves vulnerable; it might not be a pleasant or fun experience at all. However, the objection is that, in principle, an online friendship *can* be built on just as much information as an offline friendship—so long as we thoroughly disclose all of the information without filtering anything out due to our own biases.

The objection correctly diagnoses that a central limitation of online friendships is based on the limited set of cues that the friends have access to, but Aristotle's observation in the *Magna Moralia* about friendship reveals why the objection nevertheless fails. *We do not know everything about ourselves.* Accordingly, we could not possibly disclose everything about ourselves, even if we disclosed everything that makes us wince and cringe when we think about disclosing it to another person. In fact, as Aristotle puts it, not only are there true things about us that escape our notice, but our friends can help us discover these things; that is the sense in which our friends act as *mirrors* for us. Our friends can teach us these things about ourselves only if *they* know them, and *we* cannot possibly self-report them because *we* do not know about them. Since we do not know them, we cannot report them to our friends.

Today, there is a veritable industry of philosophers and psychologists studying whether introspection is a reliable tool for achieving self-knowledge. It is not the point of this chapter to survey this body of scholarship, so let us mention only a few brief considerations. First, philosophical criticisms of introspection as a method of achieving self-knowledge have existed since antiquity. After all, the passage from Aristotle's *Magna Moralia* says exactly that: it is impossible for us to directly study ourselves. Even before Aristotle, Plato staked out a similar position in the *Alcibiades*.[6] These philosophers get at something that we all perceive but do not often heed: we are not particularly good at knowing ourselves. Let me illustrate with a few examples. I often interact with undergraduate students who have impostor syndrome. To have impostor syndrome is to doubt one's own achievements and skills and to fear being exposed as a fraud. Very rarely, if ever, do people with impostor syndrome know that they have impostor syndrome. (Perhaps it happens only when a person is recovering.) Instead, people with impostor syndrome feel like they are an impostor. The thought in their head is not "I feel like an impostor because I have impostor syndrome." The thought is "I feel like an imposter because I really am one." We could easily imagine my friends seeing me correctly answer questions in class and then hear me doubt my own proficiency in the course material. *They* could perceive that I have impostor syndrome and inform me. We regularly count on our friends to do such things and to teach us about ourselves.

Something similar occurs with body-image issues. Of course, each one of us generally thinks that we are an expert about our own body. After all, we spend the most time with it, and we have a unique set of evidence pertaining to it because we get to experience things about our body that nobody else does. Now, let us imagine that I do not feel attractive. When I tell my friends this, they try to correct me, but I assure them that I am the expert when it comes to my own body. This sounds like a compelling slogan, but the reverse is most likely true: *I am too close to my own body to be an impartial judge.* My friends' opinions benefit from the distance that I lack. This sometimes happens when people feel unattractive at one point in time, and they look back years later on a photo from that time and remark on how attractive they look. This happens because the elapsed time has generated the sort of distance that friends usually enjoy. In other words, the passage of time might as well have made someone into a different person altogether. This is a crucial insight into the nature of friendship: we often need our friends' feedback on some situation that we have found ourselves in. The fact that we are the people in the situation is precisely the reason why we are *not* able to judge the situation well. That is where our friends come in. Our friends can be judges who see things that we cannot.

In conclusion, we can say that our offline friends have access to a fuller range of cues than our online friends do. This gives them a better understanding of who we are, and it allows us to develop deeper and richer friendships. If we thoroughly disclose information about ourselves to our online friends, we might be able to overcome the way we naturally filter out cues that we do not want people to know about or respond to, but there is no way we could overcome the fact that there are things about ourselves that we just cannot know without our friends helping us discover them.

## 2. Online Friendships Are Superior to Offline Friendships

There are arguments that online friendships are superior to offline ones.[7] These arguments are based on a different set of considerations than the arguments that support the opposite view. The first argument acknowledges that we *do* often change the way that we reveal ourselves to other people when we go online, but this change can be toward being more authentic and more fully ourselves. Consider that when we are online, we have additional opportunities to develop more deliberate, thoughtful things to say. Face-to-face communication is often marked by half-finished sentences and rapid-fire responses, but online we can take our time to craft responses. We might more easily think of things to say that reflect our values and considered judgments.

People who think that offline friendships are superior might be skeptical of this line of thinking. In their view, we are *more* authentic when we are spontaneous than when we are deliberate. However, this assumption might well be false. After all, in offline communication, we might regret something we said and feel that we did not have the opportunity to think twice before we said it. The same thing can happen online, but there are tools in place to prevent that, and general conversational expectations permit long delays between responses. These delays can engender a kind of attentiveness and discipline that improve us as friends and interlocutors; in addition, they allow us to be more precise in the things that we say. If online communication allows us to be more precise about how we feel and think, then it is hard to see how it could be considered *less authentic*: the ability to speak more precisely seems to perfectly capture the idea that deliberate and thoughtful online interactions are more authentic and reveal more fully who we are.

The mere act of writing itself can be more introspective than speech. Reading back what we have written before we send a message to our friends can prompt us not only to rethink the words that we have chosen but also to reflect on how we truly feel. The resulting message is a deeper and more accurate signal about who we are. In the previous section, we considered the way that offline friends help us learn things about ourselves that we do not even know, but when we do know something about ourselves, online friendships might be better sites for communicating our self-knowledge.

The main takeaway is that the *context of communication changes the content that is communicated*. For instance, when I am at a soccer match, my support for the team is different from what it is when I am watching the match on television. The context prompts feelings and impulses to behave differently—and to communicate different things. Similarly, we might be prompted by the context of writing to our friends to be more attentive, deliberate, thoughtful, and precise.

Online, there is a marked absence of social pressure to conform and to hide things about ourselves. This is probably the most prominent advantage of online friendships. The other advantage relies on the notion that we can be more authentic and more truly ourselves when we are online.

Here is an example that does not feature social-media technologies but will help to make some of the underlying concepts clear. Imagine soldiers fighting in the American Civil War.[8] We might expect the soldiers to be close friends with each other: they see each other often; they have to trust each other immensely and implicitly; and they know what each other is going through in a way that nobody else does. However, this might not be so. One soldier has a pen pal in Boston, who is a schoolteacher, and we could argue that these two have a greater potential for a close friendship than two soldiers do. This is because the schoolteacher and the soldier can be honest with each other in a way that the soldiers might not be able to. Consider the social pressure that prevents the soldiers from discussing certain topics and airing certain feelings. For instance, perhaps the soldier with the pen pal has grave doubts about the war, but these doubts cannot be shared without risking the morale of the unit. Perhaps the soldier is overcome by fear, and he does not feel comfortable talking to his comrades about his feelings. Perhaps he toys with the idea of deserting, and, again, cannot share these feelings. However, he can do so with the teacher. Similarly, the teacher can share whatever he is feeling and thinking that he cannot share with those around him.

The reason we feel at first that the schoolteacher and soldier cannot have a friendship as close as the one between soldiers is that there are kinds of distance between the soldier and schoolteacher. Of course, one kind of distance is *geographical*: they are in different parts of the United States. The more salient distance is the social distance: they occupy different walks of life. When we look deeper, we can see that the social distance might, in fact, *help* their friendship because it opens a space for candor, sincerity, and authenticity. Online, we can be free from some social pressures.

We can take the insights from the American Civil War example and think about its implications for the twenty-first century. Imagine Sophia, a twenty-five-year-old woman who is looking for a close friendship. She often wants to vent about her boss, but she is wary of being completely forthcoming with her work colleagues. She plays basketball on the weekends, but she has a complicated romantic past with one of her fellow players; so, she feels a lot of awkwardness when it comes to being herself with them. For her, online life could never *replace* those communities, but as for being her honest, true self and being *close* with anyone, her online friendships are superior to her offline ones. That is because offline friendships come embedded with other demands, expectations, and conventions, and these can impede bonding and self-disclosure.

It must be stated that not everyone uses social-media apps this way. People who catfish—that is, deceive others by pretending to be someone else—use the apps in a way that is completely *opposed* to what we are talking about, after all. However, this fact does not negate the advantages that online life *can* offer some people.

# 3. The Future of Friendship

The possibilities generated by new technologies should make us think more carefully about the possibility that online friendships, even if not *superior* overall to offline ones, have a unique advantage. Virtual-reality technologies enhance that advantage.

As we have seen, online friendships benefit from the fact that they are free from many social pressures. In an offline friendship, the social setting might make us uncomfortable about sharing some personal matter. For instance, we can easily imagine members of a minority group who are afraid to share their status because their larger community might punish them for it. Even if these concerns are wrong-headed or baseless, our anxieties may prevent us from opening up to the people around us. It would be too difficult to get away from them, if they react badly. So, we feel the risk is too large.

Meanwhile, we might be more comfortable with revelations in offline relationships. If we share something about ourselves that someone else online dislikes, we have the ability to filter out their comments or block them altogether. It is also much easier to try on membership in a community: with a click of a button, anyone can join a community on Reddit, and just as easily, leave it. The unique advantage these communities offer is that joining them is virtually cost-free, both financially and emotionally: we can become friends with people without having to worry about what they think of some identity that we are trying on.

Virtual-reality technologies improve online friendships in a number of ways. For instance, people with disabilities can now do things with their friends that might not have been possible before, online *or* offline. Someone who has a disability that prevents them from skiing can have that experience with their friends: with virtual-reality headsets, they can engage in shared experiences, which is one of the most important features of friendships and, until now, has been a crucial consideration in favor of the superiority of offline friendships.

Just as this door has been opened for disabled people, it has been opened for everyone. It was a real drawback of online friendships that they were once limited to text-based communication. Social-media sites have changed this: they now allow us to interact with online friends in the form of videos, photos, and audio content. Thanks to even newer technologies, people can truly *engage in shared experiences and activities* with their online friends. People all across the world devised strategies to connect with friends when the COVID-19 pandemic precluded in-person gatherings. It was no longer about merely sharing updates on Facebook. Groups of friends could watch movies together using FaceTime. Two friends could cook risotto together on Zoom.

Even so, these activities are not precisely as they would be if the friends were in the same room. There are things missing. Virtual-reality technologies change at least some of this. As these technologies improve, there might even be ways for two people to have the experience of smelling each other even though they are on different continents. The olfactometer in one headset could track what the wearer smells like, and then transmit that information to the receiving headset, triggering the release of some odor in the receiving olfactometer. It is possible for two friends to attend a virtual-reality basketball game with thousands of other people, with the experience designed such that as a user gets closer to other people's avatars, the user can hear what those people are saying more clearly; as the user backs off, the volume decreases naturally. These technologies are already reproducing important parts of what it is like for a person to engage in an activity, and we are able to do them with friends.

Think back to the *cues-filtered-out objection*. The objection states that friends respond to cues in our behavior, and this response is part of what makes friendships special. We do not have to tell our friends things about ourselves; they know these things just by observing our behavior. It is a good thing that we do not have to tell our friends these things because we ourselves might not even be aware of them. As technology improves, friends might not have to rely on self-reported cues at all. (To some extent, this is already the case: I could be on a FaceTime call with my friends, and they would have access to more than just my self-reported cues, such as my facial expressions, and they could respond accordingly.) Virtual-reality technologies in particular might help us connect with our friends as if they were right there in front of us. One user's equipment might detect all of the user's cues and then relate them to the equipment of the other user with complete fidelity.

# 4. Conclusion

It is not obvious whether online friendships are inferior to offline friendships. There are arguments on each side of the debate, and the future will no doubt change many features of online life. There are other, smaller considerations that are hard to base a philosophical argument on. For instance, consider the physicality of friendship that is lacking in online friendships. On the one hand, physicality, such as hugging, is important in many friendships and is impossible online. On the other hand, many people have deep, intimate friendships that involve no physicality at all. Few people would maintain that a healthy, happy human life could be lived without ever touching anyone else, but nobody in this debate about friendship says that we should replace all of our offline friends with online friends. If we restrict the pro-online-friendship claim to be merely that, all things being equal, online friendships are superior to offline ones, that is consistent with a concession that physicality is a nice perk of offline friendships; still, online ones could be better for the reasons discussed earlier.

The same goes for the small consideration that online friendships often take place on heavily commercialized platforms, such as Reddit and Facebook, where the *stuff* of their friendship—namely, their communication—is encouraged by the company hosting them for the sake of advertisement revenue and data collection. This is true, but it is hard to see how it challenges the depth and quality of a friendship. It is also hard to see how this is different from many offline friendships, although certainly, it is easier for offline friends to meet in non-commercialized spaces. We also should bear in mind the context: when evaluating online and offline friendships, we should attend to what point people are at in their lives and what sort of relationship they most need.

## Key Terms

**Cues**: information that is communicated verbally and non-verbally, such as through behaviors.

**Friendship**: a close relationship in which there is deep mutual affection, a tendency to assist in the welfare of the other person, and a lasting desire to engage with the other person in shared activities.

**Interpretation**: to interpret a cue from someone is to recognize the significance of the cue and to integrate it into our understanding of that person. When appropriate, we then respond to the cue in light of our interpretation.

## Discussion Cases

### 1. Catfishing

Catfishing is the activity of creating and using a fake identity online to form a bond with someone for the sake of deceiving that person. A catfish might steal someone else's photos in order to complete the fake identity. Perhaps the motivations are financial or something more innocent. The phenomenon of catfishing is more than just an instance of deceit and dishonesty: the knowledge that some people deliberately and thoroughly lie about themselves online presents real challenges to developing intimate online friendships.

How do you think that catfishing fits into the debates around online and offline friendship? Do you think that catfishing undermines the possibility of having close online friendships, or is the phenomenon rare enough to not be a major concern? How should we cope with the possibility that our online friends might be lying to us about who they are?

## 2. Friendship

In light of the arguments in this chapter, reflect on your own online and offline friendships.

What does each kind of friendship bring to your life? Are there any online friendships that, if possible, you would convert to offline friendships? What do you think would be gained by that conversion? What do you think would be lost?

## 3. Influencers as Friends

One reason why influencers are so popular is that they have cultivated a *parasocial* relationship with their audience: a one-sided relationship marked by emotional investment that can *feel* like a friendship. It *feels* to so many of us that we know and are friends with our favorite podcasters and YouTube and TikTok stars. The glimpse into someone's personal life, through Get-Ready-with-Me videos or Twitch streams, can make us feel like we really know the influencer in question. As much as we follow their lives in great detail, they do not know anything about us.

How might the idea of an imaginal relationship, from Chapter 6, guide how we evaluate these parasocial relationships? What risks are there, both for the viewer and the influencer? What benefits? Does the one-sidedness of these relationships really mean that they cannot be friendships?

## 4. Managing Friendships

In the introduction to this chapter, we discussed Sherry Turkle's work on the changing nature of friendship. One sixteen-year-old girl, Julia, described a desire or *need* to almost constantly be in contact with her friends. This highlights an important facet of online friendships: the difficulty of managing the balance between being available and unreachable.

What are some advantages and disadvantages of technology that, in principle, allow us to be always available to other people? Does this promote burnout or deeper, more solid friendships?

## Further Reading

Aristotle. 2019. *Nicomachean Ethics*, translated by Terence Irwin. Indianapolis, IN: Hackett Publishing, 2019.

In this chapter, I quoted and relied on Aristotle's *Magna Moralia*, but the *Nicomachean Ethics* is the go-to text for his views on friendship. This text is divided into ten books, the eighth and ninth of which develop an influential taxonomy of friendship: friendships built on pleasure; those built on utility; and those built on virtue. I have cited here a great translation by Terence Irwin, which I heartily recommend to anyone interested in pursuing Aristotle's views.

Briggle, Adam. 2008. "Real Friends: How the Internet Can Foster Friendship." *Ethics and Information Technology* 10: 71–79.

Briggle defends the view that online friendships have unique advantages. Briggle is responsible for the soldier-and-schoolteacher example that is meant to draw our attention to the way that distance from our friends can help create a space for us to be more open and honest about what we feel. I also credit him with the argument that the methods of online communication can prompt us to be more deliberate, thoughtful, and precise with our friends.

Cocking, Dean, and Steve Matthews. 2000. "Unreal Friends." *Ethics and Information Technology* 2: 223–31.

I credit the understanding of friendship that is used in this chapter to Cocking and Matthews. Their compelling argument that friends interpret each other's cues and that such cues are naturally filtered out online, even when we try to avoid filtering them out, is an influential one in the philosophical debates about online friendship, and it is an important one in this chapter. They are responsible for the insight that the *context of communication changes the content that is communicated.* They also quote Aristotle's *Magna Moralia*, as I do here.

Elder, Alexis. 2014. "Excellent Online Friendships: An Aristotelian Defense of Social Media." *Ethics and Information Technology* 16: 287–97.

Elder continues the trend set by Cocking and Matthews, with whom she disagrees, of importing Aristotelian ideas into a discussion of online friendships. This highlights Aristotle's enduring importance in the philosophy of friendship. She argues that online friendships preserve most of what makes friendships so valuable to us. I channel her analysis briefly in this chapter when I explain that there are other considerations (e.g., the physicality consideration and the commercialization-of-friendship consideration) that might at first appear to count in favor of offline friendships but ultimately are not decisive.

Harris, Michael. 2017. *Solitude: In Pursuit of a Singular Life in a Crowded World.* New York: Basic Books.

Harris provides a well-written, journalistic survey of some of the reasons why we should disconnect from social media, including the argument that solitude causes us to be better friends because we approach friendships with a stronger and more developed sense of self. This theme is also taken up by Turkle. His arguments are mostly presented in the form of interviews, some of which feature prominent active philosophers, and in the form of a memoir of his own disconnection from social media.

Riesman, David, Nathan Glazer, and Reuel Denney. 1950. *Lonely Crowd: A Study of the Changing American Character.* New Haven, CT: Yale University Press.

This book was written long before the advent of social media, but it provides an interesting analysis of the transformation of Western culture into one that is more *other-directed* and less *inner-directed*. To be other-directed is to live at the whims of how other people live and work; it is characterized by a desire to be loved and a readiness to accommodate other people to win approval. Many of these features are amplified by tendencies on social media.

Turkle, Sherry. 2011. *Alone Together: Why We Expect More from Technology and Less from Each Other*. New York: Basic Books.

Turkle is a sociologist at MIT, and her approach to online friendships differs greatly from philosophical work on the subject because her evidence tends to be qualitative data, such as the quotations from various teenagers that I have included in the first part of this chapter. The most insightful chapter of this book, as far as the ethics of social media is concerned, is the ninth chapter, which is about the effects of growing up tethered to each other (and to our parents).

## Notes

1. I borrow this definition from Cocking and Matthews 2000.
2. See Turkle 2011.
3. Turkle 2011, 176.
4. Turkle 2011, 177.
5. This section is influenced by Cocking and Matthews 2000.
6. See *Alcibiades* 132a–134e in Cooper 1999.
7. This section is inspired by Briggle 2008.
8. I borrow this example directly from Briggle 2008.

# Chapter Eight: Quitting

After working through a whole book on the ethics of social media, we come to the question of whether we should quit and delete our social-media accounts. We have already surveyed some reasons on both sides of the debate. The benefits of social media, such as the advantages of online friendships, give us a reason to stay. The many downsides give us reasons to leave. However, some important questions remain for us to focus on, such as whether we are permitted to have relationships with companies that do evil things. That is what this chapter is about.

We shall have to paint with a broad brush here. It might be that we have a duty to delete our Facebook accounts but not a duty to delete our LinkedIn accounts, for instance. Which social-media platforms we might permissibly stay on will, in the end, depend on whether each one satisfies whatever broad principle we settle on. If it turns out that we should delete our account on each platform that engages in wrongful conduct, then we might have to delete our Instagram accounts but not our Tumblr accounts, if indeed the former engages in bad behavior, but the latter does not. The goal of this chapter is to work through how contemporary philosophers have approached various broad principles and discussed the ethics of consumption. The goal is not to outline the behavior of each extant social-media company and determine which is good and which is bad.

## 1. One Reason to Quit: Our Own Well-Being

The first and most pressing reason to delete our social-media accounts is that being on these platforms is detrimental to our happiness and well-being. We ought to delete our accounts for the same reason we ought to get good-quality sleep and eat nutritious food: doing so is good for us. Ancient philosophers, such as Plato, Aristotle, and Epictetus, believed that morality in the first place is concerned with our duties to ourselves. In general, we ought to promote our own well-being by obtaining what is good for us and avoiding what is bad for us. Today's psychological research bears out the claim that the time we spend on social-media platforms is bad for us. This is in addition to the *opportunity cost*: the time that we spend on social-media platforms *could have been spent* doing other, more meaningful things.

The research really is damning. I have included in this chapter's Further Readings detailed descriptions of methodologies and findings. Here, it is sufficient to say that one 2019 study associated passive social-media use, such as scrolling, with fatigue, loneliness, and concentration loss, all of which, as the researchers noted, are symptoms of depression.[1] Another 2019 study showed that even when researchers controlled for the mental-health histories of participants, there were still associations between social-media use and poor mental health.[2] (In other words, we observe the same associations no matter what one's mental health was like earlier in life.) Lastly, one 2016 study found that, among adolescents, social-media use is associated with anxiety, depression, low self-esteem, and poor sleep quality. An interesting finding in this last study was that the negative consequences were worse for those who were emotionally invested in social-media platforms.[3]

A keen reader might notice the word "association" and seize on it. These associations do not establish that social-media use *causes* these negative health outcomes. (The researchers are well aware of this fact.) It is not out of the realm of possibility that anxious and depressed people reach for their phone more often and are on social-media platforms more regularly. Thankfully, we *are* armed with randomized controlled trials that do yield conclusions about causation, and they tell us that social-media use causes negative outcomes for our well-being. One 2018 experiment found that undergraduates who had their social-media use drastically reduced for three weeks saw reductions in loneliness, depression, anxiety, and the fear of missing out.[4] This study was designed to sort people of different backgrounds into different groups, some of whom had their social-media time limited, and some of whom did not. Members of the groups were the same in relevant respects, except for the time they spent on social-media apps. It follows from this fact that the difference in outcomes must be attributable to and caused by the time on social media. This is precisely what we would expect. Another 2019 study found that those who used digital media for five or more hours a day had substantially worse psychological well-being than those who used it for less than an hour a day.[5] ("Digital media" is a category that includes social media but also includes video games and the internet more generally.) The research on social-media use clearly supports the claim that we would be better off quitting social media—or at least drastically reducing the time that we spend on it.

There is more on the line when it comes to our lives than just our happiness and well-being. For instance, we might find that our competence as citizens in

## 1. One Reason to Quit: Our Own Well-Being 175

democracies has been undermined by social-media platforms. Certainly, in the chapter on echo chambers, we talked about the way that democratic institutions have been eroded, according to many philosophers. We are the victims of this erosion, to the extent that we rely on such institutions to protect our rights and advance our interests. The point that I am making now is slightly different: we might notice in ourselves that we are worse at reasoning about and thinking through the viewpoints of those we disagree with because of our exposure to filtered and user-tailored content on social-media apps. Quitting would help us escape from echo chambers. We could similarly promote our well-being by escaping other social-media ills: for instance, we might protect our privacy by quitting, and we might boost our productivity at work by not wasting so much time on YouTube, Reddit, and so on.

Some philosophers object to this approach. They do not deny that we have duties to ourselves, and they do not deny the clear findings of psychologists. Instead, their objection is based on the notion of **privilege**. It is hard to define "privilege" precisely, and it is virtually impossible to present a definition that captures what everyone means by the term. However, the general idea is that *to have privilege* is to have a social advantage that other people lack. Those who have privilege often take their privilege for granted; they are unaware of their own privilege. For instance, without the legal recognition of same-sex marriages, heterosexual people have privilege because they have access to an important institution, marriage, that gay and lesbian people do not have access to.

Some people allege that the whole debate about quitting social media is steeped in privilege.[6] There is something accurate about this. After all, not everyone has the luxury of being able to stop using social media so easily. There are people whose livelihoods rely on maintaining some social-media presence. We can think of owners of small businesses, as well as people whose entire businesses are digital and based on Instagram, TikTok, or Facebook. The fact that running a business on social-media platforms comes with virtually no overhead cost and can be done effectively without any marketing budget means that it is attractive to many people who would otherwise never overcome the difficult barrier to entry that brick-and-mortar businesses have. Moreover, I have met many undergraduate students who lamented the feeling that they *had* to have a serious social-media presence: not just on account of the pressures from peers, but because employers preferred to hire people with a certain number of followers. Many employers see it as a valuable upside of prospective employees at a restaurant or movie theater to have thousands of eyeballs on TikTok following their movements and habits. Meanwhile, a college professor in a philosophy department can quit every social-media platform, not suffer any loss to his or her earning potential, and still write a book on the subject.

There is more to the privilege-based objection than simple financials. Consider the way that members of minority groups often turn to online forums for security and community. For instance, members of minority groups who live outside large urban centers might not be able to easily find other members of their communities, and the problem compounds if they live in an environment that is discriminatory. Offline, they might often feel like they must hide who they really are. In their case, online life can provide a valuable source of support and companionship. It is much easier for people in majority groups to stop using social media: they do not have any such things to lose. Think of people who live under oppressive governments or who do not have easy access to alternatives to state-run media coverage. They, too, benefit from communicating on social-media platforms.

There is another important aspect of the research on well-being and social-media use that we should consider. There are demographics that do not seem to be so negatively affected by social-media use: for example, older people. One 2021 study showed that older people do not report the same reductions in well-being as younger people due to social-media use.[7] In this case, it is probably not a causal relationship: being older *itself* does not protect someone from social-media-induced reductions in well-being. Instead, it is likely, as the researchers suggest, because older people use social media less intensely (i.e., with less frequency and with less investment). This squares with the result from a study that I mentioned earlier that attributed some negative effects of social-media use to emotional investment in an app. Even more relevant to the discussion of privilege is a 2018 review of many studies of the effects that social-media use can have on lesbian, gay, and bisexual individuals.[8] The researchers found that the results were mixed. On the one hand, as we might expect, social-media sites were important places to seek support and share experience. On the other hand, the most commonly reported social experience was cyberbullying, which was found by the researchers to lead to depression and suicidality. We might conclude the following: while members of minority groups have reasons to stay on social-media platforms that members of the majority group do not have, there are reasons for them to quit too.

Ultimately, the problem with the privilege-based objection is that it does not seem to directly answer the question of whether we ought to quit social-media platforms. It merely states that some people give up more than others by quitting.

As such, the privilege-based objection is not really an objection to the view that we should quit at all. The observation that quitting social media is easier for one person than it would be for another, on account of the first person's privilege, does not, by itself, tell us whether there is an obligation for any of us to delete our Facebook accounts. The observation *could* yield an answer to that question if it came paired with an argument that people should not take advantage of any of the benefits conferred on them by their privilege, but no such argument seems forthcoming. In conclusion, it *is* true that some people can quit social media with fewer downsides, but this does not mean that there is no duty to quit. Similarly, even though it is true that some disabled people might find it harder to climb stairs than able-bodied people, it does not follow that able-bodied people should not take the stairs. Privilege, while present, does not tell us what not to do.

The observation concerning privilege *does* broaden this debate, however: it reminds us that if the goal of quitting social-media platforms is to enrich our lives, then we ought to weigh the costs and benefits. A philosophy college professor might have fewer reasons to continue using social media than someone whose entire livelihood relies on Instagram and who cannot easily pivot to a different career. Quitting social media might make the former better off but the latter worse off, all things considered. To the extent that we are talking about duties to ourselves and the promotion of our own well-being, that consideration surely matters. We might rephrase the general view, accordingly: no longer are we claiming that *everyone should quit social media*; now, we are claiming *if quitting improves one's life, then one should quit*. This conclusion seems to better reflect the argument in the first place.

## 2. Consequences and Individual Causal Inefficacy

There is another way to argue that we have a duty to leave social-media platforms. This argument relies on **consequentialism**. Consequentialism is the theory that what makes actions right or wrong is their consequences. An action that promotes good consequences is good, and one that promotes bad consequences is bad. For instance, if I lied to my friend and you wanted to assess whether I acted correctly, you would consider not my intentions but only the outcomes, such as whether my friend was better off. This approach is exclusively focused on the consequences of actions.

Social-media companies do all sorts of bad things. They violate privacy; they promote eating-disorder content to young girls; they erode our democratic institutions—and they know that they do. In some cases, it is part of their business model. Many social-media platforms violate our privacy in order to sell our data, and they sell our data in order for their business to make money. We saw in Chapter 3 that a whistleblower revealed Meta *knowingly* showed eating-disorder content to young girls on Instagram, despite knowing about the bad consequences of this content for the girls' mental health.[9] They persisted in their behavior because it succeeded at getting people to stay on the platform for longer periods of time. In this way, it was good for their business.

A consequentialist approach to ethics surely says that this behavior of social-media companies is wrong. Moreover, it says that *we* users are wrong if we do not quit, since these businesses survive only because of their users. The exact business model varies from case to case: perhaps some are funded by advertisement revenue that would dry up if users were not frequenting the site; perhaps some are funded by users who pay a monthly fee for access. At any rate, if users did not visit these sites and deleted their accounts, then the sites would have to either change their business model or go out of business. Either way, the world would be a better place if users quit, at least to the extent that it would curtail the effects of the social-media companies acting badly.

The first approach surveyed in this chapter concerned duties to ourselves, and that was consequentialist, too, in the strict sense. It focused on the way that quitting promoted good consequences for the person who did the quitting. Now, however, we are talking about the way that quitting is required because it promotes good consequences *overall*: for society or, at least, everyone who is affected. This kind of consequentialism is called **utilitarianism**: utilitarians evaluate an action by focusing on the overall consequences for everyone. If an action promotes the best consequences possible, then it is the right action to take. For instance, if a government is considering whether to ban some harmful substance, utilitarians would weigh *all* of the consequences: the harms that are done by the substance and the harms that would be done by the ban to the companies that sell the product. Many of us reason as utilitarians do when we think about donating to charities: if we look at how much good a charity does in the world rather than the charity's good motives, we think as utilitarians do. It does seem that either putting social-media companies out of business or boycotting them until they change their ways is what a utilitarian would deem the right action because it seems to be what would promote the best consequences overall.

## 2. Consequences and Individual Causal Inefficacy 179

Of course, social-media companies do not do *only* bad things, and since we are evaluating the consequences *overall*, we need to take the good into account as well. However, the good things seem to be easily separable from the bad things. If what we like about these technologies is that they allow us to stay in contact with long-distance friends, we hardly need the privacy-violating, echo-chamber-creating infrastructure that is provided to us by Facebook, Instagram, TikTok, and so on. We could survive with iMessages and without Facebook. It might well be that TikTok or other platforms do not do *anything* good for us at all besides providing us with pleasure, distraction, and enjoyment, which can be easily found elsewhere.

Along similar lines, we might lament how much social pressure keeps us from quitting. Yet, every person who quits contributes to the dissolution of this pressure.[10] Sometimes we use Reddit or another platform because someone else uses it. If I quit, then I cannot be the *someone else* who prompts you to use that platform. This is just a negative reason for quitting: if I quit, then I am *not* the reason for someone else to join. There is another side of the coin too: by quitting, I might contribute to the creation of a new convention about what we do with the time or resources that I previously spent on social-media sites. For instance, perhaps instead of communicating by direct messages on X, now you and I communicate on Signal or iMessage. This shows other people that communicating without established social-media platforms is feasible. We contribute to the creation of a new convention.

One problem that we might have with this line of reasoning is that driving social-media companies out of business or causing them to change does not seem like the sort of thing that individuals are obligated to do, even if we grant that the consequences would be good. There are different ways of articulating this objection. We can claim that people who advocate for quitting are making a *political problem* seem *personal*, with the implication that it really is impersonal. We could also note that there are different kinds of obligations: collective obligations and individual obligations. This second framing is more promising since it is implausible to say that problems caused by social-media companies are not personal problems. It is *my* privacy that is being violated. *I* am the one at risk of being misinformed and polarized. *I* am the one whose mental health is jeopardized. There is nothing wrong with calling this problem *personal*, even if it is also political.

The distinction between collective and individual obligations is important. The distinction rests on the fact that even though some action might be morally required *for us as a group*, it does not follow that it is morally required for *me* to do it. An example can be helpful. Let's grant for the sake of the argument that the government has a responsibility to build bridges and repair roads. This responsibility is justified on a variety of grounds, some of which are utilitarian: it is better overall for the government to do these things; therefore, it ought to do them. However, let's say that the government *fails* in its obligation. It does not follow that *I* ought to repair the roads and build the bridges. There are jobs that belong exclusively to the government, even though the world would be better off if *I* made some progress on them in comparison to the case in which nobody at all attends to them. The thought behind this argument is that the problems posed by social-media companies ought to be handled by politicians whose job it is to protect our democratic institutions, rights to privacy, and so on. The government's failure does not make me responsible for protecting democracy.

It is not obvious that this argument succeeds, though. The distinction between collective and individual obligations plausibly exists. The infrastructure example illustrates that fact. Yet, this argument falls short when it comes to establishing the boundaries between the two kinds of obligations. For instance, we might all agree that the government has a responsibility to educate my children. We might agree to this on utilitarian grounds, as well as for other reasons. However, if the government fails to educate my children, it surely *is* my responsibility to ensure that they are educated anyway. If we grant this point, then we have now admitted that there are some collective obligations that individuals inherit when the government neglects its obligations. We would have to figure out whether the duties to force social-media companies to change are the sort that individuals inherit.

Another objection to the utilitarian argument for quitting social media asks whether quitting is the most effective way to bring about the desired outcomes. This is a hard-hitting criticism because, according to the utilitarian, if there exists an obligation to quit social media, it exists because quitting promotes the good consequences that we have in mind, such as reforming Facebook, TikTok, and so on. It is possible that even if quitting would effectively promote reform, our time and effort are still better spent lobbying elected officials to pass appropriate legislation. In a moment, I shall discuss some of the reasons for doubting that quitting effectively promotes reform but let me quickly note that this view interestingly combines collective and individual obligations. This view amounts to the claim that only the government has an obligation to ensure that social-media companies are reformed, but that individuals have an obligation to ensure that the government carries out *its* obligations.

## 2. Consequences and Individual Causal Inefficacy    181

A final objection to the consequentialist argument for quitting social media involves the application of the principle of **individual causal inefficacy (ICI)**. ICI is the notion that we as individuals cannot effect the sort of change that we have been talking about so far. Defending the use of this principle is consistent with thinking that social-media platforms regularly engage in evil behavior and that the world would be better off without them. It is also consistent with thinking that the obligation to do something about this problem rests with the government. Ultimately, however, when you or I quit Facebook, we simply are *not* promoting the sort of outcome that we aim to promote: getting Facebook to change or putting Facebook out of business. ICI gets off the ground as an objection because we have been focusing exclusively on the consequences of our actions. If our actions do not, in fact, promote the sorts of consequences that we have been talking about, then our position falls apart.

ICI is commonly invoked in other fields of ethics. When philosophers talk about climate change, some say that a moral obligation for individuals to reduce greenhouse-gas emissions does not exist.[11] We can grant that greenhouse-gas emissions contribute to climate change, that climate change will be profoundly harmful, and that we have moral obligations to not harm other people. Yet, on account of ICI, we simply do not have an obligation to reduce our emissions. Governments do, and businesses do, but not us individuals. The reason is that an individual's emissions do not produce *more* harm than there would be because of how little a person emits. Consider an analogy. Let's say that a flood is rushing toward a village and when it hits, it will cause five deaths and the destruction of three houses. Now I witness the flood and throw a teaspoon of water in the flood. The flood causes harm, and I have contributed to the flood. However, even with a teaspoon of water added to the flood, the harms are the same: five deaths and the destruction of three houses. Perhaps if I had added a million teaspoons of water, I would have caused more deaths, but I did not. I added such a small amount that *no different harms came about*. Defenders of ICI in climate-change ethics say the same thing: large businesses ought to limit their emissions because they emit so much that they make a difference. Individuals do not, in fact, bring about any harms even though their emissions are real, and such emissions do contribute to climate change through the greenhouse effect. It is not that the harms created by the individual are insignificantly small; it is that the emissions are so small that they do not produce any additional harms at all.

ICI can be applied to discussions of quitting social media. In 2023, Facebook had three billion users; Instagram had more than two billion, as did YouTube. If you quit social media, the principle of ICI says that you do not have any effect on the business at all. It is not merely that you have a small effect. You have no effect at all. Your action does not promote the good consequence that you aim to promote. To see why, let's consider an analogy with another application of ICI: this time, in animal ethics.

The factory-farming industry produces a variety of harms, both to the animals who are slaughtered and to the environment.[12] One way of responding to these harms is by thinking that we as individual consumers have an obligation to not give these companies our money. We should vote with our wallets and make it known to the factory-farming industry that they will go out of business if they do not change their evil ways. The problem is that the industry does not have a way of responding to signals from individual consumers. There are many stages between when a cow is slaughtered and when the beef ends up on your plate, and the information that you send with your consumption decision as an individual does not make its way to the people slaughtering the cows. If you opt to *not* buy meat from Walmart, then you send a market signal that Walmart might register *if* it has such an acute grasp of its consumers that it notices even one consumption decision and the reasons for it. However, Walmart bought the meat from some wholesaler, who in turn bought the meat from a processing plant, who in turn bought the meat from someone else. We add further nuance to this account if Walmart has a three-year contract with the meat wholesaler, and the store cannot make any changes to its orders. Perhaps if you were an exceptionally influential person, your consumption decisions might be so prominent and so noticeable that the market signal you send would make its way all the way back to the factory farm. The defenders of ICI accept this point. After all, ICI gets off the ground because of consequentialism: *if* your action has an overall good effect, *then* your action is required. What the defenders of ICI say is that it is deeply unlikely that you are the sort of person who is going to make that kind of difference, and if you are not that sort of person, then utilitarian reasons have no purchase on you.

Before we turn back to the social-media context, let me present another brief analogy. Suppose that a politician is running for an important elected office on an extremely evil policy platform. The platform is evil by virtue of all the harmful consequences that it would have if implemented. Now say that this evil

## 2. Consequences and Individual Causal Inefficacy   183

politician is elected after receiving one million more votes than was necessary to win the office in question. Adding or subtracting *my* vote from the total votes that the evil politician received makes *no* difference to the election outcome. No different harms would exist or stop existing. We are not claiming that this one individual vote makes a tiny difference. This vote does not make *any* difference. This analogy illustrates the principle of ICI without any of the details associated with market signals.

On social-media platforms, it is not obvious that any given user being on the platforms gives rise to any different harms. It is even less obvious that quitting social media will register any market signal at all in the eyes of the business whose platform the user is quitting. Of course, the ICI argument does not say anything about whether the government should do anything about social media, whether influential people should quit, whether quitting would be good *for me*, or whether my quitting would help coax my friends into quitting by contributing to a new social convention of communicating differently. (Would a market signal be registered if my whole circle of friends quits? It depends on the size of the group.) ICI is a principle that is meant to be applied rather tactically: it undermines only the connection between an individual's action and the outcome that utilitarian theories are concerned with.

This application of ICI does not seem off-base. Social-media companies have no real way of reading market signals so closely. Information about how one user's behavior affects a platform's bottom line is proprietary, about which we can only speculate, but it seems to be a safe bet that the companies have contracts for advertisement revenue that are not so sensitive that they become null and void if one user leaves the platform. There is most likely no room in any of these revenue-generating contracts for one user to disrupt business. Furthermore, each major platform has more users sign up for the platform each day: for instance, Facebook reportedly adds about half a million new user accounts a day. It is hard to see the company sweating the loss of one user in the face of such a large daily gain.

Of course, we could start talking about quitting *en masse* and turning the wave of half a million new users into a net loss. Large droves of users leaving would send a clear market signal. How large the exodus needs to be is unclear, but the general fact that such an exodus is possible is consistent with ICI, which claims only that *individual* actions are *causally inefficacious*. They do not promote the effect that we think that they do. Nevertheless, there are ways of objecting to ICI.

The first objection to ICI is that the principle says something implausible about individual action. Defenders of ICI concede that large-scale actions promote the consequences that utilitarians are interested in, but they deny that individual actions do. However, large-scale actions *just are* individual actions compounded. It is hard to maintain that individual actions do *nothing* if we think that compounding them does *something*. This reply turns on the idea that if there is a large market signal sent by groups exiting social-media platforms, then there must be *some* market signal that an individual sends. If a big act is efficacious, then a small act must be efficacious too, at least to some very small degree, since the big act is just a composite of small acts. This debate depends on the nature of social-media businesses and how inefficient the markets they belong to are. There is another way of replying to this line of thinking that eschews these questions altogether; let's consider this now.

## 3. Complicity in Evil

Consequentialist arguments capture something important about the way that we reason about ethics: we balk at the thought of continuing to support businesses when we know that they are going to spend their revenue to promote bad outcomes for the world. Perhaps these are the bad outcomes caused by social-media companies, or perhaps they are caused by oil companies or factory farms. Either way, we have seen how to approach the debate around the ethics of consumption when we focus on outcomes. Another way to think about this subject has nothing to do with whether our actions promote bad outcomes. Instead, it is about whether we have an obligation to *avoid being complicit in evil*. This way of thinking sidesteps ICI altogether.

Many of us have the sense that it is wrong to associate with bad people or bad things. This is an important feature of moral life that some theories attempt to capture. Consider the way that we often cut ties with people in our lives when we notice that they have heinous vices. It makes no difference whether the person with whom we are cutting ties would change their behavior due to the severance of ties. We might hope that the cessation of contact will prompt them to change their ways, but many people think that we are obligated to end the association in any event. In other words, the promotion of good and bad outcomes is not the only thing that matters. Similarly, we express outrage when companies from whom we buy products are revealed to be evil. When faced with two products of equal quality, few people would be indifferent if it were revealed that the maker of one product does great things and the other does bad things. Few people would feel comfortable knowing that they voted for a malevolent politician, even if the politician was elected by such a large margin that one vote would have done precisely nothing.

Philosophers sometimes present this approach to ethics as relying on an *obligation to avoid being complicit in evil*. This obligation holds even when our complicity does not promote any bad outcomes and even when the end of that complicity does not promote any good outcomes. I have already presented some cases where this rule is invoked; for instance, there might exist an obligation to *not* vote for an evil politician, even if one correctly believes that the politician would get elected without one's vote. Other cases when this rule might apply are those in which the principle of individual causal inefficacy is usually appealed to. Those who believe that we should not be complicit in evil often believe that it is wrong to buy meat from factory farms. In fact, they say that we should not eat factory-farmed meat even if we came by it in a circumstance that did not involve giving the factory-farm industry any money. Imagine that a grocery store threw out a perfectly unspoiled factory-farmed steak. If someone stumbled upon it, they could eat it without the consequentialist objecting. After all, as far as the market is concerned, the steak was thrown into the garbage. If we think that it is wrong to be complicit in evil, on the other hand, then eating the thrown-out steak *is* wrong. It is wrong because we are getting pleasure from the enormous harm done to the slaughtered animal. We did not commit the slaughter, but we did partake in the fruits of it, and we did so knowingly.

Let's consider the rule that we ought to avoid being complicit in evil more broadly. You might be familiar with this rule from popular discussions online and in the news media concerning artists. For instance, we hear that a singer has done something heinous, and we resolve to boycott their music. Usually, what is going on here is that a prominent person, or perhaps *the* most prominent person, involved in the creation or marketing of a product has done something that is both conspicuous and evil. Part of the problem with avoiding complicity in evil is that people doubtless do inconspicuous, evil things, but the very fact that they are inconspicuous makes it hard for us to notice them and, therefore, comply with the rule. Further, it is hard for us to have a principled way of objecting to the behavior of a prominent person—for instance, in the case of music, the singer—but not objecting to the behavior of people behind the scenes who might have done evil things. Consider two different cases. In the first case, we look at the behavior of people behind the scenes, such as the countless editors and producers, and we see that most of them are good people, but a prominent person has done something bad. In this case, our rule that we ought to avoid being complicit in evil compels us to avoid association with this vast number of *good* people—just because the prominent person has behaved badly. In another case, we notice that there are bad people behind the scenes, regardless of whether the prominent person has done bad things. If we begin to apply this rule consistently and end associations with every product that has some bad people involved in its production, the consequences for our lives would be dire.

That is generally the problem with avoiding being complicit in bad things. The rule is so demanding that there is virtually no food we could eat and no way that we could transport ourselves. Consider that virtually every step of even a small commute is facilitated by petroleum companies. Even those who drive electric vehicles are not immune: the vehicles themselves are made in a way that emits greenhouse gases, and so are the roads. It is virtually impossible to buy food from sources that do not harm the environment, even if we manage to avoid buying food that harms animals. Consequently, the rule is simply too demanding, as I said: we could hardly go anywhere or eat anything. Those are just the necessities. There would certainly be no opportunity for any kind of luxury or entertainment.

There is a way to correct this defect. Instead of simply avoiding complicity with evil, we consider first *how essential the harm is to a thing*.[13] If no evil or harm is essential to a product, then it is morally permissible for us to buy it. In the case of social-media platforms, that would mean that if there is nothing essentially evil about Facebook, Instagram, Tumblr, and so on, then it is morally permissible for us to continue using these apps. Consider an example. You are at a grocery store, and you see a box of spinach. In order to know whether it is morally permissible for you to buy that spinach, you have to ask yourself two questions. The first is whether there is any evil or harm involved in it. The answer to this question seems to be yes, as it would be for virtually anything that you could buy. After all, consider the greenhouse gases emitted during transportation. The second question you must ask yourself is whether any of these harms are *essential*. If they are, then we have to discover the degree to which they are essential. In this case, it seems that there are no harms essentially involved in the spinach: none in the nature of spinach; none in the production; none in the transportation; and none in the consumption. We could easily imagine spinach being transported without greenhouse-gas emissions, for instance. So, even though there *are* harms involved in the transportation of spinach, there are no *essential* harms.

If this view of things is right, then there does not seem to be an obligation to quit social media. None of the harms caused by the major platforms are essential to their service. It might be hard for us to imagine a lucrative business model for some of these platforms if they did not violate our privacy and use all of the attention-grabbing powers available to them, but that does not mean that the harms are *essential*. (Consider that spinach might be transported in gas-guzzling trucks because that is the least-expensive option, which means that the vendors enjoy a larger profit margin. Nevertheless, the harms of climate change are not an essential part of buying and eating spinach. So, it is morally permissible to consume spinach.) Perhaps the harms are *more essential* to the services provided by social-media companies than the analogous harms of transporting spinach are in the vegetable-buying case. Even if they are more essential than those other harms, it does seem that they are still sufficiently distant from the essence of the services provided by social-media companies that we would not have to conclude that there is an obligation to leave social media.

There are other ways to support the same conclusion. For instance, it might well matter that there is no evidence that Instagram *intends* to do all of the evil things that it does. It seems that Meta was well aware of the way that Instagram was harming young girls, but they persisted in doing it because it earned them more money on account of how compelling eating-disorder content is. However, I do not think that we could say that the company *intended* to harm young girls. Instead, it *intended* to make a lot of money. There are cases where it is even clearer that Facebook had no bad intentions. For instance, the United Nations has said that Facebook was used to spread hate speech in Myanmar, which led to the genocide of Rohingya Muslims. It is hard to deny that Facebook's platforms were used that way, but there is no evidence that Facebook intentionally helped spread such hate speech. This might be a reason to say that although Facebook may promote bad outcomes, it is not evil in the sense that requires us to sever all ties with the platform.

## 4. Conclusion: Should We Quit?

We have seen some pretty compelling reasons to quit social media, and we have seen some arguments against those reasons. The arguments we should probably bear in mind the most are those that call into question our relationship with social media:

even amid the debate about whether we should quit to promote good outcomes or to avoid complicity in evil, there is no disputing the fact that time spent on social media is bad for us. It is true that some people, such as members of minority groups, have more to gain from being on social media because it provides them with a source of community and support that might be otherwise hard to come by, and it is equally true that some people have more to lose because they lack the privilege that others have. In the former group, there are still reasons to leave: psychological research has uncovered the pervasiveness of cyberbullying in online life and its bad effects. As for the latter group, we who have privilege might be required to quit in order to create new conventions around communicating with others, which could reduce the costs of leaving social media for those without privilege. If quitting social media prompts the platforms to change, then perhaps others will stay on the platforms because they would then be not so unhealthy. If so, we have not reduced the cost of leaving social media, but we *have* reduced the harms for those who stay.

One important question that we should ask ourselves concerns what, if anything, we as users bring to social-media platforms. It is tempting to think of us as just providing eyeballs for the advertisements that populate social-media sites. In other cases, maybe we pay a monthly fee to the site. In either case, we indirectly or directly provide the company with income. In Chapter 2, on the attention economy, we went one step further and highlighted the way that our attention is a commodity: in a sense, we are the goods that are being sold in transactions between the social-media companies and whomever they are considering hosting advertisements from.

Let us end this chapter with a final consideration. We might be akin to test subjects. Social-media companies are constantly revising their algorithms. In using these sites, we are having these algorithms tested on us. This might be something worth watching out for in the future: as apps become better at accomplishing the ends that they set for themselves, we might find that they are better at producing harms to society. We might then wonder how they became so good, and we would have to recollect the way that *we* became the data points that allowed these companies to succeed.

## Key terms

**Consequentialism**: the theory that what makes actions right or wrong is their consequences. An action that promotes good consequences is good, and one that promotes bad consequences is bad. For instance, if I lied to my friend, and you wanted to assess whether I acted correctly, you would consider not my intentions but only the outcomes, such as whether my friend was better or worse off because of the lie. This approach is exclusively focused on the consequences of actions.

**Individual causal inefficacy (ICI)**: the claim that the actions we take as individuals do not have consequences within some defined domain (e.g., climate change). Therefore, it is an objection to consequentialist reasoning because it denies that our actions have an effect at all.

**Privilege**: a social advantage that other people lack; those with privilege often take this advantage for granted or are unaware of it. For instance, without the legal recognition of same-sex marriages, heterosexual people have privilege because they have access to an important institution, marriage, that same-sex couples do not have access to.

**Utilitarianism**: a kind of consequentialism. Utilitarians evaluate an action by focusing on the overall consequences for everyone. If an action promotes the best consequences possible, then it is the right action to take. For instance, if we are considering whether it is right for the government to ban some harmful substance, utilitarians would weigh all of the consequences: the harms that are done by the substance and the harms that would be done by the ban.

# Discussion Cases

## 1. Quitting Facebook

Some social-media sites, such as Facebook, make it quite difficult to delete accounts. Sometimes, they mislead users by making it seem that *deactivating* an account is the same thing as truly *deleting* it. Plus, deleting all of your information from a site is difficult because some of your content is shared with other people, such as the photos that you and ten other people are tagged in. Some sites have made it so that you have to wait thirty or sixty days before your account is deleted. This is allegedly so that you have the chance to change your mind. In reality, it is a way to prevent you from deleting your account on the spot and increase the cost (in terms of time) of deleting your account altogether.

Should social-media companies make it easy for you to quit? Are they allowed to make it as hard as they want? What sorts of behaviors are they not allowed to engage in as they try to prevent you from quitting?

## 2. Giving Up, or Standing Up?

In 2023, after Twitter was purchased by Elon Musk and transformed into X, thousands of scientists left the platform.[14] Their reasons varied, but many of them were protesting Musk's intention to curtail efforts to combat misinformation on X. To the extent that we can speak about these scientists as a monolith, it seems right to say that they were standing up for a healthier information environment. When they left the platform, what they left behind was a space where, proportionally, more users spread misinformation, and there were fewer expert voices to correct them. Some people might say that the experts gave up the fight against misinformation and conceded to the users spreading misinformation.

Do you think that some people might have a responsibility to use social media? When we leave a platform to protest the bad things that the company in charge of the platform is doing, is there anything that we can or should do for the sake of the people we are leaving behind?

## 3. The Big Question

Reflect on your own experience with social-media apps and the arguments laid out in this chapter.

Should you quit? What would be the advantages and disadvantages?

# Further Reading

Aalbers, George, Richard J. McNally, Alexandre Heeren, Sanne de Wit, and Eiko I. Fried. 2019. "Social Media and Depression Symptoms: A Network Perspective." *Journal of Experimental Psychology* 148 (8): 1454–62.

The researchers determined that passive social-media use, such as scrolling, was associated with the symptoms of depression. They did not determine that whether the social-media use caused these symptoms. (Perhaps the symptoms of depression caused the passive social-media use.) The participants were all undergraduate students: the number of women slightly more than doubled the number of men. The participants were prompted seven times a day for two weeks to report how they felt as they used social-media platforms without posting, sharing, or commenting—that is, passively.

Budolfson, Mark B. 2015. "Is It Wrong to Eat Factory-Farmed Meat? If So, Why?" In *The Moral Complexities of Eating Meat*, edited by Ben Bramble and Bob Fischer, 80–99. Oxford: Oxford University Press.

Budolfson provides a good introduction to the principle of individual causal inefficacy as well as to the idea of avoiding complicity in evil. He also refines the latter idea by introducing the notion of the *degree of essentiality of harm* when talking about some act, product, or service. While Budolfson does not talk about social media at all, I strongly recommend his paper to anyone who is interested in learning about the ethics of consumption. Budolfson does a good job deflating many of the typical arguments that one hears, some of which I surveyed in this chapter.

Escobar-Viera, César G., Darren L. Whitfield, Charles B. Wessel, Ariel Shensa, Jaime E. Sedani, Andre L. Brown, Christian J. Chandler, Beth L. Hoffman, Michael P. Marshall, and Brian A. Primack. 2018. "For Better or for Worse? A Systematic Review of the Evidence on Social Media Use and Depression among Lesbian, Gay, and Bisexual Minorities." *JMIR Mental Health* 5 (3). https://doi.org/10.2196/10496.

This is a review of eleven studies that were done between 2003 and 2017 on the effects that social-media use has on members of the LGB community. The results were mixed. On the one hand, social-media platforms do appear to be important places for such individuals to get support and share experiences. On the other hand, the most commonly reported social experience was cyberbullying, which, as the researchers found, was associated with depression and suicidality. Participants also reported that constant surveillance of their social-media presence became a stressor that could lead to depression.

Glaser, April. 2018. "The Problem with #DeleteFacebook," *Slate*, March 21, 2018. https://slate.com/technology/2018/03/dont-deletefacebook-thats-not-good-enough.html.

Glaser's opinion piece in *Slate* is a good, accessible introduction to some of the basic lines of reasoning in the debate concerning quitting social media. She argues that the debate is steeped in privilege because there are many people who would lose too much if they did quit, and she argues that the problems posed by social media to society exist for the government, not individuals, to solve.

Hunt, Melissa G., Rachel Marx, Courtney Lipson, and Jordyn Young. 2018. "No More FOMO: Limiting Social Media Decreases Loneliness and Depression." *Journal of Social and Clinical Psychology* 37 (10): 751–68.

The researchers conducted a randomized controlled experiment on 143 college undergraduates. Students were assigned to different groups: some could use social-media apps as usual; others had to limit their use of a certain platform to ten minutes a day. (The platforms in question were Snapchat, Instagram, and Facebook.) The researchers found that there were significant reductions in anxiety, fear of missing out (FOMO), loneliness, and depression. This study is important because its design helps us determine the *causal relationship* between reduced well-being and social-media use: if the only difference between the various groups was the reduced social-media use, then the only viable explanation for improved well-being is that the social-media use *causes* reductions in well-being (i.e., anxiety, depression, FOMO, and loneliness).

Liao, S. Matthew. 2018. "Do You Have a Moral Duty to Leave Facebook?" *New York Times*, November 24, 2018. www.nytimes.com/2018/11/24/opinion/sunday/facebook-immoral.html.

Liao is a bioethics professor at NYU; his short article in the *New York Times* is a great introduction to the ethics of quitting social media, on account of both its brevity and accessibility. He defends the view that there is no obligation to quit social media because the company has not crossed any so-called red lines: Facebook has done bad things, but it did not intend to do them, so it has so far avoided outright wickedness. Consequently, there is no obligation for us to quit.

Riehm, Kira E., Kenneth A. Feder, Kayla N. Tormohlen, Rosa M. Krum, Andrea S. Young, Kerry M. Green, Lauren R. Pacek, Laraina N. La Flair, and Ramin Mojtabai. 2019. "Associations between Time Spent Using Social Media and Internalizing and Externalizing Problems Among US Youth." *JAMA Psychiatry.* 76 (12): 1266–73. https://doi.org/10.1001/jamapsychiatry.2019.2325.

The researchers determined that social-media use among adolescents was linked to mental-health problems. (The researchers say that it is associated with "internalizing problems" and they provide anxiety and depression symptoms as examples; they also say that it is associated with "externalizing problems," and they give bullying and attention difficulties as examples.) This was a large study of 6,595 adolescents.

Sales, Nancy Jo. 2017. *American Girls: Social Media and the Secret Lives of Teenagers.* New York: Random House.

Sales does a remarkable job portraying how social-media technologies are part of the lives of today's youth. She interviewed hundreds of young girls for this book, and readers will find it eye-opening to see how the girls talk about the apparent impossibility of quitting social media, the feeling that social pressure keeps them on the platforms, and the way that living on the platforms harms them.

Schimmele, Christoph, Jonathan Fonberg, and Grant Schellenberg. 2021. *Canadians' Assessments of Social Media in Their Lives.* Statistics Canada. https://doi.org/10.25318/36280001202100300004-eng.

The researchers looked at results from the 2018 Canadian Internet Use Survey to determine the negative results that Canadians between the ages of fifteen and sixty-four report due to their use of social-media apps. The researchers found loss of sleep, reduced physical activity, concentration problems, anxiety, depression, and negative feelings around other people, such as envy, frustration, and anger. The researchers found that older people were far less likely to report these things than younger people, which they attribute to the greater intensity with which young people use social media.

Simpson, Robert M. 2022. "The Ethics of Quitting Social Media." In *The Oxford Handbook of Digital Ethics,* edited by Carissa Véliz, 685–704. Oxford: Oxford University Press.

Simpson provides a good look at both the privilege-based objection to the claim that we should quit social media (with which he disagrees) *and* the argument that we should quit in order to promote reforms (with which he agrees). He talks about the importance of *mass quitting*, which reflects one of the considerations outlined in this chapter: namely, that we need people to quit in large numbers to effect the sort of change that we want to see in social-media platforms. When Simpson discusses the argument that we should quit in order to *not* be complicit in evil, he considers it mostly from the point of view that no longer being complicit might promote good outcomes. Also, Simpson thinks that at the heart of the privilege-based objection is the thought that social-media platforms as they are currently constituted are, for all intents and purposes, an unchangeable part of modern life.

Twenge, Jean M., and Keith Campbell. 2019. "Media Use Is Linked to Lower Psychological Well-Being: Evidence from Three Datasets." *Psychiatric Quarterly* 90: 311–31.

The researchers found that greater digital-media use, which includes using social media as well as playing video games and browsing the internet, was associated with lower psychological well-being. The researchers measured such markers of well-being as happiness, depression, suicide ideation, and suicide attempts. This study is helpful because of the way that it organized participants into different groups in accordance with how much they used digital media. Those who used digital media lightly (i.e., for an hour or less a day) had substantially higher psychological well-being than those who used it heavily (i.e., for five or more hours a day). The research was done on adolescents.

Woods, Heather Cleland, and Holly Scott. 2016. "#Sleepyteens: Social Media Use in Adolescence Is Associated with Poor Sleep Quality, Anxiety, Depression and Low Self-Esteem." *Journal of Adolescence* 51: 41–49.

The researchers found associations between social-media use and poor sleep quality, anxiety, depression, and low self-esteem. The outcomes were worse for those who used social-media platforms at nighttime and for those who were emotionally invested in the apps and sites that they were using. The participants were 467 Scottish high-school students between eleven and seventeen years of age.

## Notes

1. Aalbers et al. 2019.
2. Riehm et al. 2019.
3. Woods and Scott 2016.
4. Hunt et al. 2018.
5. Twenge and Campbell 2019.
6. See Simpson 2022 for a thorough discussion of the privilege-based objection to the duty to quit social media.
7. Schimmele, Fonberg, and Schellenberg 2021.
8. Escobar-Viera et al. 2018.
9. See *Wall Street Journal* 2021a, 2021b.
10. This discussion is influenced by Simpson 2022.
11. See Sinnott-Armstrong 2005.
12. See Budolfson 2015.
13. This approach comes from Budolfson 2015.
14. Valero 2023.

# Conclusion

The ethics of social media is a flourishing field of philosophical thought, as new as the technologies themselves are. One of the chief aims of this book has been to introduce readers to the power that philosophy has to illuminate parts of our world when it turns its attention to them. Echo chambers, misinformation, online friendships, and many other important topics discussed in this book are just some of what needs our attention.

In time, we will discover new problems with social-media platforms. The eight chapters of this book catalog the problems discussed most often and urgently in philosophical books and journals, but these technologies move fast enough that in a few years, the list might be longer. One emerging issue, for instance, is influencer culture: the way that the online landscape is increasingly dominated by large personalities whose job is to create and comment on social-media content. Life on social-media platforms did not look this way even ten years ago. Influencers are discussed as misinformation conduits in Chapter 5. In light of their role in spreading misinformation during the COVID-19 pandemic, that is justified. One day, it might be important for philosophers to discuss the ethics of influencer culture itself.

This book is by no means the final word on any of the issues discussed here. It is among only the first words, and my hope is that it has been an intellectually exciting, rewarding, and fun introduction to the topic. Social-media technologies are, after all, fun and exciting. They are also important: our deteriorating civil discourse and information environment demand our urgent attention. While these threats are not as obviously existential as nuclear warfare or climate change, much is on the line. Philosophers have something important to contribute to our understanding of these problems and to the discovery of their solutions.

# Bibliography

Aalbers, George, Richard J. McNally, Alexandre Heeren, Sanne de Wit, and Eiko I. Fried. 2019. "Social Media and Depression Symptoms: A Network Perspective." *Journal of Experimental Psychology* 148 (8): 1454–62.

Alter, Adam. 2017. *Irresistible: The Rise of Addictive Technology.* New York: Penguin Press.

Aristotle. 2019. *Nicomachean Ethics.* Translated by Terence Irwin. Indianapolis: Hackett Publishing.

Arthur, Charles. 2012. "Google Admits Tracking Safari Users." *Guardian*, February 17, 2012. https://www.theguardian.com/technology/2012/feb/17/google-admits-tracking-safari-users.

Associated Press. 2023. "Google Settles $5 Billion Privacy Lawsuit Over Tracking People Using 'Incognito Mode.'" December 29, 2023. https://apnews.com/article/google-incognito-mode-tracking-lawsuit-settlement-8b30c9397f678bc4c546ab84191f7a9d.

Auxier, Brooke, Lee Rainie, Monica Anderson, Andrew Perrin, Kumar Madhu, and Eric Turner. 2019. "Americans and Privacy: Concerned, Confused and Feeling Lack of Control Over Their Personal Information." *Pew Research Center*, November 15, 2019. https://www.pewresearch.org/internet/2019/11/15/americans-and-privacy-concerned-confused-and-feeling-lack-of-control-over-their-personal-information/.

Basak, Rajesh, Niloy Ganguly, Shamik Sural, and Soumya K. Ghosh. 2016. "Look Before You Shame: A Study on Shaming Activities on Twitter." In *Proceedings of the 25th International Conference Companion on World Wide Web: WWW'16 Companion*, 11–12. Geneva, Switzerland: International World Wide Web Conferences Steering Committee.

Baumeister, Roy F. 1997. *Evil: Inside Human Violence and Cruelty.* New York: Henry Holt.

Beard, Keith W. 2002. "Internet Addiction: Current Status and Implications for Employees." *Journal of Employment Counseling* 39 (1): 2–11.

Bhargava, Vikram R., and Manuel Velasquez. 2021. "Ethics of the Attention Economy: The Problem of Social Media Addiction." *Business Ethics Quarterly* 31 (3): 321–59.

Billingham, Paul, and Tom Parr. 2019. "Online Public Shaming: Virtues and Vices." *Journal of Social Philosophy* 1: 1–20.

Briggle, Adam. 2008. "Real Friends: How the Internet Can Foster Friendship." *Ethics and Information Technology* 10: 71–79.

Bublitz, Jan C., and Reinhard Merkel. 2014. "Crimes Against Minds: On Mental Manipulations, Harms and a Human Right to Mental Self-Determination." *Criminal Law and Philosophy* 8 (1): 51–77.

Budolfson, Mark B. 2015. "Is It Wrong to Eat Factory-Farmed Meat? If So, Why?" In *The Moral Complexities of Eating Meat*, edited by Ben Bramble and Bob Fischer, 80–99. Oxford: Oxford University Press.

Burnham, John F. 1987. "Medical Practice à la Mode: How Medical Fashions Determine Medical Care." *New England Journal of Medicine* 317 (19): 1220–21.

Byrne, Donn E. 1971. *The Attraction Paradigm*. New York: Academic Press.

Cadwalladr, Carole, and Emma Graham-Harrison. 2018. "Revealed: 50 Million Facebook Profiles Harvested for Cambridge Analytica in Major Data Breach." *Guardian*, March 17, 2018. https://www.theguardian.com/news/2018/mar/17/cambridge-analytica-facebook-influence-us-election.

Campbell, Douglas R. 2023a. "In Defense of (Some) Online Echo Chambers." *Ethics and Information Technology* 25 (3): 1–11.

Campbell, Douglas R. 2023b. "Cancel Culture, Then and Now: A Platonic Approach to the Shaming of People and the Exclusion of Ideas." *Journal of Cyberspace Studies* 7 (2): 147–66.

Carey, Brandon. 2023. "Misinformation and Epistemic Harm." *Social Philosophy Today* 39: 89–100.

Castro, Clinton, and Adam Pham. 2020. "Is the Attention Economy Noxious?" *Philosophers' Imprint* 20 (17): 1–13.

Chen, Xinran, Joanna Sin Sei-Ching, Yin-Leng Theng, and Chei Sian Lee. 2015. "Why Do Social Media Users Share Misinformation?" In *JCDL '15: Proceedings of the 15th ACM/IEEE-CE on Joint Conference on Digital Libraries*, New York, 111–14.

Chomanski, Bartlomiej. 2023. "Mental Integrity in the Attention Economy: In Search of the Right to Attention." *Neuroethics* 16: 8–19.

Cocking, Dean, and Steve Matthews. 2000. "Unreal Friends." *Ethics and Information Technology* 2: 223–31.

Cohen, Shlomo. 2013. "Nudging and Informed Consent." *American Journal of Bioethics* 13 (6): 3–11.

Conly, Sarah. 2013. "Coercive Paternalism in Health Care: Against Freedom of Choice." *Public Health Ethics* 6 (3): 241–45.

Cooper, John, ed. 1999. *Plato: Complete Works*. Indianapolis: Hackett Publishing.

De Ridder, Jeroen. 2021. "What's So Bad about Misinformation?" *Inquiry* 67 (9): 2956–78. https://doi.org/10.1080/0020174X.2021.2002187.

Diddi, Arvind, and Robert LaRose. 2006. "Getting Hooked on News: Uses and Gratifications and the Formation of News Habits among College Students in an Internet Environment." *Journal of Broadcasting and Electronic Media* 50 (2): 193–210.

Dunt, Ian. 2014. "Nudge Nudge, Say No More. Brits' Minds Will Be Controlled without Us Knowing It." *Guardian*, February 5, 2014. https://www.theguardian.com/commentisfree/2014/feb/05/nudge-say-no-more-behavioural-insights-team.

Eddy, Kirsten. 2024. "6 Facts about Americans and TikTok," *Pew Research Center*, April 3, 2024. https://www.pewresearch.org/short-reads/2024/04/03/6-facts-about-americans-and-tiktok/. Updated December 20, 2024.

Elder, Alexis. 2014. "Excellent Online Friendships: An Aristotelian Defense of Social Media," *Ethics and Information Technology* 16: 287–97.

Emery, David. 2016. "Did Donald Trump Claim Global Warming Is a Hoax?" Snopes.com, September 27, 2016. https://www.snopes.com/fact-check/donald-trump-global-warming-hoax/.

Escobar-Viera, César G., Darren L. Whitfield, Charles B. Wessel, Ariel Shensa, Jaime E. Sedani, Andre L. Brown, Christian J. Chandler, Beth L. Hoffman, Michael P. Marshall, and Brian A. Primack. 2018. "For Better or for Worse? A Systematic Review of the Evidence on Social Media Use and Depression among Lesbian, Gay, and Bisexual Minorities." *JMIR Mental Health* 5 (3). https://doi.org/10.2196/10496.

Eyal, Nir. 2019. *Indistractable*. Dallas, TX: BenBella Books.

Ferreira Caceres, Maria Mercedes, Juan Pablo Sosa, Jannel A. Lawrence, Christina Sestacovschi, Atiyah Tidd-Johnson, Muhammad Haseeb Ul Rasool, Vinay Kumar Gadamidi, Saleha Ozair, Krunal Pandav, Claudia Cuevas-Lou, Matthew Parrish, Ivan Rodriguez, and Javier Perez Fernandez. 2022. "The Impact of Misinformation on the COVID-19 Pandemic." *AIMS Public Health* 9 (2): 262–77. https://doi.org/10.3934/publichealth.2022018.

Fitzpatrick, Caroline, Robin Burkhalter, and M. Asbridge. 2019. "Adolescent Media Use and Its Association to Wellbeing in a Canadian National Sample." *Preventive Medicine Reports* 14: 1–6. https://doi.org/10.1016/j.pmedr.2019.100867.

Flynn, Kerry. 2020. "Joe Rogan Spread Dangerous Misinformation about Fires. Now He Says He's Sorry." *CNN*, September 18, 2020. https://www.cnn.com/2020/09/18/media/joe-rogan-apologizes/index.html.

Gage, Brandon. 2022. "Anti-Vax Activist Claims COVID-19 Vaccines Cause AIDS." *Salon*, April 3, 2022. https://www.salon.com/2022/04/03/anti-vax-activist-claims-19-vaccines-cause-aids_partner/.

Gates, Bill. 1995. *The Road Ahead*. New York: Penguin Books.

Glaser, April. 2018. "The Problem with #DeleteFacebook," *Slate*, March 21, 2018. https://slate.com/technology/2018/03/dont-deletefacebook-thats-not-good-enough.html.

Goldberg, Jeffrey. 2020. "Why Obama Fears for Our Democracy." *The Atlantic*, November 16, 2020. https://www.theatlantic.com/ideas/archive/2020/11/why-obama-fears-for-our-democracy/617087/.

Grodzinsky, Frances, and Herman Tavani. 2010. "Applying the 'Contextual Integrity' Model of Privacy to Personal Blogs in the Blogosphere." *International Journal of Internet Research Ethics* 3: 39–47.

Harris, Michael. 2017. *Solitude: In Pursuit of a Singular Life in a Crowded World*. New York: Basic Books.

Holte, Alex J., and F. Richard Ferraro. 2020. "True Colors: Grayscale Setting Reduces Screen Time in College Students." *Social Science Journal* 60 (2): 274–90. https://doi.org/10.1080/03623319.2020.1737461.

Horwitz, Jeff. 2021. "The Facebook Whistleblower, Frances Haugen, Says She Wants to Fix the Company, Not Harm It." *Wall Street Journal*, October 3, 2021. https://www.wsj.com/articles/facebook-whistleblower-frances-haugen-says-she-wants-to-fix-the-company-not-harm-it-11633304122.

Hunt, Melissa G., Rachel Marx, Courtney Lipson, and Jordyn Young. 2018. "No More FOMO: Limiting Social Media Decreases Loneliness and Depression." *Journal of Social and Clinical Psychology* 37 (10): 751–68.

Illing, Sean. 2020. "'Flood the Zone with Shit': How Misinformation Overwhelmed Our Democracy." *Vox*, February 6, 2020. https://www.vox.com/policy-and-politics/2020/1/16/20991816/impeachment-trial-trump-bannon-misinformation.

Johnson, Bobbie. 2010. "Privacy No Longer a Social Norm, Says Facebook Founder." *Guardian*, January 11, 2010. https://www.theguardian.com/technology/2010/jan/11/facebook-privacy.

Johnson, Simon. 2024. "JK Rowling calls trans football manager 'straight, white, middle-aged bloke.'" *Telegraph*, May 12, 2024. https://www.telegraph.co.uk/news/2024/05/12/jk-rowling-bully-transgender-womens-football-sutton-united/.

Konrath, Sara H., Edward H. O'Brien, and Courtney Hsing. 2011. "Changes in Dispositional Empathy in American College Students Over Time: A Meta-Analysis." *Personality and Social Psychology Review* 15 (2): 180–98.

Kurtz, Sheldon F., and Michael J. Saks. 1996. "The Transplant Paradox: Overwhelming Public Support for Organ Donation vs. Under-Supply of Organs: The Iowa Organ Procurement Study." *Journal of Corporation Law* 21: 767–806.

Larmore, Charles. 1999. "The Moral Basis of Political Liberalism." *Journal of Philosophy* 96 (12): 599–625. https://doi.org/10.2307/2564695.

Lee, Chei Sian, and Long Ma. 2012. "News Sharing in Social Media: The Effect of Gratifications and Prior Experience." *Computers in Human Behavior* 28 (2): 331–39. https://doi.org/10.1016/j.chb.2011.10.002.

Lewandowsky, Stephan, Ullrich K. H. Ecker, John Cook, Sander van der Linden, Jon Roozenbeek, and Naomi Oreskes. 2023. "Misinformation and the Epistemic Integrity of Democracy." *Current Opinion in Psychology* 54: 101711. https://doi.org/10.1016/j.copsyc.2023.101711.

Lewis, Paul, 2017. "'Our Minds Can Be Hijacked': The Tech Insiders Who Fear a Smartphone Dystopia." *Guardian*, October 6, 2017. https://www.theguardian.com/technology/2017/oct/05/smartphone-addiction-silicon-valley-dystopia.

Liao, S. Matthew. 2018. "Do You Have a Moral Duty to Leave Facebook?" *New York Times*, November 24, 2018. https://www.nytimes.com/2018/11/24/opinion/sunday/facebook-immoral.html.

Marin, Lavinia. 2021a. "Sharing (Mis) Information on Social Networking Sites. An Exploration of the Norms for Distributing Content Authored by Others." *Ethics and Information Technology* 23 (3): 363–72.

Marin, Lavinia. 2021b. "Three Contextual Dimensions of Information on Social Media: Lessons Learned from the COVID-19 Infodemic." *Ethics and Information Technology* 23: 79–86.

Merritt, Anna C., Daniel A. Effron, and Benoît Monin. 2010. "Moral Self-Licensing: When Being Good Frees Us to Be Bad." *Social and Personality Psychology Compass* 4 (5): 344–57.

Mill, John Stuart. 1991. *On Liberty and Other Essays*. Edited by John Gray. Oxford: Oxford University Press.

Nadkarni, Ashwini, and Stephan G. Hofmann. 2012. "Why Do People Use Facebook?" *Personality and Individual Differences* 52 (3): 243–49. https://doi.org/10.1016/j.paid.2011.11.007.

Ng, Eve. 2020. "No Grand Pronouncements Here ... Reflections on Cancel Culture and Digital Media Participation." *Television & New Media* 21 (6): 621–27. https://doi.org/10.1177/1527476420918828.

Nguyen, C. Thi. 2020. "Echo Chambers and Epistemic Bubbles." *Episteme* 17 (2): 141–61.

Norlock, Kathryn J. 2017. "Online Shaming." *Social Philosophy Today* 33: 187–97.

Norris, Pippa. 2023. "Cancel Culture: Myth or Reality?" *Political Studies* 71 (1): 145–74.

Nussbaum, Martha. 2004. *Hiding from Humanity: Disgust, Shame, and the Law.* Princeton, NJ: Princeton University Press.

Pariser, Eli. 2011. *The Filter Bubble: How the New Personalized Web Is Changing What We Read and How We Think.* New York: Penguin Press.

Parsell, Mitch. 2008. "Pernicious Virtual Communities: Identity, Polarisation, and the Web 2.0." *Ethics and Information Technology* 10: 41–56.

Paul, Kari, and Dani Anguiano. 2021. "Facebook Crisis Grows as New Whistleblower and Leaked Documents Emerge." *Guardian*, October 23, 2021. https://www.theguardian.com/technology/2021/oct/22/facebook-whistleblower-hate-speech-illegal-report.

Pelley, Lauren. 2024. "Ontario's First Measles Death in Decades Offers Grim Reminder That Unvaccinated Kids Are at Risk." *CBC*, May 18, 2024. https://www.cbc.ca/news/health/measles-vaccination-rates-1.7207834.

Postmes, Tom, Russell Spears, and Martin Lea. 1998. "Breaching or Building Social Boundaries? SIDE-Effects of Computer-Mediated Communication." *Communication Research* 25 (6): 689–715. https://doi.org/10.1177/009365098025006006.

Puri, Anuj. 2021. "The Right to Attentional Privacy." *Rutgers Law Record* 48 (1): 206–21.

Rachels, James. 1975. "Why Privacy Is Important." *Philosophy and Public Affairs* 4 (4): 323–33.

Raudsepp, Lennart, and Kristjan Kais. 2019. "Longitudinal Associations between Problematic Social Media Use and Depressive Symptoms in Adolescent Girls." *Preventive Medicine Reports* 15: 1–5. https://doi.org/10.1016/j.pmedr.2019.100925.

Raz, Joseph. 1986. *The Morality of Freedom.* Oxford: Clarendon Press.

Reviglio, Urbano. 2019. "Serendipity as an Emerging Design Principle of the Infosphere: Challenges and Opportunities." *Ethics and Information Technology* 21 (2): 151–66.

Riehm, Kira E., Kenneth A. Feder, Kayla N. Tormohlen, Rosa M. Krum, Andrea S. Young, Kerry M. Green, Lauren R. Pacek, Laraina N. La Flair, and Ramin Mojtabai. 2019. "Associations between Time Spent Using Social Media and Internalizing and Externalizing Problems among US Youth." *JAMA Psychiatry* 76 (12): 1266–73. https://doi.org/10.1001/jamapsychiatry.2019.2325.

Riesman, David, Nathan Glazer, and Reuel Denney. 1950. *Lonely Crowd: A Study of the Changing American Character.* New Haven, CT: Yale University Press.

Ronson, Jon. 2015. *So You've Been Publicly Shamed.* New York: Riverhead Books.

Sales, Nancy Jo. 2017. *American Girls: Social Media and the Secret Lives of Teenagers.* New York: Random House.

Satz, Debra. 2010. *Why Some Things Should Not Be for Sale: The Moral Limits of Markets.* Oxford: Oxford University Press.

Schimmele, Christoph, Jonathan Fonberg, and Grant Schellenberg. 2021. *Canadians' Assessments of Social Media in Their Lives.* Statistics Canada. https://doi.org/10.25318/36280001202100300004-eng.

Schkade, David, Cass R. Sunstein, and Reid Hastie. 2007. "What Happened on Deliberation Day?" *California Law Review* 95 (3): 915–40.

Shakya, Holly B., and Nicholas A. Christakis. 2017. "Association of Facebook Use with Compromised Well-Being: A Longitudinal Study." *American Journal of Epidemiology* 185 (3): 203–11. https://doi.org/10.1093/aje/kww189.

Simpson, Robert M. 2022. "The Ethics of Quitting Social Media." In *The Oxford Handbook of Digital Ethics*, edited by Carissa Véliz, 685–704. Oxford: Oxford University Press.

Sinnott-Armstrong, Walter. 2005. "It's Not My Fault: Global Warming and Individual Moral Obligations." In *Perspectives on Climate Change*, edited by Walter Sinnott-Armstrong and Richard B. Howarth, 221–53. New York: Elsevier.

Soroka, Stuart, Patrick Fournier, and Lilach Nir. 2019. "Cross-National Evidence of a Negativity Bias in Psychophysiological Reactions to News." *PNAS* 116 (38): 18888–92.

Spears, Russell, Tom Postmes, and Martin Lea. 2002. "The Power of Influence and the Influence of Power in Virtual Groups: A SIDE Look at CMC and the Internet." *Journal of Social Issues* 58: 91–108.

Spinello, Richard A. 2011. "Privacy and Social Networking Technology." *International Review of Information Ethics* 16 (12): 41–46.

Srikanth, Anagha. 2021. "12 Prominent People Opposed to Vaccines Are Responsible for Two-Thirds of Anti-Vaccine Content Online: Report." *The Hill*, March 21, 2021. https://thehill.com/changing-america/well-being/prevention-cures/544712-twelve-anti-vaxxers-are-responsible-for-two/.

Sunstein, Cass R. 2017. *#republic: Divided Democracy in the Age of Social Media.* Princeton, NJ: Princeton University Press.

Tannenbaum, David, Craig R. Fox, and Todd Rogers. 2017. "On the Misplaced Politics of Behavioural Policy Interventions." *Nature Human Behavior* 1. https://doi.org/10.1038/s41562-017-0130.

Tavani, Herman. 2007. "Philosophical Theories of Privacy: Implications for an Adequate Online Privacy Policy." *Metaphilosophy* 38 (1): 1–22.

Thaler, Richard H., and Cass R. Sunstein. 2008. *Nudge: Improving Decisions about Health, Wealth, and Happiness.* New Haven, CT: Yale University Press.

Tharoor, Ishaan. 2021. "The Indisputable Harm of Facebook." *Washington Post*, October 26, 2021. https://www.washingtonpost.com/world/2021/10/26/indisputable-harm-caused-by-facebook/.

Thomason, Krista. 2021. "The Moral Risks of Online Shaming." In *The Oxford Handbook of Digital Ethics*, edited by Carissa Véliz, 145–62. Oxford: Oxford University Press.

Thomson, Judith J. 1975. "The Right to Privacy." *Philosophy and Public Affairs* 4 (4): 295–314.

Tran, Jasper L. 2015. "The Right to Attention." *Indiana Law Journal* 91: 1023–64.

Tronto, Joan. 1994. *Moral Boundaries: A Political Argument for an Ethic of Care.* New York: Routledge.

Turkle, Sherry. 2011. *Alone Together: Why We Expect More from Technology and Less from Each Other.* New York: Basic Books.

Twenge, Jean M., and Keith Campbell. 2019. "Media Use Is Linked to Lower Psychological Well-Being: Evidence from Three Datasets." *Psychiatric Quarterly* 90: 311–31.

Valero, Myriam V. 2023. "Thousands of Scientists Are Cutting Back on Twitter, Seeding Angst and Uncertainty." *Nature*, August 16, 2023. https://www.nature.com/articles/d41586-023-02554-0.

Vogels, Emily A., Risa Gelles-Watnick, and Navid Massarat. 2022. "Teens, Social Media and Technology 2022." *Pew Research Center*, August 10, 2022. https://www.pewresearch.org/internet/2022/08/10/teens-social-media-and-technology-2022/.

Walker, Mason, and Katerina Eva Matsa. 2021. "News Consumption across Social Media in 2021." *Pew Research Center*, September 20, 2021. https://www.pewresearch.org/journalism/2021/09/20/news-consumption-across-social-media-in-2021/.

*Wall Street Journal*. 2021a. "Teens & Young Adults on IG and FB." September 29, 2021. https://s.wsj.net/public/resources/documents/teens-young-adults-on-ig-and-facebook.pdf.

*Wall Street Journal*. 2021b. "Teen Girls [sic] Body Image and Social Comparison on Instagram—An Exploratory Study in the US." September 29, 2021. https://s.wsj.net/public/resources/documents/teen-girls-body-image-and-social-comparison-on-instagram.pdf.

Warren, Samuel, and Louis Brandeis. 1890. "The Right to Privacy." *Harvard Law Review* 4 (5): 193–220.

Wechsler, Henry, Jae Eun Lee, Meicun Kuo, and Hang Lee. 2000. "College Binge Drinking in the 1990s: A Continuing Problem. Results of the Harvard School of Public Health 1999 Alcohol Study." *Journal of the American College of Health* 48: 199–210.

Wells, Georgia, Jeff Horwitz, and Deepa Seetharaman. 2021. "Facebook Knows Instagram Is Toxic for Teen Girls, Company Documents Show." *Wall Street Journal*, September 14, 2021. https://www.wsj.com/articles/facebook-knows-instagram-is-toxic-for-teen-girls-company-documents-show-11631620739?mod=hp_lead_pos7&mod=article_inline.

White, Abbey. 2024. "Country Singer Chely Wright Calls New York Times Op-Ed Speculating About Taylor Swift's Sexuality 'Upsetting.'" *Hollywood Reporter*, January 7, 2024. https://www.hollywoodreporter.com/news/general-news/taylor-swift-essay-new-york-times-chely-wright-1235781149/.

Wittgenstein, Ludwig. 1958. *Philosophical Investigations*. Translated by G. E. M. Anscombe. Oxford: Blackwell Publishing.

Wood, Allen W. 2005. "Exploitation." In *The Oxford Companion to Philosophy*, 2nd ed., edited by Ted Honderich, 283–84. Oxford: Oxford University Press.

Woods, Heather Cleland, and Holly Scott. 2016. "#Sleepyteens: Social Media Use in Adolescence Is Associated with Poor Sleep Quality, Anxiety, Depression, and Low Self-Esteem." *Journal of Adolescence* 51: 41–49.

Woolf, Nicky. 2016. "Documents Show AT&T Secretly Sells Customer Data to Law Enforcement," *Guardian*, October 25, 2016. https://www.theguardian.com/business/2016/oct/25/att-secretly-sells-customer-data-law-enforcement-hemisphere.

Wu, Tim. 2016. *The Attention Merchants: The Epic Scramble to Get Inside Our Heads*. New York: Vintage Books.

Xunzi. 2015. *Xunzi: The Complete Text*. Princeton: Princeton University Press. Edited and translated by Eric L. Hutton.

# Index

addiction, 42–43
advertising: attention economy, 37, 43, 188; cookies and, 18–19; nudging, 57–58, 61; revenue, 52, 58, 178, 183
algorithms, 42–43, 84, 87, 94
Amazon, 16–18
anonymity, 8, 18
Apple, 19, 25, 30, 48, 88
Aristotle, 153, 156–57, 159–60
attention economy: access transactions, 37; addiction to, 42–43; clickbait, 52–53; coercive paternalism, 47–48; distractions and, 43–45; echo chambers, 40; libertarian paternalism, 48–49; low levels of knowledge, 41; misinformation, 40–41; moral risks, 38, 41; as noxious market, 40–42, 45–46, 49–50; social antibodies, 46–47; Tiktokification of, 53; value of, 49; violation of privacy, 41
attention merchants, 37, 40–41, 43, 45
autonomy: bodily integrity, 44; informed consent and, 11; limited control of information, 17; mental integrity, 44; right to privacy, 9–13, 26; self-determination, 9–10; simplifying hypothesis, 12

Bannon, Steve, 110
bent testimony, 115
bias, 3, 157, 159. *See also* confirmation bias
Billingham, Paul, 142
binge-watching, 61
bodily integrity, 44

Brandeis, Louis, 14–15
brand loyalty, 95
Brennan, William, 14
buy-in effect, 61–62

Cambridge Analytica, 17, 19, 29
canceling: consequences of, 131–34; defining, 131; de-platforming, 135; directing community attention, 143; imaginal relationship, 135; as moral criticism, 143; politicization of, 132; public shame, 131–35; revising, 137; risk to co-deliberation, 135–36
caring culture, 132, 144–45
celebrities, 25–26, 30–31
children and teens: impacts on well-being, 67–71, 154–55, 178; misinformation, 126; personal information, 10, 31; sense of self, 154; social media risks, 41–42, 70–71, 174; TikTok use, 53, 126
choice, 16, 48, 58
choice architecture, 58–66, 70–71
co-deliberation, 135–37
coercive paternalism, 47–48
complicity in evil, 184–87
confirmation bias, 85–86
consent, 16–20. *See also* informed consent
consequentialism, 177–82, 184
conspiracy theories, 68, 93, 109, 113, 118–19
consumer sovereignty, 3, 87–89
content: algorithmic filtering, 84–85, 87, 94; attention economy, 40; manual filtering, 84–85, 87, 94; nudging, 58, 60–61, 64, 66–69

209

contextual-integrity (CI) model of privacy, 21–26
control: choice, 16; consent, 16; correction, 16; data collection, 13–14; limited, 15–20; personal information, 8–9, 13–14; RALC model, 15–18, 21, 26
cookies, 18–20
correction, 16
cyberbullying, 85, 144, 176
cybercascades, 108, 111–15

data mining: contextual integrity, 24; cookies and, 18–19; data patterns, 16–17; harmful outcomes, 17, 41; informed consent, 11, 29; lack of control over, 13–14; privacy violations, 7, 11, 13–14, 17–19, 24, 41, 57; RALC model, 17, 21; selling, 11, 17–18
deindividuation, 85
democratic processes: dysfunctional political communities, 94–95; echo chambers, 40, 83, 91, 94–95, 175; erosion of, 91–92, 175; misinformation harms, 108–10, 119, 122; noxious markets, 40; polarization, 92–93; public reason, 92–94
de-platforming, 135, 143
design principles: consumer sovereignty, 3, 87–89; serendipity, 88–89, 99; user behavior and, 2–3
disinformation, 108
disproportionality, 135, 152n13
distractions, 43–45
doxxing, 26

echo chambers: banning dissidents, 84; benefits of, 96–99; confirmation bias, 85; conspiracy theories, 93; consumer sovereignty, 87–89; content filtering, 84–85, 87, 94–95; cost-free expulsion, 86, 96–97; discrediting in, 83, 97–99; dysfunctional political communities, 94–95; escape from social pressures, 97; harmful outcomes for individuals, 41, 83, 89–91, 98; harmful outcomes for society, 40, 91–95, 175; polarization, 85–87, 89; psychological factors for, 84–87; quitting, 175; technological factors for, 84–85, 88, 97; undermining of public reason, 93
e-commerce sites, 61–62
ethics of care, 132, 144–45
exploitation, 43

Facebook: business use, 175; Cambridge Analytica scandal, 17, 29; choice architecture, 60; content filtering, 84; cookies, 18; data collection, 17; deleting account, 64, 189; echo chambers, 179; harm to children, 42, 68; misinformation, 121; nudging, 58, 63, 65–66, 68–69; user health, 68–69. *See also* Meta
filter bubbles, 83, 88, 94, 96
filtering: algorithmic, 84–85, 87, 94; consumer sovereignty, 87; echo chambers, 84, 86–87, 95; manual, 84–85, 87, 94
4Chan, 113, 121
friendships: context of communication, 162; cues and interpretations, 157–59, 161; cues-filtered-out, 159, 165; defining, 153; influencer culture, 167; mirroring, 156–57, 159; narcissism, 154; self-creation, 155–56; self-knowledge, 154–57, 159–61; social media impacts, 154–55; social pressures, 163–64; superiority of offline, 153–61;

# Index

superiority of online, 161–64; virtual-reality technologies, 163–65

Gates, Bill, 87, 107
general social-media sites, 117, 119
Google, 19

Haugen, Frances, 68

imaginal relationship, 134–35
individual causal inefficacy (ICI), 181–84
influencer culture, 111, 113, 115, 153, 167, 197
informational cybercascades, 112–14
informed consent: autonomy and, 11; cookies and, 18–20; corporate dishonesty, 19–20; data collection, 11, 29; decision-making and, 10; privacy and, 10–11, 13; terms and conditions of use, 19–20
Instagram: business use, 175, 177; cyberbullying, 144; echo chambers, 88, 179; mental health impacts, 68–69; nudging, 58, 66, 71; plane-tracking information, 30; pro-anorexia communities, 88, 102; risks to children, 41–42, 64, 68–69, 178

language-games, 117–18
libertarian paternalism: attention economy harms, 48–49; choice architecture, 58; nudging, 48–49, 57–59, 63–64, 67–68
LinkedIn, 116–18
low levels of knowledge, 39–41

magnitude gap, 133–35, 140
mandated-choice nudge, 63
manipulation, 64–66, 81n6
markets, 37–41. *See also* noxious markets

mental health: canceling, 131, 134; echo chambers, 90; social media impacts on, 70, 154–55, 174, 178; teens and, 68–69, 71, 154–55, 178
mental integrity, 44
Meta: attention economy, 43; cookies, 18; harm to young girls, 41–42, 73, 178, 187; research on user health, 68–69; third-party access to data, 19. *See also* Facebook
Mill, John Stuart, 132–33, 135–37, 140, 142
misinformation: anti-vaccine, 97, 99, 107; attention economy, 41; bent testimony, 115; conspiracy theories, 109, 113, 118–19; cybercascades, 108, 111–15; duty to remove, 120–22; general social-media sites, 117–19; harms to democracy, 40, 108–10, 122, 124–25; harms to the information environment, 108, 110–11; identification of, 122–23; influencer culture, 111, 113, 115, 197; institutional spread of, 115–16; language-games, 117–19; personal harms, 41, 108–10; purposeful social-media sites, 116; quitting social media, 190; sharing, 115; social harms, 40; social media policies, 107
misinformation conduits, 111
Musk, Elon, 30, 190

narcissism, 154
Netflix, 60–61, 64
non-intrusion model of privacy, 14–15
notifications: color of, 2–3, 60; nudging, 60, 63, 65–66, 73; opting in/out, 48, 70
noxious markets: attention economy, 40–42, 45–46, 49–50; harmful

outcomes for individuals, 39–41; harmful outcomes for society, 39–40; low levels of knowledge, 39–41
nudging: advertising revenue, 58; buy-in effect, 61–62; choice architecture, 58–66, 70–71; conspiracy theories, 68; content promotion, 58, 60–61, 64, 66–69; default-options, 60–61; endless scrolling, 60, 66; ethics of, 62–66, 70; freedom of choice, 63–64; impact on well-being, 68–69; informing people, 59–60; intuitions on, 64–65; libertarian paternalism, 48–49, 57–59, 63–64, 67–68; mandated-choice, 63; manipulative, 64–66, 81n6; moral permissibility, 62–66; notifications, 60, 63, 65–66; ownership, 62; positive influences, 59–60; publicity principle, 63, 69; screen time limits, 70–71; social-media technologies, 57–58; towards the bad, 66–70
Nussbaum, Martha, 133, 142

Obama, Barack, 65, 109
online caring, 132, 144–45
online shaming: canceling, 131–35; directing community attention, 143; distance from victim, 133; imaginal relationship, 134–35; impact on victim well-being, 133–35, 140–41; institutional solutions, 140–41; magnitude gap, 133–35, 140; risk of co-deliberation, 135–37; risk of disproportionality, 135; self-licensing, 133; spoiled identity, 142; tyranny of, 132–33, 135, 140; value of, 141–42

Parr, Tom, 142
personal information: contextual integrity, 21–23; control over, 8–9, 13–14; cookies and, 18–19; data selling, 11, 17–18; doxxing, 26; harm avoidance, 9, 17; informed consent, 10; limited control of, 17–20; privacy and, 7–13, 17–20; reasons to reveal, 20; rules of appropriateness, 21–24; rules of distribution, 21–25; shared with partners, 17; social relationships and, 8–9, 13
phone hacking, 25–26, 30–31
Plato: *Alcibiades*, 138, 160; on concepts of value, 3; on friendship, 153; *Laws*, 92–93, 153; *Lysis*, 153; on moral improvement, 140–42; on reconciliation, 92–94; *Republic*, 12; on shamelessness, 137–41
polarization, 85–87, 89, 102
privacy: autonomy and, 10; contextual-integrity (CI) model, 21–26; informed consent, 10–11, 13; non-intrusion model, 14–15; personal information, 8–13, 17–20; RALC model, 15–20; right to, 7–9, 11–12, 14, 26; simplifying hypothesis, 11–12, 26; as social norm, 7–8, 14; social relationships, 9, 21
privacy violations: attention economy, 41; data collection, 7, 11, 13–14, 17–19, 24, 41, 57; doxxing, 26; harmful outcomes for individuals, 33; low levels of knowledge, 41; personal information, 12; rules of appropriateness, 24; rules of distribution, 22–23, 25; sonal information, 15
private shame, 132, 143
privilege, 175–77
problem of the moral limits of markets, 37
publicity principle, 63, 69

public reason, 92–94
public shame: canceling, 131–32; de-platforming, 143; directing community attention, 143; endorsement of social norms, 142–43; risk of disproportionality, 135; self-licensing, 133; social tyranny of, 132–33, 135; spoiled identity, 142. *See also* online shaming
purposeful social-media sites, 116

quitting: complicity in evil, 184–87; consequentialism, 177–82, 184; escape from echo chambers, 175; individual causal inefficacy, 181–84; individual vs. collective obligations, 179–80; privilege-based objection, 175–77; social pressure against, 179; utilitarianism, 178–80; well-being and, 173–76

RALC model. *See* restricted access/ limited control (RALC) model of privacy
Raz, Joseph, 65
Reddit, 31, 60, 101
reputational cybercascades, 114–15
restricted access/limited control (RALC) model of privacy, 15–20
Riesman, David, 154
right to attention, 43–45, 49
Ringley, Jennifer, 23–24
risk of disproportionality, 135
risks: attention economy, 38, 41; to children and teens, 41–42, 64, 68–69, 178; data collection, 13; informed consent, 11; low levels of knowledge, 41; privacy violations, 41
Rogan, Joe, 111

Rowling, J. K., 131, 148
rules of appropriateness, 21–24
rules of distribution, 21–25

Sacco, Justine, 131, 133, 135, 143, 147
scrolling, 37, 42, 45, 60, 66, 174
self-licensing, 133
serendipity, 88–89, 99
shame: absence of mutual respect, 136; effects of, 132–34, 140; for moral improvement, 137–42; private, 132, 143. *See also* online shaming
sharing: misinformation, 115; online friendships, 163–64; personal information, 7–9, 13, 23–24, 118
simplifying hypothesis, 11–12, 26
social antibodies, 45–47
social contagions, 45–46
social identity model of deindividuation effects (SIDE), 85, 105n1
social-media sites: addiction to, 42–43; autoloading features, 61; benefits of, 1–2; business use, 175, 177; curation, 157; deindividuation, 85; design values, 2–3; distractions and, 43–45; general, 117–19; harmful uses, 2, 41–42; influencer culture, 197; lack of contextual integrity, 22–23; mindset and, 3–4; negative effects on well-being, 66–67, 178; purposeful, 116; risks to children, 41–42, 64, 68–69, 178; thought-terminating clichés, 1–2; violation of privacy, 17–19, 24, 41, 178
social relationships, 8–9, 13, 21
Socrates, 137–42
spoiled identity, 142
Sunstein, Cass, 68, 91, 93–94, 109
supernormal stimuli, 45

Tenpenny, Sherri, 107
terms and conditions of use, 19–20
testimony, 111–12
Thaler, Richard, 68
TikTok: attention economy, 53; business use, 175; community building, 145; data mining, 16–17; echo chambers, 179; endless scrolling, 37, 45, 60; misinformation, 119, 126; nudging, 58, 71, 74; pro-anorexia communities, 102; screen time limits, 71
Trump, Donald, 17, 29, 101, 125
Turkle, Sherry, 154
Twitter. *See* X (formerly Twitter)

utilitarianism, 178–80

Warren, Samuel, 14–15
*The Washingtonienne* blog, 24–25
well-being: impact of polarization, 89–90; mental health issues, 68–71; misinformation harms, 108–9; negative effects on, 66–69; quitting social media for, 173–76; subjective/objective, 67; teenage girls and, 41–42, 64, 68–69; victims of public shaming, 133–35, 140
Wittgenstein, Ludwig, 117

X (formerly Twitter): caring culture, 144–45; content filtering, 89; endless scrolling, 60; misinformation, 107, 121, 190; nudging, 58; plane-tracking information, 30; shamers on, 134
Xunzi, 3

YouTube: autoloading features, 61, 66, 70; children on, 31; content filtering, 84–85, 88–89; cyberbullying, 144; misinformation, 107, 119, 121; nudging, 58, 61, 66

Zuckerberg, Mark, 7, 14, 88